Dear Megan

OTHER TITLES IN THE CAPITAL CARES SERIES:

Children of Jonah: Personal Stories by Survivors of Suicide Attempts edited by James T. Clemons

The Fearless Caregiver: How to Get the Best Care for Your Loved One and Still Have a Life of Your Own edited by Gary Barg

Fourteen Friends' Guide to Eldercaring: Inspiration, Practical Advice, Shared Experiences, Space to Think by Fourteen Friends, LLC

Is Your Parent in Good Hands? Protecting Your Aging Parent from Financial Abuse and Neglect by Edward J. Carnot, Esq.

Last Rights: Taking Care with Your Final Journey by Pat Cochran

Love, Honor & Value: A Family Caregiver Speaks Out about the Choices and Challenges of Caregiving by Suzanne Mintz

Dear Megan

Letters on Life, Love, and Fragile X

Mary Beth Busby & Megan Massey

Capital Cares Series

CAPITAL BOOKS, INC.
Sterling, Virginia

Capital Books, Inc.
P.O. Box 605
Herndon, Virginia 20172-0605

ISBN 10: 1-933102-23-3 (alk.paper)
ISBN 13: 978-1-933102-23-8

Library of Congress Cataloging-in-Publication Data

Busby, Mary Beth.
Dear Megan : letters of life, love, and Fragile X / Mary Beth Busby and Megan Massey.— 1st ed.
p. ; cm. — (Capital cares series)
ISBN 1-933102-23-3 (alk. paper)
1. Fragile X syndrome—Miscellanea.
[DNLM: 1. Personal Narratives—Collected Correspondence. 2. Fragile X Syndrome—Collected Correspondence. QS 677 B979d 2006] I. Massey, Megan. II. Title. III. Series: Capital cares book.

RJ506.F73B87 2006
618.92'858841—dc22

2006007305

Printed in the United States of America on acid-free paper that meets the American National Standards Institute Z39-48 Standard.

First Edition

10 9 8 7 6 5 4 3 2 1

Proceeds from the sale of this book will be donated to FRAXA Research Foundation.

To our beloved sons,

Jack and Jacob Massey
and
Robert and Jack Busby

Robert Busby, 1992

Jack Massey, age 16, 2005

Jack Busby, 1998

Jacob Massey, age 13, 2004

Advance Praise for *Dear Megan* . . .

"When reflecting on Mary Beth's and Megan's book, two sayings jump into my mind: Jesus, in the Gospel According to John, '. . . and you will know the truth and the truth will set you free;' and Boris Pasternak, in *Dr. Zhivago*, '. . . the irresistible power of the unarmed truth.' Their book is about the freedom and power of telling the truth. *Dear Megan* is written for parents of special needs children; however, it is also for all brave enough to follow their example."
—The Right Reverend Jane Holmes Dixon

"A brave exchange of hopes, fears and, ultimately, wisdom, expressed with unflinching honesty. These letters of women trying to find their way through excruciating circumstances will move and inspire all who read them. *Dear Megan: Letters on Life, Love and Fragile X*, is an uncommon achievement."
—Mary Jane Clark, author and mother of Fragile X child

"Mary Beth Busby and Megan Massey have written an important and highly original book on Fragile X—'the most common known inherited cause of mental retardation.' They know their subject intimately—as only mothers of Fragile X children can. Written as letters between the two mothers, 'Dear Megan' is highly readable, informative, ground-breaking and unforgettable."
—E. J. & Roger Mudd

"It is important to understand Fragile X and how it impacts the lives of children and parents. Megan and Mary Beth are brave to share their deeply personal story of adversity, love, and triumph during their journey to discover the answers to Fragile X. This is a wonderful book. "
—U.S. Senator Chuck Hagel (R-NE)

"The immediate and everlasting love and connection between Fragile X carrier women, and indeed all mothers with special needs children, is simply amazing. *Dear Megan* is like a support group for all of us to share our triumphs and despairs together"
—Kelly Randels, mother of Fragile X son

"Finally a book for special needs parents that addresses the Fragile X community. I found great solace and a sense of relief in reading the letters. I realize now that as a Fragile X mom, I am not alone in this journey. These extraordinary children can teach us more about ourselves and life than we ever thought possible. An inspirational read."
—Anne Souder, mother of Fragile X son

Contents

Acknowledgments

I promised Kathleen Hughes, the wonderful publisher of Capital Books, that Megan and I would try to refrain from thanking our third grade teachers in our acknowledgments. But there are certain friends and supporters we want to thank, beginning with Kathleen herself. She makes everything easy, and we are grateful for her faith in our book. She just said, "Yes." Her editors and designers were supportive and encouraging.

From Mary Beth Busby:

First, I thank Megan Massey, who makes the book a real dialogue, who has become one of the true joys of my life, and who reminds me that spanning our two generations, some things change, while others remain remarkably the same.

Kelly Randels has, selflessly and courageously, made an enormous contribution to this book. She tells, in graphic detail, her story of pain and loss and further pain and—finally—joy. Thank you, Kelly. You are wonderful.

Among the many people who have given selflessly of their time and encouragement to me in the process of writing this book is my very dear friend Diane Rehm, who not only has written one of the forewords, but who also assured me that I could write a book. She and John Rehm and their wonderful children, David and Jennie, have been cherished friends of the entire Busby family for thirty-eight years. There is no dearer friend to me than Diane Rehm.

Thanks also to best-selling author, Mary Jane Clark, a fellow traveler in the Fragile X orbit who truly *is* a writer but, more important, a marvelously sympathetic and empathetic friend to both Megan and me; and wonderful friends, E. J. and Roger Mudd, who have generously supported the FRAXA Research Foundation by hosting our fund-raising galas in Washington, New York, Chicago, Boston, and Pittsburgh—seven events in all. Roger and E. J.

are among the nearest and dearest friends of my husband, David's, and mine, and it would be impossible to count all of the ways in which we should thank them. I am most grateful, too, for the gracious wisdom of my caring friend, Jane Dixon.

I thank Dr. Don and Pam Bailey, who wrote a marvelous foreword, setting forth the importance of Fragile X and making the case for a book such as this one. I especially hoped that they would be willing to participate in the project because Don is one of the sure-footed, recognized researchers on Fragile X and commands the respect of the Fragile X community.

E. J. Mudd, Peyton Lewis, Ellen Atwell, and I have what we call our writers' group. We gather to critique each other's work. The writers read most of this book in stages before I was convinced it could be a book. For their loving support and guidance, my gratitude is boundless. Besides all that, our luncheon meetings enrich and enhance my life beyond measure. Thank you, cherished friends.

Indeed, I have been blessed throughout my life with friendships that have sustained me in the hard times and made the good times all the better. To all of you—and you know who you are—I thank you and love you for being in my life. I especially thank those of you who have supported FRAXA's research and who have helped with our numerous fund-raisers. Here in Washington, I could not have managed without Kitty de Chiara and her husband, Enzo, who have cochaired galas along with Diane Rehm and me, and who have generated astonishing support for FRAXA's research. Also, I so appreciate the Maryland Fragile X Resource Group, good and valued friends.

I especially thank my Aunt Regina and my cousin Jan and her husband, Dale Hartig. They and their sons have truly accepted our boys and made them special members of their family. And David's brother, Phil Busby, has been every boy's dream uncle. My gratitude to him and to his wife, Carolyn, will be everlasting.

Without Katie Clapp and Mike Tranfaglia, there would be no Fragile X Research Foundation (FRAXA). Surely there would be more ongoing research than there was when David and I first learned about Fragile X in 1982, but without Katie and Mike's having started FRAXA with Kathy May in 1994, I am certain that the research would be nowhere near the present stage where we find ourselves on the cusp of a viable treatment. Katie and Mike's commitment and energy is truly a wonder to behold, and David and I are grateful to them for allowing us to ride on their bus. I have monumental regard and affection for these people.

To all of the researchers who labor in the Fragile X vineyard, to our endlessly supportive friends at the National Institutes of Health, and to those congressional staffers who have welcomed our visits and our requests for increased support for new research, I can't thank you enough. No one has ever said to David or me, "No, you can't. No, we won't do that." It's always been, "OK, let's see what we can work out." Bettilou Taylor and Ellen Murray, clerks of the Appropriations Subcommittee on Labor, Health, Human Services and Education, have always been approachable and receptive, as have the Fragile X champions—Senators Hagel and Stabenow, former Senator Edwards, Congressmen Delahunt and Radonovich, Congresswoman Hart, and former Congressman Watkins. Sometimes, our tax dollars truly are at work on positive projects.

In my own research on the research, Drs. Steve Warren and David Nelson, the co-discoverers of the Fragile X gene in 1991, were good enough to vet my chapter on the history of Fragile X; and Dr. Herb Lubs, who first saw the Fragile site on the X chromosome in 1966, was generous in giving me the real story of that event. I also had helpful input from Mike Tranfaglia, Jennifer Darnell, Don Bailey, and Ted Brown.

The first National Fragile X Foundation's International Fragile X Conference David and I attended was in Portland, Oregon, in 1996. Louise Gane held a one-on-two session of Genetics 101 with David and me at a table in the sidewalk café at the hotel. Her generosity and patience in going over (and over) material she had clearly covered with countless parents was typical of her dedication, for which we are grateful. Dr. Randi Hagerman and Dr. Ted Brown, too, have always been there for parents, giving tirelessly of their time and extraordinary expertise. I sincerely thank you all for this. I am, and will always be, most appreciative of Robert and Jack's marvelous caregivers and employers at McCall's Communities, New Horizons Unlimited, Wellspring Ministries, and ServiceSource.

With all of the support I have received throughout my life, none approaches that of the wonderful David Busby, the love and light of my life. If there has ever been someone who could turn lemons into lemonade, it is David Busby, whom I adore.

A huge part of what has always made David special to me is the fact that he brought to our marriage, from his first marriage, two spectacularly beautiful, loving, and fun daughters, Hopie and Alison. How could I have known in 1962 that not only would they bring myriad joys to my life, but that they would also provide us with the five grandchildren we could never have had otherwise: the steadfast and resourceful Timothy, the creative and mesmerizing Patrick, the musically gifted and patiently loving Nick, the curious and insightful writer Christian, and the joyous and perceptive Hope.

Finally, to my late parents and to my dear Robert and Jack, thank you for defining my life and giving me a rare opportunity to participate in a project than can make a difference. Robert and Jack, your mom loves you both, big time!

From Megan Massey:

Mary Beth, thank you for the privilege you have given me to respond to your letters. It has been an honor. I have learned so much from you and with your light I can see a glimpse into the future. You are an inspiration to me.

Along this journey of raising my precious children, I could not have made it through without the unfailing grace of God. I am grateful to my parents, Diane and Bill, who raised my two older sisters, Heidi and Kristy, and me in a positive, loving environment. Never did one day go by without either of you telling us how much we were loved. You have always encouraged us and believed in us. I know that love is being passed on to all of your grandchildren.

John, your devotedness, and faithfulness give me enormous encouragement. Your wisdom and patience is so admirable. You are always ready to advocate and pursue the needs of our children with me. You make our life so easy. Thank you for allowing me to live the life one can only dream of.

To my girlfriends, especially Sue, Helen, Joni, Gayle, Dallas, and Sandy. I am so blessed to have each and every one of you in my life. Even my parents often comment on the incredible support system I have in Scottsbluff, Nebraska. What would I do without you? You have made my journey through "Holland" a lovely one. You are my Rembrandts, my tulips, and my windmills. You give me the confidence to endure. "Continue to let your lights so shine before men, so that they may see your good works and glorify your Father in Heaven" (Matthew 5:16). You are all my prayer warriors and I love you.

To the "Great Aunt Sandy," Boppe, and Bucko, you are extraordinary. The time you commit to the boys, weekend field trips, stops in Kentucky to see Jack, and any other kind of outing you can think of have really been highlights in the lives of Jack and his brother, Jacob. Your commitment to help FRAXA find a treatment or a cure is fantastic.

There are so many teachers, therapists, and mentors who have made a difference in the lives of Jack and Jacob. Linell Wohlers and Lori Blehm, your commitment to our family, the countless individual education plans, all the time you have put forth to improve the education and quality of life for our kids is a gift we can never repay. And we aren't done yet!

Dr. Kent Lacey and Dr. James Massey, we have needed you every step of the way. Your knowledge and medical expertise has been an essential guide to our understanding of the continuing health of the boys. Thank you for your professional help and your personal interest.

Holly and Heather, raising our children and keeping our sanity could not have been accomplished without you. John and I always wanted twins, and God provided.

Mary Jane Clark, thank you for your friendship. It warms my heart every day to know that Jack and your son, David, are pals. To my cousin Anne Souder, a fellow resident of Holland with her Fragile X child, our circumstances are a joy to share together.

"Hey, Hagel!" as Jacob would say. That is U.S. Senator Chuck Hagel. You have been instrumental in accelerating the process of research for Fragile X syndrome, getting it into high gear. The blurb for the book was definitely a highlight in putting this all together. You have heard this before, but you are, without a doubt, our Fragile X hero.

To the Stewart Home School, in Frankfort, Kentucky, where Jack has been attending school for the past two years; I will be forever grateful to you. Sandy Bell, Lisa, David, Gretchen, Nancy, and other staff have provided an opportunity for Jack to become the shining star that God intended him to be. The Stewart Home School is a piece of heaven on earth. I am just sure of that! This school provided an answer to my prayers and happy endings to my letters to Mary Beth.

My mother deserves the big prize for she has jumped on board the Fragile X train and refuses to disembark until a treatment or a cure is found. You amaze me with all your ideas that to me seem so impossible. But you always pull them off so graciously. I hope that our relationship shows how much I treasure you, and how much your words of wisdom and support mean to me. I will be eternally grateful for having you as a mother.

To all of those who read through the pages of our story, I pray these letters will touch your heart and bring you hope and understanding.

Most important to Jack and Jacob: you give great meaning to my life.

Foreword by Diane Rehm

Rarely have I been privileged to read such a personal book, a book in which two mothers, one I have known for forty years, the other I have only recently met, share their experiences of raising children who have severe limitations. Their stories, separated by many decades, come together in this series of extraordinary letters, in which each woman shares her journey, from realization to denial to anger to mourning, and, finally, if this can ever be said of parents whose children will forever be less than what they'd dreamed of, to acceptance.

Most people have never heard of Fragile X syndrome. Had I not known the Busby family, it would have been many years before I came to realize how prevalent the genetic disorder is in our society, and how devastating it is to families. But I was fortunate enough to come to know and love the Busbys, Mary Beth and David, their boys, Robert and Jack, and David's daughters, Hope and Alison. And to learn from them, not only about Fragile X, but also about what it means to be a committed parent, working and extending their caring circle of love to their affected boys and to David's totally "normal" girls.

If you were to meet either of these two mothers, you would scarcely believe they were troubled by anything more than the usual day-to-day anxieties that any of us faces. You would also be struck by their exquisite beauty, their delicacy, their near-fragility. But the strength these two women share has been ongoing and monumental. They are constantly addressing the needs of the young people in their care, who are barely able to function on their own. At the same time, Mary Beth and Megan have carried on with their own everyday social activities, always including their children in the company of others.

When you read their letters, you will understand the profound commitment it takes to be a parent of a child/adult with Fragile X. You will understand the heartache, the struggle, the effort it has taken these two women to parent their children. And you will understand the gift they have given each other, and us, the readers, in sharing their story.

—Diane Rehm, Washington, DC
March 26, 2006

Foreword by Pam and Don Bailey

Fragile X syndrome affects families in many ways. As the most common known inherited cause of mental retardation, learning disabilities, and autism, it reaches not only into the lives of the affected children and their parents, but to the greater extended family network. Parents who have given birth to a child with Fragile X syndrome are likely to have more children with the trait. The siblings of the carrier parent are also likely to be carriers, as are cousins, aunts, uncles, nieces, and nephews.

Relatively speaking, Fragile X syndrome is a new discovery. Previously known as Martin-Bell syndrome, named for two researchers who documented large families with an unusually high incidence of mental retardation, the cause of the problems in affected individuals was unknown until the early 1990s, when the gene for Fragile X was discovered as part of the National Human Genome project. Researchers soon learned that lack of a certain protein interfered with the brain's ability to function properly.

Since that time, what we know about the Fragile X gene has exploded. Physicians and genetic counselors can now test for the condition and provide parents with information that can help them understand their risks of having an affected child. Children can be diagnosed with a single blood sample. We are able to provide much information to physicians and families about physical, behavioral, and intellectual characteristics. Although there is no cure for Fragile X syndrome, and medical treatment options are minimal, the fast pace of discovery is encouraging for those who are looking for a cure.

While our understanding of how the gene works has grown at a remarkable rate in the past twenty years, in contrast we know very little about how to live with children who have Fragile X syndrome. Except for the support of each other, parents, caregivers, and educators are left on their own to figure out what is best for their children. Traversing the road of parenthood can be difficult even in typical circumstances, but the comfort and advice from those who have traveled these roads is never far away. However, for parents of children with disabilities, the roads are not the superhighways that most parents travel, but the lonely side roads, not much more than a footpath. Enter Mary Beth Busby and Megan Massey, both mothers of two boys with Fragile X syndrome.

Mary Beth's boys were born in the mid-1960s before Fragile X had even a name. Megan's boys were born thirty years later when Fragile X had been named and the gene isolated. The beginnings of their journeys were not terribly different, as each discovered first that one son had mental retardation and then also the other. Separated by almost a generation and light years of knowledge about Fragile X syndrome, they were joined by the similarity of their situations. Mary Beth and her husband, David, traveled the road alone. However, as Megan and husband, John, traveled their road, they discovered they had a guide, and that guide was Mary Beth. This book, a series of letters between Mary Beth and Megan, witnesses the rapid changes in knowledge about Fragile X and the changing landscape of services to children with disabilities. The book allows us to take an unfiltered peek into the souls of these two amazing women as they bushwhack the trail and make it smoother for others who will follow. They do not skirt the tough issues, addressing topics such as the desire to have more children, in vitro fertilization and abortion, home versus residential treatment, quality of life for both their children and themselves, effects on siblings and other family members, public embarrassment, and a host of other thorny issues.

Hopefully, scientific research will one day soon eradicate this disease and the need for this book will cease. But for researchers, this book reminds us of the urgency of our work. For families, we find guidance and companionship in the journey. Many thanks to Katie Clapp, Kathy May, and others who are mentioned in this book, and to all the children and adults with Fragile X syndrome who are on the frontlines marching down that side road, making it wider, smoother, and less lonely. And especially, thanks to Mary Beth and Megan, who are paving the path with paper and pen.

—Pam and Don Bailey MD
June 2005

Introduction

Every mother has a story, and of course each is unique. This one is two mothers' stories: Megan Massey's and mine. It's about our experience as mothers of four sons with Fragile X syndrome, the most common form of inherited mental retardation. Megan has two sons with Fragile X, as do I. When my boys were born in New York, Robert in 1964 and Jack in 1965, Fragile X had not yet been identified as a genetic abnormality. When Megan's sons, Jack and Jacob, were born in Scottsbluff, Nebraska, in 1989 and 1991, Fragile X, while having been identified by a few researchers, was hardly even a blip on the screens of practicing pediatricians. I don't say that having two children with Fragile X has restricted my life, simply that it has defined it. Megan agrees, and I must say that she embraced the challenge to a far greater extent than I did when David and I first received the diagnosis in 1982.

This book, from two generational perspectives, is about dealing with the tragedy of having two mentally retarded children, as well as the privilege of joining a crusade to cure Fragile X. I won't say that becoming involved with FRAXA Research Foundation has *made* Megan's and my lives, but it has certainly enriched them beyond any expectation. The promise of the current research is such that we are full of hope that soon there will be a viable treatment and, one day, a cure. While I am aware of the lateness of the hour when it comes to a treatment that might benefit my own sons, I think of them as catalysts for vast improvement in the chances of younger children like Jack and Jacob Massey and—even more—of future children who will be born with Fragile X.

This is also the story of Kelly Randels, a young mother of one son with Fragile X. Kelly is willing to share her story, which compellingly tells of the frustration and agony of the preimplantation genetic diagnosis (PGD) and donor egg processes, as well as the promise of the potential success that these procedures offer in this brave new age of medical discovery. As I write this, Kelly is happily mothering her second child, a result of a successful donor egg procedure, following two unsuccessful ones.

This book deals with everything from dealing with children to dealing with the school system, to marriage, to entertaining, to putting on a fund-raiser. I don't apologize for this. For one thing, lots of us Fragile X carriers are known to multitask. The explanation for this, I suppose, is that we have trouble concentrating on one thing and find it less stressful to scatter our attention and focus. So, while a book on kids and lobbying that also includes recipes may seem bizarre, to me it's all of a piece. One of the most important things that I hope we can convey to young mothers of young Fragile X children is that they need to get a life—a life beyond those kids. Their children must not consume their parents' entire lives. If they do, we all pay for it down the line.

I hope this book will appeal to any young mother who is overwhelmed with trying to be too many things to too many people, to anyone interested in how easy it is, when you have a worthy cause, to gain access to the political system in Washington whether one lives in Washington or Scottsbluff. Megan and I would perhaps think of this book, too, as a cautionary tale for young women who are thinking of being married. It is the story, after all, of so many young couples who marry with the notion that because they seemingly have it all, their lives will go along a kindly certain path. That path isn't supposed to include one party in the marriage harboring an unknown gene that could result in having handicapped children. As my friend E. J. Mudd's poem (which is in the book) says, young people tend to marry for richer, for better, in health.

This book is not a downer. Megan and I don't think of it, or of our lives, that way, and we hope it will come across as a view from the other side—the easier, skiing downhill side— for young parents of children with Fragile X. It may seem more like a "how-not-to," than a "how-to." But we simply didn't have the information in the 1960s, or even in the '90s, that we now have in the twenty-first century. Still, I think that Megan and I can help. I hope this book might assure young parents that at least some of the symptoms—like head banging and hand flapping—do subside, and better still, the memory of the head banging fades and becomes diffused into a blur of nonspecific stress, rather than horrific episodes.

Getting the word out about Fragile X is where I started with the project, and it's Megan's reason for embracing it. Even with the great strides in the last twenty years, since David and I first learned of the condition, there are still too many people who ask, "Fragile what?" If Megan and I can tell a few more people "what," I will feel this book is worthwhile.

As a final note, both Robert and Jack Busby now live in group homes: Robert in Ada, Oklahoma, and Jack in Fairfax, Virginia. They both have workshop jobs: Robert an an auto detail shop and Jack as a mess attendant at the Marine Barracks in Washington, D.C.

1

Welcome to FRAXA

Dear Megan,

I can't tell you how much David and I enjoyed visiting with you and John at the FRAXA fund-raiser, and I'm so glad we arranged that special time together beforehand. I will tell you right here and now that both David and I were blown away by the blond, athletic good looks of the Masseys. I have to tell you, too, that I couldn't get over that adorable short haircut of yours. If I didn't know full well that it's about thirty years too late for me to wear my hair that way, I'd fly out to Nebraska to your hairdresser. Never mind coming to see you, my friend, it's that hairdresser of yours!

If I hadn't known that you have two Fragile X boys, if I hadn't known that you'd been through the horrendous diagnostic procedure, if I had simply run into you somewhere at some unrelated event, I would have thought to myself, "Now there's a handsome young couple who have it all, who have it all together, who enjoy the outdoors with their children, and who have only good things before them." Reading this, I assume you're thinking, "Oh, yeah, right." I know that you're feeling totally overwhelmed with your situation. How well I remember this very stage you're in, when you've been given this devastating diagnosis that has irreversibly changed your life. Well, hear this: you and John come across to me—and I'm pretty perceptive, I think—as a couple I like, a couple I admire,

Mary Beth Busby

and a couple I want to know better. Plus, I get a sense of this marvelous spunk and feistiness on your part, as well as a sense of strength and a real sense of fun in John. So, of course I was thrilled to have your letter. Let's do be friends.

One of the things I look forward to at each fund-raiser or conference is the opportunity to meet new friends among the Fragile X parents. Needless to say, this is a club that none of us wanted to join—this fellowship of parents with similarly handicapped children—but I have to tell you that with each passing month, the Fragile X friendships I've made become more precious to me.

Though it was twenty-five years ago, I remember so well going to see my dear friend Sheila Harris as she was dying of cancer. She said to me, "You know what? At this stage, the people I most want to talk to are those who have had cancer and survived it. They're the only ones who can give me any hope." While, needless to say, there's only a modest parallel here, I do feel that to talk with someone who has literally walked down the same road as you have, and survived enough to talk about it, can be helpful. I hope so anyway.

I suppose that one reason I took such a strong liking to you was that precious picture you showed me of your boys. I know this sounds spooky, but they even look something like my boys when they were the ages of yours. With the obvious difference of your boys being blond, your Jack has the darker hair, as our Robert does; though Jacob doesn't wear glasses, as our Jack has since he was three, there's still a resemblance. I truly relate to them–—and to you.

I wish we lived closer together, so that we could get together more often than I'm sure we will. Nebraska is hardly an easy drive from Washington, DC, but we're going to hope that John's work will bring him to Washington in the not too distant future, and that you'll manage—somehow, some way–—to come with him.

So, let's keep in touch, Megan.

Warmly,

Mary Beth

PS. The next time you pick up your FRAXA newsletter, look again at the quotation from American anthropologist Margaret Mead that Katie Clapp and Mike Tranfaglia chose to put on each and every copy of each and every issue:

> "Never doubt that a small group of thoughtful, committed citizens can change the world. Indeed, it's the only thing that ever has."

The wonderful thing about that quote, which I have begun to note is used by other groups as well, is that it truly can apply to us all. We may be a small "club," this Fragile X parents group, but we are indeed committed. And with God's help, we'll always be thoughtful in all that we do to make our children's lives count. ✉

Dear Mary Beth,

Thank you for your sweet letter. It helps so much to share experiences with others. You mentioned in your letter that looking at my husband and me, you never would have thought we had two boys with Fragile X syndrome. (You ought to see me on the bad days . . . it isn't pretty!)

Anyway, just as I'm sure it was for you, we never had that in our plans, but isn't it interesting how God has different plans for us? I wouldn't trade them in for anything, but it sure has been difficult at times.

FRAXA is such a wonderful organization, a group of people who really want to make a difference for children and adults with Fragile X. And I understand everyone on the board are parents . . . wow! . . . that speaks volumes. I'm so glad my Aunt Daphne found FRAXA on the Internet.

MEGAN MASSEY

We would love to get together sometime and see you. My mother sent me an article the other day that was in "Dear Abby" back in November of 1989. Gosh, Jack would have been seven months old at that time! Anyway the title is "Raising a Child with Disabilities Isn't Horrible—Just Different." It is a piece by Emily Perl Kingsley titled "Welcome to Holland." Have you ever read it? It compares the experience of raising a child with disabilities to that of planning a trip to Italy, flying overseas, and then the flight attendant comes on the intercom and says, "Welcome to Holland." Holland you say, but I was suppose to go to Italy. All my life I have dreamed of going to Italy. Well, you are in Holland, and there you must stay.

So you must go out and buy new guide books, learn a whole new language, and meet a whole new group of people you would never have met.

It's just a different place. It's slower paced than Italy, less flashy than Italy. But after you've been there for a while and you catch your breath, you look around, and you begin to notice that Holland has windmills, Holland has tulips, and Holland even has Rembrandts!

But everyone you know is busy coming from and going to Italy, and they're all bragging about what a wonderful time they had there. And for the rest of your life, you will say, "Yes, that's where I was supposed to go. That's what I had planned. And the pain of that will never, ever, ever go away, because the loss of that dream is a very significant loss.

But, if you spend your life mourning the fact that you didn't get to Italy, you may never be free to enjoy the very special, the very lovely things about Holland.

I'm glad you and David are right here in Holland, along with John and me.

I would love to know, when you have a chance, when and how you and David learned about Fragile X.

Talk to you soon, I must go meet Jack's bus.

Megan ✉

2

What the Blind Palm Reader Saw

Hi, Megan!

Gosh, I never thought I'd ever in my life be starting a letter with "Greetings from East Holland," but here I am saying just that. I loved that story, and you know what else I loved about it? I loved knowing that your wonderful mother sent it to you. I wonder how long she had kept it aside, waiting for the right time to pass it on to you.

I'm sorry it's taken me this long to get back to you, but then you asked a short question that requires a long answer. I've been thinking about your question, and the trouble with thinking about how all this Fragile X stuff started with us is that I've had to dredge up some memories that I had thought safely buried for all time to come. It goes back farther than you might imagine, to 1958.

I read somewhere that it's a bad sign when you go to a palm reader and she asks for the money up front. Maybe I should have seen that on that day in 1958 when I drove with a carload of my high school classmates to Pauls Valley, Oklahoma, to have our palms read by a blind lady we'd heard about. Even at that young age, I was supercynical about such things, but I thought it would be a fun day in the country with my girlfriends—especially since by then, we'd all been off to college for a year and hadn't seen much of each other. And it was fun. We giggled about getting lost trying to find the place, giggled about how crazy we were to be taking this excursion, and then we giggled all the way back home to Oklahoma City about various things she predicted—-such as that both Carolyn and Martha would have twins, which they did, as it turned out. And this was before the days when women waited until later to have their kids and then started taking all these hormones that produce multiple births.

Even at that time, as young and idealistic as I was, I remember being struck by something she told me. She said that I was going to have a long and basically happy life, a very happy marriage, that I would travel a lot, and that I would have tragedy connected with my children. Actually, I can't remember whether she said with my children, or one child, but she definitely predicted tragedy. She also said that my parents would disapprove of my marriage at first but would later come to be happy about it. She hit a bull's-eye on that one too. For a blind lady, she "saw" plenty. Years later, when "all this" turned out to be the story of my life, that day in Pauls Valley, Oklahoma, came back to me—big time.

Another defining moment came when I was pregnant with Robert. We were at a service at St. Thomas church in New York, where we were living. There I was on my knees, praying for my baby to be OK, when all of a sudden, I had this awful, sickening feeling that he/she wouldn't be. Not only that, but the sense I had was that this baby would be mentally retarded. Maybe that experience accounts for the fact that when he was finally diagnosed at age two, I wasn't nearly as shocked as David was.

Perhaps one reason I was concerned about having a retarded child was that Hope Busby, my wonderful mother-in-law, whom I truly adored with my life, had told me repeatedly (and continued to tell me long after the diagnosis of both boys—tact not being her strong suit) that as long as she could remember, David had said that the one thing in life he could never handle would be having a retarded child. So, here I was about to give him just that. I just remember this creepy feeling that something was wrong with this baby. I suppose I was thinking more of Down syndrome, because of Annie, the precious toddler daughter of our closest friends, T George and Sheila Harris. In those days, they didn't do amnio—at least, if they did, I didn't know anything about it. I never heard the term "amniocentesis" until years later. Even if they were doing amnio, they wouldn't have bothered doing it on me, as I was only twenty-four and twenty-five when the boys were born.

When Robert David Busby Jr., was born on March 1, 1964, we really did have cause for concern. The cord was wrapped around his shoulder during labor and his heart kept stopping. Nowadays they would simply switch gears and do a Caesarian delivery, but in those days, that was considered to be a last resort. Even though the resident on duty kept telling David he thought a Caesarian was what they should do, the doctor, who was in the middle of another delivery, kept poking his head in and saying everything was fine. After a twelve-hour labor, our baby was delivered with high forceps. He looked like a mess even to me, but was pronounced "fine."

For years, David and I blamed the obstetrician for Robert's problems. Even after the original diagnosis of Fragile X on both boys in 1982, we continued to think that the reason Robert was more handicapped was because he had suffered brain damage at birth. He may have, but the cold fact is that now—just this year, actually—we finally had blood drawn and sent up to Dr. W. Ted Brown at the New York State Institute for Basic Research, to do the DNA test that shows the number of CGG (cytosine, guanine, and guanine) repeats. It turns out that Robert is a full mutation, whereas Jack is a mosaic. I gather this means that Jack has some normal cells on that gene which produces some of the Fragile X protein. Ted had done a complete workup on the boys in 1983. At that time, we only had the old cytogenetic test, which didn't show CGG repeats.

I must say, every time I see one of those ads on TV for those lawyers who are dying to sue your doctor, I thank God that we didn't sue the doctor who delivered Robert. We were so sure "it" was all his fault. When I think of the pain it would have caused him and that hospital, and also of the fact that "it" was mostly because of Fragile X, I feel kind of silly for having even entertained the notion. Not that we ever seriously discussed it, maybe because we knew in our heart of hearts that Robert's problems were caused by more than a lousy, ill-timed, ill-attended, high forceps delivery.

What we, of course, didn't realize when the boys were very young—because Fragile X was not yet a blip on our horizon, or anyone else's—was that Jack was higher functioning because he is a mosaic. Robert's Fragile X gene, on the other hand, carries the full mutation. We had always assumed that Robert's lower functioning level was because he had suffered brain damage at birth; but we had long since realized that with Jack's obvious deficits, we could no longer blame Robert's problems on the doctor. Gosh, it was nice when we could. It's just so neat and tidy and comfortable to be able to blame a specific person. Works very well for me. And now, all these years later, to find out that I really should have been blaming my poor dear mother? No thanks, this doesn't work well at all.

I know, Megan, you're wondering why on earth I waited all of these years after the DNA test became available to get it done. After all, I had it done on myself (eighty repeats) and even on my mother (seventy repeats), on her deathbed and without her knowledge, so why not the boys? Well, duh. It was lots more fun to blame the doctor for Robert's greater degree of retardation. The poor doctor is probably one of several people to whom I may owe an apology. I say "may" because I still think Robert suffered some brain damage at birth, a double whammy along with the full mutation for Fragile X.

I think that God has a way of giving us what we can handle when we can handle it. Not before and not after. That's why I try never to pass judgment on the way other people handle their own situations. I needed to be able to blame the doctor for as long as I blamed him. Since I had left him for another doctor for my pregnancy with Jack, there was never any confrontation (thank God!), no letter, no nothing. But I have to admit that it gave me some degree of comfort to be able to blame him. It sure beat blaming my parents and grandparents.

My parents went to their graves believing that my boys' mental retardation was due to a "Busby gene." Since David's brother, John, had various mental disorders that prevented him from living a normal, happy life, my parents decided that our boys' problems were related to poor Johnny's problem. As far as they knew, there had never been any mental disorder whatsoever in either of their families.

I know, Megan. It's bizarre that we never did tell my parents about Fragile X. What can I tell you? It was indeed nuts. When we got the diagnosis in 1982, I made the huge mistake of telling my brother before telling my parents. I was totally shattered by the realization that it was my gene and that I had sort of visited this plague, this stigma of mental retardation, upon the whole Busby family—especially Hopie and Alison, David's wonderful daughters from his first marriage. I really needed for my brother to help me deal with it with Mother and Daddy. What he did instead was to totally withdraw from any involvement. He said that there was no way we would ever tell them this, that (I'll never forget his words): "It would send them to an early grave." He was so adamant about it that I was cowed to such an extent that I felt even worse and simply crawled into my little shell of remorse, sadness, self-pity, and paralysis.

Though my father lived for another fourteen years and my mother lived for eighteen years after the diagnosis of Fragile X in 1982; and though my father was at the time still practicing law, and though my mother was involved in the lives of all four of her grandchildren, we never told them. And you know what? They never asked. They never asked us if we had ever learned the cause of the boys' retardation. I guess they thought they knew, and that since it was a "Busby problem," why bring it up? I don't know, really. I do know that during those years, it was very painful for me to carry it alone, without their support. I really did feel alone, and terribly sorry for poor Mary Beth. She was so miserable and sad and sure that no one could possibly understand just how miserable. I mean, you can't imagine, Megan, how pathetic this poor little Mary Beth felt. I could have been the founding chairman of Victims Anonymous. And, besides, the fetal position can be amazingly comfortable.

The frustration that you young parents feel, knowing exactly what's wrong, that it's simply a matter of this one gene and this one missing protein, is—in some ways—worse than what I felt. I honestly didn't think we'd ever find out what was wrong with our boys. More than frustration, I just felt this sadness over what might have been. I don't know, maybe I was just too tired and too sad to feel frustrated.

I used to rock the boys and sing to them a lot. One song I used to sing to them was on one of the records they had. As you well know, these little guys like to hear the same song over and over and over ad infinitum. This old British song called "The World Turned Upside Down," went something like this:

If buttercups buzzed after the bee
If boats were on land, churches on sea
If ponies rode men and if grass ate the cows
If cats should be chased into holes by the mouse
If the mamas sold their babies to the gypsies for half a crown
If summer were spring and the other way round
Then all the world would be upside down.

How well I remember rocking my boys and singing that song, with tears streaming down my face—not once, not twice. Too many times. What made me cry was thinking of mamas selling their babies, with the next thought always being, "But no one would buy my babies. Who would want these babies? Who would even take them if I tried to give them away?" And I would cry. Then I would cry some more. And I would feel excruciating guilt for having those dreadful thoughts. And then I would cry some more.

My crying, through all those years, was never the sobbing, wailing kind of crying. It was never tears of rage or frustration, or even of desperation. It was just quiet tears of sadness—sadness over what was and what might have been, sadness over not having a daughter, who—of course—would have been the perfect daughter (yeah, right!) to enjoy in my old age, and sadness for my boys for what I knew was turning out to be massive limitations to their own futures.

The only thing that saved me—and I really mean this—was the strength of David Busby. He would not let me wallow in self-pity for very long. He could not bear seeing me cry. He would not let me ignore all the goodness, all the fun in our lives. Nor would he let me drift away from making love to him.

I remember that after both the 1966 diagnosis of mental retardation for Robert and the 1982 diagnosis of Fragile X for both boys, making love was the last thing I wanted to do. I just wanted to curl up in the fetal position and feel very, very, very sorry for Mary Beth. I remember that when we made love, I would cry. After all, making love had made these babies, had, in effect, caused us all this grief. It got to the point that each time we made love, David would gently stroke the corners of my eyes, feeling for tears and gently wiping them away. But what saved us both is that he insisted that we keep up with our sexual relationship. What saved us both is that I really did and do like sex. What saved us both is that because we didn't let it go, those tears in the corners of my eyes have long since disappeared. I truly think that if our sex life had gone by the wayside, the marriage itself would have cooled to the temperature of last week's ashes.

Good grief! I never thought I'd be writing to anybody about my sex life. Are we talking, "Move over, Dr. Ruth" here, or what? This is not my style, but I have to say that it is a huge part of what's made my life, and my marriage, fun and workable. If I could help just one couple with a handicapped child to stop and think of the long-term ramifications of simply ignoring or eliminating one of the major elements in a relationship, then it's worth saying. I have heard that there are marriages that are perfectly happy with no sex at all, and I have no doubt that this is true. But this ain't one of them, and, honey babe, I don't think yours is either.

The other thing that our lives require to a unique degree is patience. Parents of handicapped children simply have to develop a special brand of patience. Not only do we have to be patient with our kids' retarded pace of development, but also we have to be patient with the researchers' progress. It's a waiting game, and the innings play on at what sometimes seems to be a glacial pace. Before this last decade, it was simply a matter of accepting what was and dealing with the trials of each day. The progress that's been made in recent years, though, makes the wait seem even more intolerable, now that the cure is within our grasp. And yet, wait we must. I know you're thinking, Megan, that it's easy for me to say. After all, my boys are old enough that I don't think of the "cure" in terms of affecting them. I can assure you that if my boys were the ages of yours, I'd be even more of a wild woman, sort of camping out on the doorstep of a different researcher each month.

At my advanced stage of life, I'm just thrilled that we, who labor in this vineyard, have a chance to turn tragedy into triumph, to ensure that eventually, most children born with Fragile X can have an even chance to get into a fair lane on the track. I say, "most" because there will of course be those babies born without prenatal or postnatal care, babies who will fall through the cracks because their symptoms are subtle enough that health professionals simply miss it. They will, however, someday be the exceptions, and their number will diminish with each passing year of this new century. Clearly, we have many miles to go before we let the researchers sleep. Curing a genetic disease is not here yet. It will be, I'm convinced, but it's not here yet. What *is* here, though, what is new in this last decade, is that there are therapeutic treatments that can enhance the lives of all Fragile X children. That, too, is improving as we speak. In our day, we didn't have anything but Ritalin, which helped Robert but not Jack. So, you just have to realize how many more options you have nowadays. And be patient.

In a strange sense, parents of Fragile X children are better able to be patient while waiting for the research breakthroughs because of that special brand of patience we've been obliged to develop while raising these children. Teaching them everything, from feeding themselves to tying their shoes to wiping their bottoms to academic work, simply takes longer, is more difficult, and requires us to develop patience beyond anything we could have imagined.

We just have to take each small victory as a huge triumph and rejoice in its having occurred at all. And that, my friend, is patience.

And now, I have to get out of here before really answering your question about how long Fragile X has been around. I've (typically, right?) been focusing on my own experience with it. I promise, I'll answer your real question, and soon.

Hugs to you and John and the boys,
MBBB

PS. "The trouble with the gene pool is there's no lifeguard." (From a bumper sticker)

Dear Mary Beth,

What the palm reader saw . . . that is so intriguing. Thank you for sharing that with me. It is so helpful to see you have had experiences similar to mine. I never went to a palm reader—I would have been too chicken! However, looking back I do see things in my life that really helped prepare me for all of this.

I can just picture you as a young woman, traveling in a car with your friends. I bet the wind was blowing and the sun was shining. I imagine the day as a great one. And how you must have laughed at what she said! And maybe you never gave it another thought until Robert David Busby was developing in your womb.

Jacob (L) and Jack Massey

Oh, I am so blessed to have met you at the FRAXA Gala. You and David seem so perfect for each other and seem to have all this figured out. Like the steps that need to be taken to find a treatment or a cure for Fragile X. You no longer have to be concerned with potty training, IEPs (individual educational plan), and therapy for your children. Now you can focus on the real problem at hand. To look at you at the gala and know that you have survived all that I am going through brings me great comfort. You are so gracious and beautiful, inside and out. After reading your letter, I feel an even closer bond. You have two boys with Fragile X too! And your first son was named after David, just like my first son was named after John. Only we call him Jack, to lessen any confusion. And Jack is the name of your second son. This might get a little confusing. We named our second son Jacob.

Anyway, I must tell you that being a woman of faith, I feel the same way you must have felt about the palm readers. However, the Lord works in mysterious ways. I remember being pregnant with Jack and being prayerful about a healthy baby. I said to God in my prayer, "I could handle a little handicap, but not a lot." Where could that have come from? Maybe that is the way we are helped to prepare ourselves for what is in our future. You mentioned the overwhelming feeling you had in the St. Thomas church in New York. These must have been examples of the Holy Spirit working within us.

My Jack, my firstborn was a Caesarian birth. He was just too big. I pushed for two and one-half hours, and finally the obstetrician said we must try something else. I remember him leaning over my face. He must have thought I might be really disappointed. I couldn't have cared less. I would have done anything to get out of my misery. Jack was eight pounds nine ounces and twenty-three inches long. Dr. Bussinger told me he had never delivered a baby that long. My Jack was never in any danger during delivery. He was just happy where he was.

We didn't notice any problems until he was maybe two days old. Really! I mean two days, not two years. The pathologist thought something in his blood didn't look right. I don't even remember what it was they were testing. It was just the routine blood work. My brother-in-law, who is an ear, nose, and throat surgeon in our town, assured me that the pathologist would not find anything. He was just trying to ease my concerns. But in the end it was he who felt something just wasn't right with Jack. Jack was about two years of age when he shared that concern with us.

Jack suffered from *numerous* ear and sinus infections. He did start sleeping through the night at two weeks of age. That should have been a red flag right there! What normal baby does that? His ears drained green mucus from the time he was two months old until he was about six years old! He started getting teeth at eight weeks. I remember my sister-in-law saying we didn't need a doctor, just a dentist. Jack had a number of sinus surgeries. He had his adenoids removed, he had numerous sets of tubes in his ears, and he was even born with a hydrocele (water on the testicles) and an umbilical hernia. This was probably caused by the low muscle tone these kids have! I am a registered nurse and was teaching pediatric nursing in the practical nursing program at our community college at the time. The knowledge that gave me was just enough to be dangerous! I had learned about Fragile X in nursing school and promptly forgot about it because it would never happen to me.

Our Jack was actually misdiagnosed at age four with Sotos syndrome.[1] It was a subjective diagnosis. No blood test, just signs and symptoms. We

1 Sotos syndrome is a rare genetic disorder characterized by excessive physical growth during the first two to three years of life. The disorder may be accompanied by mild mental retardation; delayed motor, cognitive, and social development; hypotonia (low muscle tone); and speech impairments. Children with Sotos syndrome tend to be large at birth and are often taller, heavier, and have larger heads (macrocrania) than is normal for their age. Symptoms of the disorder, which vary among individuals, include a disproportionately large and long head with a slightly protrusive forehead, large hands and feet, hypertelorism (an abnormally increased distance between the eyes), and down-slanting eyes. Clumsiness, an awkward gait, and unusual aggressiveness or irritability may also occur. Although most cases of Sotos syndrome occur sporadically, familial cases have also been reported.

had this diagnosis for four years. I even became involved with the Sotos Syndrome Support Association and we attended a conference in Chicago.

My cousin Anne Souder (my mom's twin sister's daughter) was experiencing similar delays with her young son, Alec. My geneticist referred her to a geneticist in Arizona, and Alec was diagnosed with Fragile X. I quickly called my doctor and told him about her results and he said, "You mean we never tested for Fragile X?" "We?" I thought, I didn't know I was supposed to be consulted in finding a correct diagnosis for our child! I found it rather funny. We were never bitter or mad about that. It has all been time well spent. Jack, at age eight, was receiving all the services he needed. The hardest decision was to test Jacob after we found out Jack had Fragile X.

Here I was, careening from one diagnosis to another. In both cases, the doctors told me less and more than I could absorb.

Jacob was just six years old. We thought all of his behaviors were a result of imitating Jack. He had delays but not nearly to the extent his older brother did. Jacob was and still is very social and loving. His father describes him as a combination of Roger Rabbit and the Tasmanian devil. After a month of contemplation (wasted worries) we finally tested him. Jacob had Fragile X, and we were told that he was a mosaic. Isn't that amazing? Your Jack is also a Fragile X mosaic—another bond we're discovering we have.

Your family story doesn't surprise me. The older I get, the more it seems almost every family is dysfunctional in some way. I used to prefer to think my family put the "fun" in dysfunctional! My father led me to believe that we went to too many physicians, and if we were only better disciplinarians and parents, our kids would be fine. He often said, "They just need to come to Grandpa Hamsa's boot camp."

My father was an orthopedic surgeon and one of the best in the state of Nebraska, I might add. He was awesome. The nurses loved him and he was very supportive and appreciative of their work. That is probably one of the reasons I became a nurse. My father was enthusiastic, smart, funny, kind, and gentle. However, genetics was not one of his strong suits. I don't think he really believed in all of the jargon we were throwing at him. He used to tease us about the different diagnoses we were coming up with. After all we lived with a Sotos syndrome child for four years and now both the children have Fragile X.

About this same time, my middle sister, Kristy (who is not a carrier for Fragile X), had her third child. His name is Robby. He was born profoundly deaf. Robby and Jacob were about three weeks apart. Everyone in the family got on board the deaf train. My parents and my two older sisters along with their families live in Omaha. They were so supportive of Robby. They took sign language classes and attended workshops on deafness. I took sign language classes here as well at the community college. I never had to use it with my boys. I did it so I could communicate with Robby. You might be thinking that I was feeling a little left out and quite frankly I may have been. I was frustrated that some of my loved ones ignored the fact that Fragile X was in our family.

In the beginning, my hero was my mother's oldest sister, Gail. She happens to live right next door to my mom and dad. She was so genuinely interested and concerned. She marched right down to the genetics clinic at the Munroe-Myers Institute in Omaha and was tested. She was not a carrier. My mother has a younger sister, Susie, who tested positive as did her youngest daughter, who was in her thirties when she found out she had Fragile X. My mom's twin, Aunt Daphne, was also a carrier as were her two girls, Anne and Lisa.

I have started to ramble and time is running out. The kids will be home soon and the peace and quiet will end. Your tears and the difficult time you had was sad for me to read about. We are both fortunate to have supportive spouses. I have been so blessed to have John. I think you told me 80 percent of marriages with special-needs children end in divorce. Not this one! We are committed for the long haul. It is a journey we can be thankful for, some days more then others! I know God gave us these children for a reason and they are created in His image. This has helped me immensely. Don't get me wrong, I have had

Jack (L) and Jacob Massey

tears too. Just mourning the loss of the child I planned on. But my two boys have taught me way more about life and what is important then any other "normal" child could ever have. I truly believe that. Humility has been a big lesson!

And yes, you are so right. Fragile X parents are better able to be patient while waiting for the research breakthroughs. FRAXA is a prime example of that statement. Parents working together, making a difference in the areas that will solve the mystery of Fragile X.

It is a red-letter day at my house when I have a letter in the mailbox from Mary Beth Busby!

Love,

Megan 🖂

3

Dropping Bread Crumbs

Dear Megan,

OK, now I'm back with a bit more time and, hopefully, some more information. I didn't know whether to laugh or cry when I got your letter. For you to ask me, of all people on the face of this planet, how long Fragile X has been around and to give you some background on it gave me a sense of someone asking Jack Busby, my youngest son, to give a clinical description of one of his asthma attacks. No way am I qualified to do that. I do hear you, though, when you say that the doctor told you more than you could absorb, and told it too quickly, for you to be able to "get it." The thing that was even more frustrating for us in 1982 when we got our diagnosis was that they didn't even have information to hand out to patients. Now material is available, which of course is not to say that most doctors have it or give it out to parents.

I realize that part of the reason you want me to tell you what I know is that you know that I really don't know much and that what little I do know is pretty basic stuff—just the bare bones—and presumably easy to absorb. You're right about that. I would also urge you to spend some time reading the FRAXA listserv. I can't possibly convey to you how different things today are from the days when we got our diagnosis on the boys. To think that any day of the week, you can log on to www.fraxa.org and hear from other parents going through exactly what you and John are going through, is truly marvelous. You have to get used to hearing the kids referred to as "fraggles," and some of the other shorthand, but, gosh, it's such a great service for parents.

The booklet on Fragile X , put out by the National Institute of Child Health and Human Development (NICHD), is excellent, and I'm sending you several of those. I hope you'll share them with all of your health professionals, as well as with the boys' teachers. I know you also have our FRAXA brochure, plus the enormously helpful information from the National Fragile X Foundation. But I know what you mean. You want more. You want to be able to answer your friends' questions—friends, that is, who have the nerve to ask you. My experience over the years has been that so many people don't ask much about it. I've never been sure whether it's because they're not interested or because they think it's painful for me to talk about. Or, in my case, it may be because they think I'm going to ask them for money if they're too interested. After all these years of fund-raising for FRAXA and other causes, I think I may have become the sort of woman who causes people to think that if they see me coming, they'd better check to be sure their wallet is in place. Given a choice, however, I rather prefer my friends' checkbooks to their wallets.

Basically, people who do ask you want to know what causes Fragile X. I think people tend to think of birth defects as unfortunate accidents of nature. Now that we have the map of all of the genes in our bodies, however, we can begin to understand what causes Fragile X. It may be the simplest genetic disease to understand, in that it's just a malfunction of one gene on the X chromosome. This gene is called the FMR1 gene, and the protein you need to make it function is called FMRP. Dr. David Nelson, who—along with Drs Steve Warren and Ben Oostra—cloned the Fragile X gene in 1991, told me there are 1,114 genes on the X chromosome, and the FMR1 gene is just one of them. To think that all of our kids' other forty-five chromosomes are "fine" and that only one of the 1,114 genes on the X chromosome is "not fine" makes you feel all the more unlucky. But there we are. And, oh, Megan, we just have to keep reminding ourselves that there are a lot of other genes, too, that could have been "not fine."

Now, to complicate things a bit more—and I never would say to anyone that Fragile X is simple—Robert and Jennifer Darnell and Steve Warren state in their article, "The Fragile X Mental Retardation Protein, FMRP, Recognizes G Quartets" (*Mental Retardation and Developmental Disabilities Research Reviews,* volume 10:49-52, 2004) that there are other genes involved, genes that also are controlled by the FMRP protein. These other genes may account for some of the symptoms that some Fragile X kids have and others don't—things like seizures, macro-orchidism, flat feet, and the long, thin faces and big ears that some of them have. This provides important insight into the function of the FMRP protein, making it all the more necessary to figure out a way to get that protein to function again.

I don't know how much history of Fragile X you really want to know, but you can just skim over this if it's too much. I am afraid I just want to know everything—even things I can't understand. I didn't know I was that way until I got into this research stuff. So I'll tell you what I have learned.

Fragile X does have a much longer history than would seem apparent, especially considering how few people have ever heard of it. In 1943, two doctors in England, James P. Martin and Julia Bell, studied a family with more than one mentally retarded male. I suppose we might say that Martin and Bell began dropping bread crumbs. They noted that their subjects all had the long, thin face, the large ears, and the enlarged testes (referred to in journals as macro-orchidism[1]) that have become familiar symptoms. Their article was published in the *Journal of Neural Psychiatry*. The entire history of Fragile X is described in a 1994 article by Renata Laxova, M.D., Ph.D., in *Advances in* Pediatrics, vol. 41, pages 305-342. Dr. Laxova is a professor of Medical Genetics and Pediatrics at the University of Wisconsin at Madison. I obtained the article through the Mosby document service. If you would like, I'll send you a copy. It's quite a lengthy article, about thirty-five pages, so it may be more than you care to slog through at this point.

I gather that not a lot had been written about mental retardation before 1943, though in 1938, L. S. Penrose, a British researcher, had noted that a lot more males than females were in institutions for the mentally retarded. At the time, it was thought that families found it easier to keep their mentally handicapped daughters at home, where they were capable of doing simple chores. Nobody knew then that there was such a thing as X-linked mental retardation and that there really were more retarded males than females.

The predominance of X-linked male retardation, we can now recognize, is because a male child has one X chromosome, which he gets from his mother, and one Y chromosome, which he gets from his father. A female child, on the other hand, has two X chromosomes, one from each parent. Hence, if a female child inherits an X chromosome with a premutation for Fragile X from one parent, she still gets a presumably "good" one from the other parent and is, therefore, less handicapped—if handicapped at all. If a male child, however, inherits his mother's X with the Fragile site, he's going

1 Macroorchidism is a condition manifested by larger than normal testicles, which many—if not most—Fragile X males have. It hits along with puberty, though rather than a hormonal thing, it's a connective tissue thing. Interestingly, knock-out mice (mice from which the FMR1 gene has been removed for research purposes) develop enlarged testicles too. Also interestingly, Fragile X males have decreased sex drive, according to Dr. Michael Tranfaglia of the FRAXA Research Foundation, but they are not sterile. "In fact their sperm has only premutations in it, so they can have perfectly normal kids," says Dr. Tranfaglia, "though all the girls will be carriers."

to be, in all likelihood, mentally handicapped. In other words, whether you and I might have passed along our "good" one or our "bad" one to our boys was the luck of the draw.

In 1966, a young scientist at the Yale Child Study Center, Herb Lubs, saw chromosome studies on a family with two sons exhibiting developmental delay. This family had been referred for genetic studies. When these studies were read by Joan Samuelson, the chief technologist of the cytogenetics lab—who, by the way, still retains that position—she brought the results to Dr. Lubs. He likes to give Joan Samuelson credit for seeing something unusual on the X chromosome of those two boys. She didn't know what it was, but there seemed to be a break at the twenty-seventh section of the long arm of the X chromosome. That's down at the bottom. It just didn't look right, that's all, and both she and Herb Lubs knew it. They were catching a glimpse of those bread crumbs dropped by Martin and Bell more than twenty years earlier.

Herb Lubs's overall career goal at the time was to apply the principles of Mendelian genetics[2] to clinical medicine. Hence, he was fascinated with the

2 Gregor Mendel is considered to have been the father of genetics—that is, by those who don't consider that Charles Darwin was with his *Origin of the Species*, which gave us the theoretical underpinning of modern biology. Darwin's theory, dealing with large populations of living things, did not explain how traits are passed from one generation to the next. Mendel, an Austrian monk, wrote a paper called "Experiments in Plant Hybridization," published in 1865. He provided the basis for the mathematical analysis of inheritance, using crossbreeding of garden peas. Mendel died in 1884, and it was two decades later before his work was rediscovered. Even though he was not recognized in his own lifetime, he now has his very own adjective, as in Mendelian genetics. Not too bad a legacy.

I read this about Mendel in a marvelous little book called *The First Hundred Years* by David Micklos, with Susan Zehl, Daniel Schechter, and Ellen Skaggs, which the Cold Spring Harbor Laboratory published in recognition of the strides that have been made in the field of genetics. I picked it up at a conference at the Branbury Center at Cold Spring Harbor one year.

And now another footnote that, to me, is simply interesting. I recently read a review (I read few books but lots of reviews) in the *New York Times* of a book on psychiatry. The reviewer, Andrew Solomon, who has written about depression, said that Hippocrates, in the fifth century BC, said that mental illness was a medical problem based on an organic dysfunction of the brain, which—now get this—could be addressed with oral remedies. Plato, on the other hand, argued that mental illness was a philosophical problem, and that character was determined by early experience, rather than by biology. This argument shifted in the Middle Ages, when some believed that mental illness was a religious problem and that "madmen" were possessed and should be exorcised. Thus began the different perceptions of mental illness. There were and are those who believe it's a biological problem and those who feel that it's a result of experience or perhaps lack of religious "health." That's all fascinating to me because old Hippocrates, back in the fifth century BC, was clearly onto something. I'll bet he would not have been a bit surprised when, in the twentieth century AD, it became possible to look at a slide and see that Fragile site on the X chromosome. He also, I'll bet again, would not be surprised to learn that in the twenty-first century, it appears there will indeed be oral remedies. Does what goes around come around? You bet.

notion of a family with X-linked mental retardation. His next step was a 1967 trip to North Carolina for his subjects' Fourth of July family reunion. His great good fortune was that this family, too, was interested in learning why there were such disparate levels of intelligence among its members. All I can say is that Herb is lucky it wasn't my family's reunion. He would have been ridden out of town on a rail. The trip to that family reunion, where Dr. Lubs obtained numerous blood samples as well as revealing photographs, formed the basis for a genetic profile of some of the characteristics of Fragile X. His article, "A Marker X Chromosome," was published in April 1967 in the *American Journal of Human Genetics* (vol.21, pages 231-244). The result was that since the X chromosome served as a specific diagnostic tool, it provided the possibility of prenatal diagnosis in some of the families with X-linked mental retardation. I say "some" because the Fragile site seemed to occur in the studies of about one-third of these families. If this was happening now, instead of in the dark ages thirty-five years ago, the DNA test would pick it up in each and every study. Even with the limitations of the old cytogenetic test, though, this was still a giant step forward in the attempt to make a diagnosis—even if only to rule out Fragile X.

The thing that pleases me so about Herb Lubs is that he has continued his interest in Fragile X over these thirty-odd years since he first saw that microscope slide in 1966. He serves on FRAXA's board of scientific advisors, and his reviews of grant proposals have carried great weight. He loves to look at something from many different angles. I do too, but I have to have someone like Herb Lubs point those angles out to me in pretty simple terms. He's great at that.

Dr. Lubs reminds me that in the early days, a researcher studying a family might see the Fragile site on some cells using the old cytogenetic test, which was the only method available before the DNA test was developed. Then, however, upon repeating that same test, the cells would appear to be normal. This of course led to an enormous amount of skepticism over whether they were indeed dealing with "a syndrome"—especially since even the physical features were inconsistent. Not all Fragile X males have the physical characteristics we tend to associate with Fragile X, like the long, thin faces, the large ears, and the macro-orchidism. Couple that with the fact that even the chromosome studies on the same person didn't always match and you have a picture of the massive frustration with which those early researchers were dealing.

Dr Lubs says that for clinical geneticists, "an informative family remains the primary source for the discovery of new information." Reading that made me realize that if I wanted to contribute to the research effort, I had to find other ways to help, as my family simply didn't deal with Fragile X. The studies published by Dr. Lubs changed forever the notion that genes were simple beads on a string that were inherited unchanged from generation to generation. They do, indeed, change; and that's where those mystifying CGG repeats come into play.

So, just what are CGG repeats? Cytosine, guanine, and guanine—that's literally what they are. They're nucleotides, or enzymes. They, along with adenine and thymine, make up that remarkably small alphabet with which the entire human genome is spelled. The sequences in which these "letters" are arranged construct the messages that lead the body to produce key proteins. All genes in the body have all four of these letters, arranged in a different way. Steve Warren explained to me that one small part of the Fragile X gene (called FMR1) has just two of the four letters arranged in a CGG pattern. If you were to look at a chromosome study of a normal person, the X chromosome would show a string of repeats that would go CGG CGG CGG CGG CGG. etc.—on up to forty or so. In a carrier for Fragile X, those repeats would keep on going up to anywhere from sixty to two hundred.

What happens if you're really unlucky is that this repetition—CGG CGG— doesn't stop at forty or even fifty. Instead, it keeps increasing in successive generations. If it gets up to sixty or more, that fetus becomes a carrier for Fragile X, or a premutation. Then, if it gets beyond two hundred repeats, that person is "affected" with Fragile X.

Judith Benkendorf, a geneticist in Washington, describes the repeat process that could lead to a fetus being affected with Fragile X. She says it's as if you were saying, "The cow jumped over the moon, the cow jumped over the moon, the cow jumped over the moon, the cow jumped over, jumped over, jumped over, jumped over," and on and on. This FMR1 gene kind of spins out of control; and when that happens, that one gene just wears itself out and dies. Unfortunately, this is one gene you really need to have working in order for the brain to develop and function properly.

One other thing I have to add is that I rather recently learned that the higher number of CGG repeats a woman has, the greater chance that she will have an affected child. Indeed, with my eighty repeats, there was a 57.8 percent chance—more than fifty-fifty odds, right?

The first prenatal diagnosis for Fragile X was in late 1981 by the late Dr. Ed Jenkins at the New York State Institute for Basic Research in Development Disabilities on Staten Island. The year 1982 is generally regarded as the year prenatal diagnoses were first achieved. (These, of course, were from blood drawn from individuals. The molecular prenatal test wasn't available until Grant Sutherland did the first one in 1991.) In 1983, we took Robert and Jack to Staten Island for a complete workup with Dr. W. Ted Brown. As far as I know, he and Dr. Randi Hagerman at the University of California at Davis are still the best in that business, though by now there are many more clinics that do the testing. My gynecologist in Washington, by the way, now does the Fragile X carrier test on any pregnant patient who reports mental disorders in her family. Way to go, Dr. Fraga. Should this be a no-brainer for all ob-gyns, or what? The only thing better—and it truly would be better—would be to test a young woman before she becomes pregnant, so that she could know her carrier status. Whenever I get to feeling frustrated over what seems to be the snail's pace of the medical establishment's march—make that baby steps—toward informing the public and promoting testing, I have to keep reminding myself that, hey, it was only about twenty years ago that it became possible to diagnose the problem.

I was at a meeting of Don Bailey's advisory board for his newborn screening project. Both Dr. Steve Warren and Dr. David Nelson were there, and I asked them for a bit of their own history with Fragile X. They, as I've mentioned, cloned the FMR1 gene, along with Dr. Ben Oostra of the Netherlands, in 1991. They told me that although they had attended a couple of the same meetings in Vermont in 1982 and 1983, they didn't actually meet until they found themselves at Dr. James Watson's Cold Spring Harbor Laboratory in New York in 1988 for the first annual meeting on Mapping and Sequencing the Human Genome. David Nelson and Ben Oostra had a rather "abrupt" first meeting when David, having been given a key to what he assumed was his very own room, went to open the door and found the chain lock connected. It turned out that this was also the room of Ben Oostra, who had not been told to expect a roommate and who had gone to bed. David slept on a rollaway bed, and these two—along with Steve Warren—went on to drop very large bread crumbs indeed, making history.

David and Steve, in those days before most people had E-mail, did all of their codiscovery work by phone and fax, while keeping in touch with Ben Oostra in the Netherlands. David Nelson, who is at Baylor, says that the great thing about working with someone in Europe is that, with the time difference, one of them was always awake. Steve Warren remembers that at one point, the fax machine in his department at Emory University was literally smoking—as in burned up. The good news is that their intellects were also "smoking," hence, the FMR1 gene became one of the first genes to be cloned as part of the Human Genome Project.

Steve remembers that the first Fragile X meeting was here in Washington in 1983. I think I attended a little bit of that meeting. How I heard about it, I don't know, frankly. All I know is that at that point, having just gotten the diagnosis the year before, I was completely incapable of functioning in any participatory way. I'm sure I've repressed what little I did hear and see, and this is why I literally have no memory of what I suppose was a historic meeting. I saw no bread crumbs that day.

Perhaps I would have gotten involved in the research earlier if I had known that the researchers were going to meet in such neat places, like Dunk Island, Australia (where Dr. Ted Brown met his wife, Donna, who was then working for Dr. Randi Hagerman), in 1985; Sicily in 1987; New York in 1989, and Oxford, England, in 1990. An especially memorable meeting was organized by Jean-Louis Mandel and the late Isabelle Oberlé in Strasbourg, France, in 1991. It was memorable for two reasons. One reason is that it was held outside of Strasbourg in a glorious inn with a four-star restaurant that was owned by a bank and used for its managerial meetings. Depending on your priorities, however, you just might think that the most important thing about that meeting was that it took place right after Warren, Nelson, and Oostra had cloned the FMR1 gene. David Nelson says that Warren and Oostra came up with that name, FMR1. He said that Jean-Louis Mandel was amused because FMR1 is pronounced like the French word *éphémère* (ephemeral). The only problem with these meetings of researchers, Megan, is that folks like you and I can't understand a thing they say. It's literally a different language. That's why the biannual conferences that the National Fragile X Foundation has are so valuable for parents. You can hear the researchers tell a vastly simplified version of what they're doing, and you can ask your questions. Even dumb questions like mine are acceptable.

But golly, just look at all that has happened in the field of Fragile X research in the past twenty-odd years. How many bread crumbs have been dropped, and how quickly, now, they're being picked up! My poker-playing friend Ted Brown might say we're now beginning to pick up the chips.

So this, Megan, is my very long answer to your very simple question of how long Fragile X has "been around."

Just be grateful that you and John had your babies in the 1980s, rather than in the dark ages of the '60s, when the Busby boys were born. At least now, some pediatricians know about Fragile X. We had no clue.

Fondly,
Mary Beth

PS. "The true men of action in our time, those who transform the world, are not the politicians and statesmen, but the scientists." (W. H. Auden, *The Dyer's Hand*," 1962.) ✉

Dear Mary Beth,

Your explanation of Fragile X was quite helpful, as was the advice on sources to seek for more information. Plus, I can only imagine the long years of frustration for you and David, as you sought a diagnosis. And to think that you had no Internet and no listserv to help you deal with behavioral problems!

I have been on the FRAXA listserv and have found it very helpful. In fact, that is how I first met Dr. Mike Tranfaglia. I wrote him asking advice on medication for Jack. John and I were so thrilled when he wrote us back. I found myself wanting to give all the support I could to others. I am a "fixer" and want everyone to be happy. At times it was overwhelming. I would receive forty to fifty E-mails and it took a lot of time to read through it all. If I forgot to unsubscribe before leaving town, I would find myself swamped with letters I wanted to respond to upon returning home. Using the digest form, which combines all the messages into one large message sent daily, turned out to be the best solution for me.

The NICHD brochures are great. I have ordered more for myself. There are many people in my life who need to read this.

I found your statement, "the higher the number of CGG repeats a woman has, the greater chance that she will have an affected child" absolutely phenomenal! I actually have never been tested. We certainly know it came from me. Doctors tell me I'm not affected but what do they know?

Some days I hope I am affected, in that it would bring hope to others who may be diagnosed or have a girl with Fragile X. It is so less obvious in girls. I use my X as an excuse, often. Only in fun, of course. I'm hoping to get the testing done through a research study. It is rather expensive, but I must admit I'm curious.

So you don't think there is a lifeguard for the gene pool? I realize you saw it on a bumper sticker, but it is quite a thought. I think there is—we have much to learn from our kids. They have much to offer. It may not be in the traditional sense of contributing to society by being a rocket scientist, but these kids are loving and kind. Maybe I'm still in a little denial, but I feel that they definitely have a purpose and it is up to me to help them find it. Some days I think the purpose may be to drive me crazy, but our God is a kind and loving God who wants us to become more like Him.

Jack and Jacob certainly bring me to my knees!

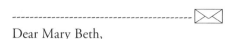

Someday we will meet our Maker and we'll have an opportunity to ask all of these questions. However, if it will be as glorious as I think, it won't even matter. And besides that, maybe it will all be solved by then. We can only hope!

Have a great week and thanks again for your support.

Megan, John, Jack, and Jacob ✉

4

Diagnosis and Dealing

Dear Megan,

Your question about what a long process it must have been, back in the dark ages of the '60s and '70s, to get a diagnosis of Fragile X, has caused me to revisit and dig around in some partially buried territory.

Trying to put myself in your place, with all you now know, I realize it's hard for you and other young mothers to imagine the many years we spent trying to figure out why our boys were mentally retarded—before the discovery of Fragile X. I'll admit it was frustrating to know that they were mentally retarded but not to know what the problem was.

I remember so well—all too well—when we got the original diagnosis of mental retardation for Robert. He was two years old, and while his development hadn't been dramatically slower than normal, it had finally become clear that something was wrong, something was not happening. This was complicated by the fact that I had never been around a child before. I had only one sibling, an older brother; my few cousins were about my age or older, and I had never even babysat. Quite simply, I hadn't thought much about what babies were supposed to be doing and when. I had the usual baby book, which I filled in enthusiastically at first, then dutifully, then reluctantly, and finally not at all. Same thing with Jack, though to a lesser degree. With Jack's book, I didn't even keep up the effort for long. It was just too depressing to read what he was supposed to be doing when he wasn't doing it. For instance, Robert didn't sit up until he was nine months old, didn't crawl until ten months, didn't walk until sixteen months. Definitely late, but not so late for the doctor to say, "Whoa, here. We've got a problem." Maybe he thought it, but he sure didn't say it. Jack was actually a bit later than Robert with those early milestones. And talking wasn't happening. Babbling, but no words. Robert didn't say a word until he was six years old.

You were asking me the other day when I first heard about Fragile X and at what stages our boys were at that point. It was in 1982, when Robert was eighteen and Jack was about to turn seventeen. Our wonderful pediatrician, Fred Burke, called me and said, "Mary Beth, I think I finally know what's wrong with the boys. I've just learned about a newly discovered birth defect called Fragile X, and I think you should get them tested for it." I remember that I was in the laundry room folding laundry when I got that call. Fred said that it was a blood test, but not a simple one because only a few labs in the country were doing it. This was back when labs were doing the old cytogenetic test, before they learned how to do the DNA test. This fact also meant that the test was not quite so accurate. Frankly, I never doubted the results of ours.

I was reluctant about having the tests done, because the boys had been through so many, many tests over the years. They had had EEGs, chromosome studies, what seemed like endless psychological tests, hearing tests, and I hated to subject them to more. I also had a gut feeling, from what Fred said, that they did have Fragile X, and I didn't know how to deal with a genetic diagnosis. My gut feeling was also that it would be trouble, but I had no idea just how much trouble. I don't even know why I had the foreboding sense that my life was about to become complicated in a way I wouldn't welcome, but I sure did have that sense.

Tulsa was one of the few places the Fragile X test was being done, and since we were soon to go down to Ada, Oklahoma, for our annual Fourth of July reunion at the Busby cabin anyway, we made the appointment for the day after the reunion.

David and I and the boys drove from Ada to Tulsa and went straight to the Children's Hospital at St. Francis, where we were received by the geneticist with great enthusiasm. She was clearly thrilled to see us. After all, here were two live ones. Fragile X was then so little known that to get families to come in for the diagnostic tests was pretty rare. She was downright elated, which of course I found pretty darned depressing. She told us a little about Fragile X, enough for me to grasp what was devastating for me: that a boy child can only get Fragile X from the mother. I felt as if I had been kicked in the stomach. I was as "down" as the geneticist was "up."

After our appointment with the geneticist, we went across the street to a Red Lobster restaurant. Jack, of course, immediately wanted assurance that he'd be able to get something besides fish, since he's allergic to shellfish and so rejects all fish. I assume the boys were well enough behaved at that lunch. I don't remember anything except that I was so depressed with the enormity of what I had just learned. This was catastrophic damage to my already fragile ego. Here I had visited this plague upon the entire house of Busby. It was all my fault. Guilty as charged. I could hardly wait to run out and buy myself a T-shirt with a big red X on it.

I didn't darken the door of another Red Lobster again for sixteen years. I couldn't even drive by one without dredging up the memory of that dreadful day—until a few summers ago, when I took Robert to a Red Lobster in Oklahoma City on our way to the airport to meet David who was arriving from Washington. It was a fine summer day, it was time for our Busby reunion, FRAXA was going great guns, and I was feeling hopeful about the research and good about my role in life. I was even feeling fortunate and thinking that Fragile X was not something that God had done *to* me, but rather something He had done *for* me—giving me a rare opportunity to make a difference. I thought, "OK, this is the day to get over this Red Lobster nonsense." I felt good all the way through the lunch at Red Lobster, especially because Robert so adores fish and was thrilled with my choice of a restaurant. Ordinarily, it's a tuna sandwich at Subway. After a pleasant lunch, we went on to the airport, and my phobia about Red Lobster restaurants was history.

You were wondering how we had raised the boys, not knowing about Fragile X. We simply raised them as two mentally retarded boys, because that's what they were. When we got the diagnosis of Fragile X, they were eighteen and almost seventeen (wonderful family planning there, having babies less than seventeen months apart. And, believe it or not, it was not an accident. We wanted four children, and I wanted to have them all by the time I was thirty. And having adored being pregnant the first time, I was ready to repeat the whole process right away. Needless to say, in retrospect, this was not a cool move.), and we had made sure that they got all the special ed services, just as we would have done if they had had Down syndrome or any other handicapping condition—even though we had no real diagnosis, no label, no brand name. Even so, there was that still, small voice that often whispered to me, "There may be something else going on here."

And now, dear Megan, a still small voice is telling me to dash to the Safeway to get something for dinner tonight. I'll get back to this diagnostic saga later on, OK?

Love to you,

MBBB ✉

Dear Megan,

As drawn out as our diagnostic process was, I have to say that I hear stories––as surely you do too, especially having lived one yourself—that, even today, are almost as bad. Worse, really. In our case, the process took so long simply because no one had ever heard of Fragile X in the 1960s and 1970s. That was a darned good excuse for not getting a diagnosis.

The best we could come up with, in those days, was a straight diagnosis of mental retardation. Of course, this was before mental retardation began to be called "developmental disability," "mentally challenged," "mental disability," or "intellectual disability."

Our closest friends in New York, where we were living when the boys were born, were T George and Sheila Harris. Sheila gave birth to the youngest of their four, Gardiner (now a crackerjack reporter for the *New York Times*), just two and one-half months before Robert was born. Sheila and I "did baby" together, which was wonderful for me but not wonderful for her, sensing—as she did, early on— that something was not right with Robert. She had reason to know, as their second child and only girl, Annie, has Down syndrome.

One day, something came up in our conversation about our sort of maybe thinking possibly we just might have some tests done on Robert, to see why he wasn't yet talking. I was clearly avoiding this like the plague and my end of the conversation was likely full of nervous chatter and avoidance of what was really worrying me. Finally, Sheila said to me, "Well, I would want to know." The minute she said that, I realized, with a cold chill, that she did know. And I knew too.

Sheila's remark brought forth in me some recognition that I could no longer avoid the process of exploring the problem. I made an appointment, through our pediatrician, with a neurologist at Columbia Presbyterian. Before we could see him, though, a whole battery of tests was required, to rule out all sorts of things such as a hearing deficit. We had to have Robert admitted to the hospital for an overnight stay, and they would not let me stay with him. Nowadays, a mother wouldn't put up with that. She would simply say, "Well, I'm staying." Who knows, maybe I could have done that back then, if I had been forceful. But I was too fragile to be forceful.

I have very few memories of those two days in the hospital, clearly having long since repressed them, but I do remember that when David and I arrived at 8:30 the next morning, they wheeled Robert into the room in a stroller with restraints. They had tied my baby down. They had just taken him for an EEG, and they had put this gucky stuff in his hair, which made it stand straight up on end. He was the scariest looking thing I'd ever seen, and it was a toss-up as to whether Robert or I was the more hysterical.

Our appointment with the neurologist was a week or two after the hospital stay. I remember despising him on sight because he was going to give us bad news. He was probably the world's nicest guy, but no one was ever going to get me to think that. Kill the messenger would have been more like my mind-set. He said what we knew he would, though David and I have remarked, and even laughed, many times since then about the way this neurologist talked in double negatives, saying things like: "There is no reason to believe that this child will not be mentally retarded." And, "There is no reason why you should not start looking around for an institution." I remember he said that we shouldn't think in terms of education because Robert wasn't educable, but that we should simply try to teach him his limits. I guess he meant so that he wouldn't run out in the traffic or walk straight into the fireplace or something.

On the way home on the subway, David was unusually strict with Robert. It was as if he had taken the doctor's admonition to heart. Maybe, in retrospect, I should thank that doctor for having participated on some level in our disciplinary tactics, which—I'm convinced—have made a difference over the years. What I think he meant for us to carry out of that office was the notion that we had to get control over Robert's behavior and to keep that control, and that you can't keep control if you never got it in the first place. Our boys really do try to behave and obey, for the most part. It's much more difficult for Robert, who does this oppositional bit, such as if you say, "Robert, I really don't want you to drink another Coke today," he will go straight, to get a Coke. Happens all the time. Come to think of it, though, I think that may be a "guy thing" that is simply magnified in these kids. I can't help noting that if David and I are pulling into a parking lot and if I say, "Hey, that looks like a good parking place right over there," there is no way on God's green earth that David Busby is going to park in that place. But, basically, when the boys understand that you really and truly and seriously mean for them to do something, they tend to get the message and try to do it. So thanks, Dr. Neurologist—I guess.

Before we left the neurologist's office, we asked if we could bring Jack to see him, and he said yes. We took Jack a couple of weeks later. The doctor said that while he understood our concern about Jack, he didn't really share it. He was a bit slow, but not alarmingly so. He said let's just watch him.

We were relieved with that little sliver of hope for Jack. I recalled that as I was leaving the hospital with Jack after he was born, our pediatrician had stopped me in the hall, looked at Jack sleeping in my arms, and said, "Now this is a good one." A chill skimmed over me as I wondered, "Is he saying that the other one, the first one, is a bad one?" This was about eight months before we got the diagnosis on Robert. So, after the neurologist's somewhat encouraging words, we were content to let Jack be for the time being. Maybe God knew how much we could take at one time.

During those first weeks after Robert's diagnosis, each morning when I awoke (this would be after having been up most of the night with first one and then the other baby), the first sensation I had was a stinging of tears in my eyes. I literally began each day crying.

Six months after Robert's diagnosis, when Robert was two and a half and Jack was one year old, we moved from New York to Washington, where we had hoped and planned to move since before we were married. The first thing we did, after finding a house to rent for a year, was to advertise in the *Washington Post* for a nanny to live in and help with the boys. Since neither boy had yet to sleep through a night—not one, ever—I was frazzled to the point of near collapse. It's difficult for me to revisit those days of being so tired all the time. I guess the only good thing was that I was too tired to do a lot of thinking about the magnitude of our problems, especially since we were not yet thinking of Jack as a problem. By that time, he had developed both asthma and dermatitis, and we thought of those as his problems. I must say, that holds true to this day. Jack's asthma and dermatitis remain our chief concerns for his health and job security—really more than his functional deficits.

Speaking of functional deficits. If I don't stop this chatter and get laundry done, David Busby will not be a happy camper tomorrow morning when he starts getting dressed. So, I'm outta here, Megan girl.

But with love,
MBBB

P.S "You must work—we must all work to make the world worthy of its children." (Pablo Casals) ✉

Dear Mary Beth,

It was so good for me to read about all your "diagnosis and dealing". Seeing you now as I do, I often think that you must have had it all figured out from the start. You are so focused and goal oriented on the mission of FRAXA. You seem so knowledgeable about the research. How did you ever have time to learn it all? And did you know about FRAXA from the time it started? How did you hear about it?

Reading about your struggles actually brought some comfort to me. It is good for me to know that you have been there too and there is some light at the end of the tunnel!

Your friend Sheila reminds me of my friend Helen. Helen actually cut out an article from the newspaper in Lincoln (which is about four hundred miles from Scottsbluff) about a family with two boys who had Fragile X. She put it in her cookie jar, where it stayed for years. Since we had received the diagnosis of Sotos syndrome for Jack, she felt it wasn't necessary to share. But in her heart, I know Helen wondered if Jack and Jacob had Fragile X. Why didn't she ever throw it away? She finally gave it to me when we received the correct diagnosis in 1997. I actually contacted the family in the article and we talked briefly, but no further relationship was pursued by either of us.

It must have been hard just labeling your boys as mentally retarded. It seems so harsh. Now we have much more politically correct terms like mental impairment or Fragile X.

I remember when my cousin Anne received the diagnosis for her son, Alec. He was five at the time. She came to visit us in Scottsbluff and we had a great weekend together, but she was adamant about the fact that she didn't want us to test our kids! She must have been very frightened and still in some denial about having a child with Fragile X.

Disregarding her advice, we tested Jack in October of 1997, and a month later we tested Jacob. Both confirmed Fragile X. John and I were never bitter. We saw it as something God had presented to us and we would find ways to meet the challenges.

One way for us to meet that challenge was to find people to help out with the boys. I was still working occasionally as a registered nurse. I always said, "Children don't run your life, babysitters do!" Thank you for your support and encouragement to continue with a search for people to help out. Sometimes I think about other moms who can do it all, but it's just a little different with two "fraggles" in your home. One of our special sitters was Betty Roberts. She was so incredible. She cooked the boys homemade meals, read them books, cuddled and rocked them (when they would let her). She drove them to preschool or wherever they needed to be. She went through all the diagnosis searching with us, but more then anything she just loved the boys and they loved her! Jack still enjoys watching *The Price Is Right* because he used to watch it with Betty.

The other gift to us was the Sweeney twins, Holly and Heather. They lived just one quarter mile up the road. They babysat for us from the time they were twelve years old until they went off to college. We brought them to New York when author Mary Jane Clark chaired the Mary Higgins Clark Gala for FRAXA at Tavern on the Green. Holly was our main gal, and her twin, Heather, sat mostly for my brother-in-law Jim and his wife Dallas, who lived next door. But usually one of them was always available. Holly went on vacations with us, attended family reunions, and even went on a Disney Cruise with my family. She was truly an angel! She is now a schoolteacher in Arizona. We sure miss her and so do the boys! Sure, we have found others, but some will never replace the ones who really touch your heart in a special way. They were so easygoing and never complained. They were always grateful for the work. They cooked, did crafts with the boys, and usually had an outside physical activity planned. They were thrifty! When they both moved away, we hoped their younger sister Lisa would fill their shoes, but not a chance! She was quite the social butterfly and had very little interest in sitting. When she did stay with the boys, we had a curfew!

Twin babysitters, Heather (L) and Holly Sweeney with Jack (L) and Jacob Massey

I always believe when God closes a door he always opens a window, and with that I trust more sitters will come around. We will persevere. I bet there will come a time when I need boy role models. When they are fifteen and thirteen, they probably shouldn't be hanging out with sixteen-year-old babes.

Take care and tell David Hello.

Love,

Megan ✉

Megan, dear one,

Your letter about your search for help for you, your house, and your boys sure brought back memories. My first memory is this sense of panic. How on earth can I keep on managing without some help? But who in her right mind would take us on? But you know what? Miracles do happen.

Until we moved to Washington from New York, I had a wonderful woman come in two afternoons a week. During the last weeks of my pregnancy with Jack, it increased to one afternoon and one full day. Mazelle Greaves always came on Wednesday around 9:30 to stay with Robert and clean our apartment. I would get on the subway and go up to Columbia Presbyterian Hospital for my ob appointment. It was always perfectly routine, and this was the most routine of pregnancies. Not a whisper of a complication here, you understand. No problem.

After my appointment was the fun part. I would get back on the subway and get off at Times Square, buy a bag of scrumptious roasted cashew nuts (this was lunch, of course) at the station, then munch them while walking to a theater to see a show I'd already picked out in the *New York Times* and to try to get a ticket for that day's matinee performance. I had phenomenal luck. I had fun. I adored the theater. I adored my husband, my baby, my life. It was the best of days, those Wednesdays in 1965. And having Mazelle Greaves at home with Robert made the fun of those Wednesdays possible. So, I guess I have to say that I learned early on that having some help is a good life plan.

Then fast-forward to our move to Washington the next year, with two babies. No help. No sleep. No fun. No choice but to look for help.

Only a few people answered our ad for a nanny, especially since we gave only a post office box number, meaning any applicant would have to write a letter. But it only takes one "right" one, and we were so fortunate that Irene Denault saw the ad and answered it. From Beverly, Massachusetts, she was temporarily visiting her sister, Flo, and Flo's husband, Mauno Laine, who lived in Alexandria, Virginia. She had thought that if the right job came along, she would like to stay in the Washington, DC area. Having worked her whole life taking care of children, she knew what she did well and she knew how to do it. After taking care of one other handicapped child for a brief time, she found the ad we had placed had some appeal. We said that we had two babies, one handicapped. She wrote us a letter expressing interest, and she came for an interview. Immediately, we knew she was heaven sent. There was a God, after all.

A vivid memory of that period was Irene's first day off. Our arrangement was that each Tuesday afternoon, after the boys' naps, they and I would drive Irene to her sister's house in Alexandria. She would spend Tuesday night and Wednesday with Flo and her husband, and they would bring her back on Wednesday evening after supper. David, at that time, was just setting up an office here in Washington, but the fact was that most of his work was still in New York. His routine was to fly up to New York on Sunday evening and work there until Thursday, when he'd return to Washington for the weekend. So, from Tuesday afternoon until Wednesday night, it was just Mama Bear and the two baby bears. And Mama Bear was a pretty grim and grizzly one.

I'm not sure what was worse—those half-hour car trips back from Alexandria or feeding the boys supper or getting them to bed. Actually, they were all the worst. It was hell. I hated being a mother. I hated my life. Especially on Tuesdays and Wednesdays. But on that first Wednesday, as evening approached, I was morally certain that Irene wouldn't come back. Why would she? Who could stand this job? I sure couldn't. When I heard her key turn in the lock and the front door open, I burst into tears of joy and gratitude and profound relief. She did come back, she did. She would stay with us after all. And she did stay for five years.

I won't say they were five wonderful years. They were five difficult years, from 1966 to 1971. They were the years of little sleep. Irene pretty much did the day shift—except that I did all of the driving, which meant school, errands, doctor appointments, and so on—and I pretty much did the night shift. Robert didn't sleep through one night, not one, until he was six years old; and Jack was up at night with asthma, itching, and general irritability during those years and beyond.

Those five years were the years, too, when we concluded that, indeed, Jack was also mentally retarded. God knows, we tried every which way to come to another, happier conclusion, but the evidence was mounting. They were the years, too, in which David slowly built up an office for the law firm here in Washington. Finally, they were the years when it became clear that we would be nut cases to try having another baby, though I desperately wanted one.

Jack Busby, age 2, with beloved nanny Irene Denault

There were, however, some good times. The one constant was the genuine joy David and I took in each other. No matter what else was wrong, he and I were right. Still are. I guess, Megan, that this has sort of set David and me apart. People have said to me, over the years, that David and I are so lucky to have each other, and it's true. We are lucky. But it's been more than luck. We've also worked very hard at this marriage. A good marriage takes a lot of time, a lot of work, and a lot of caring and sharing. I would say, indeed, that a good marriage is achieved by both parties giving 100 percent to it 100 percent of the time. There are sure to be days when one party can only give a fraction of that, but by God, that party had better make up for it early and often. So, the good times have rolled for us, even as we've rolled with the punches.

Irene stayed with us for those five difficult years, until we got the bright idea to move out to Potomac, Maryland, thinking that if we lived in a neighborhood with lots of kids, that our boys would have playmates. I don't know where our common sense was vacationing the day we decided that, but that was totally off-the-wall reasoning. Number one, there weren't a lot of kids in the neighborhood we picked, and those who were there were not about to play with our boys. Forget that. Proximity does not breed acceptance. There was one darling little girl across the street, Gina Schiattareggia, who was really sweet to them, but how was she going to play with them? They couldn't do anything of interest to her.

Irene warned us that she didn't want to move into the suburbs, and certainly not to a neighborhood with no sidewalks. She didn't drive, never had. She took the boys, first in the double stroller and then walking, for many walks in our neighborhood, to the Macomb Street playground, over to the Friendly Beasties pet shop on Wisconsin Avenue, where they became acquainted with all sorts of animals, and up to Murphy's, our wonderful but long-gone dime store. Irene used those excursions as learning experiences for the boys. She talked to them constantly, teaching them about the animals they saw at the pet store, teaching them how to behave in a store, teaching all the time. And those walks they took required sidewalks. So, for her, a life for the boys and her without sidewalks would be a vastly diminished existence.

And do you know what, Megan? Irene was absolutely right. We learned it too late, but we learned it. Indeed, to this day, whenever a young couple tells David Busby about a house they're considering buying, his first question is, "Are there sidewalks in the neighborhood?"

Sure enough, we hadn't been in the new house in Potomac for even a week before Irene announced she would be leaving as soon as we could find a replacement. When we found one, Irene left to move to Florida, where Flo and her husband, Mauno, had moved by then. Irene remains, to this day, a very special person in our lives. The boys have taken turns visiting her in Clearwater and we hear from her regularly. Now in her nineties, and even with badly failing eyesight, she's as wise and interested in the boys, and indeed the whole universe, as ever. Irene is truly one of the main constants in our lives, and her letters are a source of support and insight.

From the time of Irene's departure, we had a series of helpers with the boys, mostly couples, some of whom—not surprisingly— worked out better than others. The best couple, Barry and Lynne Israel, were remarkable young people and they both went on to outstanding careers—Barry as a high-powered lawyer and Lynne as an occupational therapist with a huge Washington practice, focusing on children with learning disabilities.

Robert Busby, age 3

Lynne Israel got what turned out to be the great idea of running a summer day camp for handicapped kids in our backyard. We had the swimming pool and the trampoline and four acres for them to run and play, so it seemed a natural. Most of her clients were kids who went to school with our boys at the wonderful school that is now called Ivymount, in Rockville, Maryland. They were nice kids, nice families, and we were all looking for summer activities. The local day camps were not exactly dying to have our kids, so "Camp Israel" turned out to be a winner. The astonishing thing is that this camp is still part of Lynne's practice, and this year she has sixty children in a DC location. Most of the children she serves are more mildly handicapped, but they all benefit from her expertise.

I will always give Barry credit for training Robert not to wet the bed. This was when Robert was ten, I guess. Everything had failed, and we still had a wet bed every morning. Lousy way to start the day. Finally, we heard about this machine that Sears had in its catalog. You put the wires under the mattress pad—as I recall—and the second any moisture hits the pad, voilà! An alarm goes off. Barry slept in the room with Robert, and the minute Barry heard that alarm, he got Robert up and to the bathroom. Miraculously, within a couple of weeks, no more wet beds.

Gosh, Megan, as I'm thinking about this, I'm wondering if they still have these bed-wetting devices? It sounds, from the way I describe it, like electric shock treatment, doesn't it? I don't know, maybe we could be charged with child abuse for using such a "shocking" tactic on our child, even though there was no "shocking" involved, only an alarm. But I have to tell you that the great thing was that once this transition was made, it really was permanent. History. By that time, too, the boys were far more manageable in all sorts of ways, and at last I could spend a day with them without ending up in a state of exhaustion and despair. Life was getting better for most of the Busbys, if not for Jack.

Gradually, David and I realized that Robert was so demanding and took so much of our emotional and physical energy that Jack was suffering from a sort of middle-child syndrome without our having a middle child. Jack was turning into the middle child, with Robert being the eldest as well as the figurative youngest. At that point, too, I'll admit that we still entertained hopes that if only Jack didn't have Robert as a negative role model, he might eventually "come out of it"—as in, come out of being retarded. Yeah, right. But we honestly and very carefully and prayerfully made the judgment that we needed to give Jack more space. We did indeed give him space. Eventually, we put a space all the way from Washington, DC, to Oklahoma between the two boys.

But that's gotta be another story for another day, Megan. What started me, after all, on "all this" was your saying that you're looking for "help." Gosh, honey, I hope you'll have half the luck I did. I almost believe it's in the lap of the gods. And boy, can it make a huge difference in your whole family's life. So, you go, girl, and pursue this project.

So, now I'm going to go on downstairs to pursue the project of dinner––or rather, to pull out leftovers. That's another great thing about David Busby. He adores leftovers.

Love,

MBBB

P.S. "Understanding is knowing what to do; wisdom is knowing what to do next; virtue is actually doing it." (Tristan Gylberd, 1954–)
And oh, Megan, I feel I've failed on all three of these counts, countless times. But we sure do learn from our failures, don't we? 🖂

5

To the White House —January 2001

Dearest Megan,

I have to tell you that this was a fun couple of days. First of all, we got both boys back to their homes. No, just kidding. That is *not* the fun part. That was the dicey part—especially since Robert had had the flu for three days and we really didn't know if he would recover in time for his trip back to Oklahoma, where he is living at McCall's Communities, a residential facility for people with developmental disabilities. I remember that one year, he didn't. He got the flu and ended up staying here at home for an extra week. After he really was over the flu, but still hadn't bounced back to health and seemed really lethargic, I took him back to Dr. Guiterman, who said, "You know, I think this young man is depressed." I said, "Oh no, don't be silly"—in effect. Believe it or not, I still hadn't gotten the message then that Fragile X kids do tend to be depressed—never mind Fragile X carriers. It took years and some really bad behavior problems before I finally acknowledged that both of my boys were depressed. Gosh, when I think how much better their lives could have been if we had treated them with medication earlier, I feel so guilty.

Anyway, back to yesterday. I got Robert out to Dulles, while David got Jack back to work. Then David dashed out to the National Institute of Child Health and Human Development (NICHD) to meet Katie Clapp who had flown in from Boston. They had a great meeting with Dr. Duane Alexander, the director of NICHD, and they agreed to co-fund some grants with FRAXA on Fragile X. That was quite a milestone for FRAXA. After that, Katie and David left the NICHD and dashed down to the White House, and I left Dulles and dashed down to the White House.

And here's the fun part, OK? As if the NICHD meeting wasn't exciting enough. David, Katie, and I were invited to the White House for an afternoon ceremony to celebrate the passage of the Children's Health Act of 2000. Actually, the whole event was planned for the Women's Health Act, which was centered around breast and cervical cancer (and boy, are those women vocal. I could learn a thing or two from them). Then, because our planned bill-signing ceremony was twice canceled (and for good reasons: one time when the president made a last-minute trip to the Middle East, and I forget the other one), they invited a few members of the Coalition for Children's Health to be at this ceremony, sort of folding the two events together. After all, the Clinton administration is winding down to a precious few days. There were somewhere between one hundred and two hundred people at the ceremony. The neat thing was that before the event began, they culled about thirty of us and took us into the Blue Room to meet the Clintons. We were included in this small group through the auspices of our March of Dimes friend Jo Merrill, from whom David and I learn so much toward understanding the ways of the Hill. We were there in the Blue Room when the Clintons' helicopter landed, right at the window, practically. They had been up to New York for a funeral. Anyway, we all rushed to the window and watched them get out. Then five minutes later, here they were, going down the line and shaking hands with each of us.

I thanked Hillary for doing the video for us for the 1999 FRAXA Gala,

KATIE CLAPP, MARY BETH AND DAVID BUSBY WITH HILLARY CLINTON, 2001

and she said, "Oh yes. Fragile X. That's a great cause." Do you love it, Megan? I did, for sure.

Then it got even better. When Hillary got up to make her remarks, she mentioned the Children's Health Act and she listed a few parts of it, including Fragile X. Isn't that neat? We were thrilled. Then the president got up and gave a great little talk. The very last thing he said was something I loved. It was about genetic research. He talked about the astonishing strides that have been made, and he said, "You know, the best stuff is still out there. Go get it." All right!!

I probably sound fairly star struck in recounting all this. Perhaps a month from now, it won't seem so heady, but I'm afraid I'm pretty full of it all today. I hope I'll never get so jaded that I wouldn't be thrilled to walk in the door of the White House.

Gosh, I feel that the year is starting well. For another thing, Jack says he doesn't want to come home this weekend. I know that doesn't sound like much, but usually our boys are lower than snakes' bellies right after the holidays, so this is a triumph. We were told that there would be a special luncheon for all of the Cathedral ushers after the service on Sunday, and I assumed that Jack would want to come. I called him about it and he said, "Well, gee, I'd love to, but we have a dance to go to on Sunday afternoon." Bull's-eye! I love it. This is my dearest hope: that my boys will have activities that they prefer over anything we might have going for them. This is good. This is progress.

Listen, honey. I want to hear how your Jack and Jacob have done through the holidays. I haven't heard from you since you called and told me about trying to get the Christmas tree decorated without too much "help." All I can tell you is that the time will come when they won't want to help. My boys seem to care that we have a tree, but they sure don't want to lift a finger toward making it happen. I trust that by now the tree has gone up and back down again, presumably without "help."

I learned a number of years ago, the hard way, that it's important to get all of the Christmas stuff put away before the boys leave to go back to school, or to their homes, or wherever it is they're going. Then they get the sense that the holidays really are over, that everything is back in its place, that we're all supposed to get to our respective lives, and so on. As I say, I learned that the hard way. I should have told you this a couple of weeks ago, right? Knowing you, though, you knew that instinctively and have had your Christmas decorations all put away for days and days. It seems that I've had to learn everything the hard way.

So why are you not surprised to hear me say that?

A very happy New Year to all the Masseys, and love,

MBBB

PS. "Whenever a fellow tells me he's bipartisan I know he's going to vote against me." (Harry S. Truman) ✉

Dear Mary Beth,

Thanks for sharing! What a thrill it must have been to be at the White House with the president and Hillary. I would love to be able to get there someday. I must be honest though; I could pass on lunch with Bill. I would much rather have lunch with George and Laura!

The boys and I survived the holidays. John and I took them up to Ten Mile Lake in Minnesota. My family has a cabin up there. It was peaceful and lots of fun. We went snowmobiling and walked on the frozen lake. I think it was educational for the boys to learn and see firsthand what happens to Ten Mile in the wintertime.

Jack wanted a stuffed Barney for Christmas. I debated and really dragged my feet on getting him one. He's eleven years old! Five-year-olds want Barney. But, I finally conceded and just purchased one. He was thrilled. It sure is easy to please these boys.

It was nice not to have the pressure of all the family dinners and commitments. Our boys get so wired at those gatherings. Sometimes it is easier to stay home, but that is not always polite!

Well, I better go. It's great to hear from you.

Love,

Megan ✉

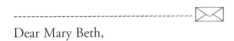

6

Washington Life

Dear Megan,

Well, honey, you're going to get your wish—at least to have George and Laura in the White House. They're very much here. Knowing you, you'll be invited there one fine day. And power to you, too!

I have to tell you something kind of amusing. I'm sure you didn't hear this, but David's sister-in-law, Carolyn Busby, was driving in her car in Norman, Oklahoma, on inauguration day, and she heard, of all people, David on *All Things Considered* on National Public Radio. An NPR reporter was at the parade-watching party that David's law firm Dorsey & Whitney[1] had for the inaugural (their office is right there on Pennsylvania Avenue—prime real estate for inaugural days). I told David that I'm sure the reporter looked around the room and picked out the oldest guy there to interview about the differences, if any, between one inaugural and another. David told him that administrations come and they go, but the lawyers all stay. I hope Katie Clapp didn't hear about the interview. I can just hear her saying, "Now, here he is on National Public Radio, so why didn't he mention FRAXA?"

Mentioning FRAXA and Fragile X is going to be my real focus this year. I am just so tired of people not knowing about it, and of course it's because we haven't been able to get any "ink"—as they say in the business. I've written to four different news organizations this month, and I will say that I've gotten responses from three of them so far. That's not to say we've gotten any stories or even any promises of stories. But they say they're interested. So, we'll hope for at least one of them to do a major story. I feel so

1 David Busby was a partner with the law firm Dorsey & Whitney before he retired and became of counsel.

strongly that people out there with undiagnosed Fragile X children need to hear about it.

Now, listen here, Amazing Megan. I am told by our friends in the Coalition for Children's Health that rather than focusing on these few big news organizations, we should instead be getting pieces in the smaller newspapers around the nation. So, here's where you come in. Don't you know anyone who knows someone with either the Scottsbluff or the Omaha newspaper? Surely in the far reaches of your brain you can come up with someone who is there, who would respond to a letter and package of FRAXA stuff from you. I'm quite certain that it's true that if we can get some pieces, and some good pieces, in those papers, this will do more than anything to spread the word. So, you go, girl, OK?

I must admit that on ceremonial occasions—even though I do no more than watch them on TV—I'm reminded all over again how much fun it is to live in Washington.

I can hardly wait for you to come to visit, and now that you're becoming a full-fledged appointee of the Federal Interagency Coordinating Council, you'll see it from a whole different perspective. I made my first trip here with my parents when I was fifteen. How old were you when you made your first trip here? I'll tell you what I remember from that first trip in 1955 and we'll compare notes.

Let's see, I remember going to Arlington National Cemetery and feeling awestruck by the sheer number of graves and by the stately quiet of the grounds there.

I remember going to National Theatre to see Deborah Kerr and Yul Brynner in *The King and I*. I remember visiting the Washington National Cathedral and thinking that while it was an extraordinarily beautiful monument, I couldn't imagine going to church there. How could I have imagined then that, years later, it would become "our church" where we worship each Sunday? Oh, and I remember dinner at Hogates. This was the old Hogates, which was much later replaced by a new one, now closed, sadly. They had the best crab cakes in town, we thought. I could fill a directory with the names of restaurants that have opened and closed in Washington in my years here.

Perhaps, when you come, we'll do some of the touristy things, and I hope we will. Chances are, though, that you will get yourself so booked with appointments on the Hill that a lot of the fun stuff will go by the wayside. We'll still hope to be able to give you a sense of this city in all its glory. Often, when I'm flying into Reagan National Airport at night, I'm struck all over again by the sheer beauty of Washington. Just this morning, I drove by the imposing Washington Monument; though too often, I don't even look at it, this morning I truly focused on it as a graceful symbol of truth and strength. Those of us who live here take this city far too much for granted, I know. We need to better appreciate the broad streets so marvelously laid out by Pierre L'Enfant, the clean neoclassic architecture, and the monuments that remind us of just how many people have sacrificed their own lives to create the system of government we have.

When I've been fortunate enough to speak at briefings on the Hill and other places around town, I sometimes say that when you have a child with a serious medical condition, it can be pretty overwhelming. Then on top of having to deal with your child's situation, you have to deal with the system. Sometimes parents feel let down by the system. But then I like to say that "today, however, we feel that the system is listening, is hearing, and is responding. Otherwise you people wouldn't be here listening to us." The fact is that flawed though the system may be, it's the best one in the whole wide world and we'd better appreciate it. Right? Right.

I should make sure to clarify for you that the only reason David or I ever get asked to speak on the Hill is because we and FRAXA—as well as the National Fragile X Foundation and the Conquer Fragile X Foundation—have been involved in the Coalition for Children's Health, which was started in 2000 by a Washington lobbying firm called Sagamore Associates Inc. The firm was originally representing one of the autism groups, which decided that the only way to get a bill passed that would jump-start its research might be to band together with other groups representing other diseases affecting children. Serena Lowe, a dynamite young woman with a vision, put this thing together and made it not only viable, but also very effective. Sagamore was able to arrange multiple briefings on the Hill, and it's truly been a win-win deal all around.

Bottom line is that we did get the bill passed, with most of the provisions the coalition promoted. Now the individual members are busy trying to get all of those provisions implemented. So the lobbying goes on. The formal coalition has now disbanded because, having gotten the Children's Health Act of 2000 passed, there was little for a coalition to do. The neat thing is that children's health is about as bipartisan as anything gets. I mean, what congressional representative or senator is going to say, "Well, I just don't really care about that? " Certainly not anyone who's planning to run for reelection. Besides, the provisions of the bill are reasonable and workable.

One thing we must do when you're here is take a drive down to see the monuments at night. We especially like to get out of the car and walk up to the Jefferson Memorial, taking time to walk clear around it on the inside, where excerpts from his speeches are engraved in the stone. That man sure did know how to turn a phrase.

Oh, you'll just love Washington. So let's try to make some plans soon, OK? You've said that John can set up some meetings here most anytime, so let's make most anytime happen pretty soon. You and John can stay in the Massey suite—otherwise known as Robert's room. The room service is lousy, but the air-conditioning works. I hope, though, that you'll come before we even need the AC. Let's move this along.

Tell Jacob that today I sent him a photo of my "little boy," Jack. Actually, Jack was a little boy not much older than Jacob when this one was taken. I thought Jacob would relate to the similarity of their names. Of course, I didn't send him the cutest photo of Jack from that age. That's the one where he's wearing boxing shorts, which Lynne Israel made for him, and the boxing gloves that Barry got him for Christmas. He has his arms raised in victory, and the look of sheer joy on his face is a treasure. That photo is in a frame on my dresser and I could never part with it. Not even for Jacob.

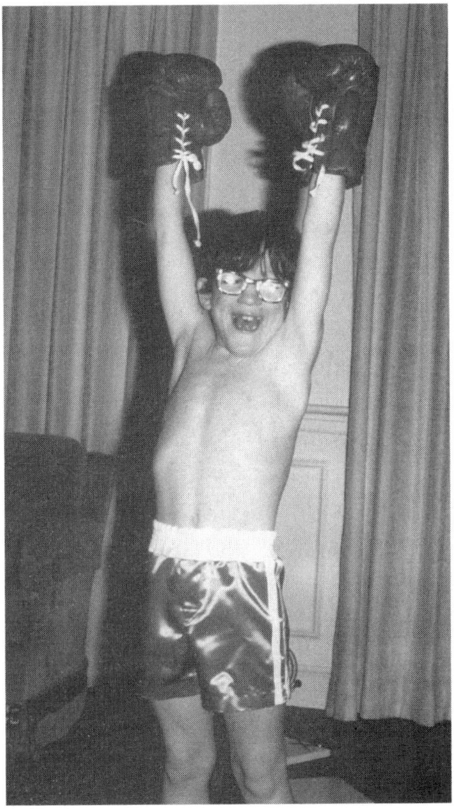

Jack Busby, the winner, age 8, 1973

I just wish my Jack had more of those moments of pure, simple joy. I don't know, maybe that's silly. I'm sure that if he had a master's degree and a great job and a wife and kids, there is no guarantee that he would have all that many of those moments either. But we'll never know, will we?

And, for heaven's sake, let Jack enjoy his Barney. I'll tell you something. Lots of perfectly normal kids love stuffed animals far beyond the years when you might think they would or should. I know that David's bright and perfectly normal grandsons adored their stuffed animals up to age ten, and likely beyond. So. Let him have it and love it, OK? You want him not to want a Barney, I know, because you want him to be beyond Barney at this stage. You want him to be "bigger" than that. Well, sorry, honey, but this is simply not a big deal—unless you make it one.

Love, love, love,
MBBB

PS. "A pessimist sees the difficulty in every opportunity; an optimist sees the opportunity in every difficulty." (Sir Winston Churchill) ✉

Dear Mary Beth,

Just a quick note to thank you for the encouragement to contact the local newspaper and television stations. I have wanted to get some publicity for Fragile X, but just needed your push to do so!

Sometimes I get subtle messages (or loud ones) from people who say, "I would never do that." Well, it isn't a big secret that there is a problem with the boys. I always figure knowledge is power, and the more people know, the more they can understand and accept others.

It is so encouraging to hear you say "go for it." I respect your opinion and kind advice. I must stand up for what I believe is right. Thank you, thank you. Your support will help me get out there and just do it! I think I'll start now.

Lots of Love,
Megan ✉

7

FRAXA's Founding

Dear Megan,

How I loved our phone visit yesterday! Scottsbluff sounded so close that for those brief, shining moments, I felt you could put down the phone and run right on over here to my house for a cup of tea. In our next life, huh?

Just having you ask me about the history of FRAXA caused me to do a double take. History? How can something that started day before yesterday have a history? I realize, though, that after all, it was in the last century that I first heard the name FRAXA, so I guess we are indeed talking "history."

Kathy May, one of the three founders of FRAXA, was also the leader of a Fragile X parents' support group in the Washington area. I sent her the little cookbook I had printed up for friends the Christmas of 1993 with some of my old Christmas letters. She called and asked if I might be willing to send one to Katie Clapp, up in West Newbury, Massachusetts. Katie and her husband, Dr. Mike Tranfaglia, founded FRAXA with Kathy in 1994. So, I did send the book—feeling kind of silly about it. I've always figured that anyone reading one of my Christmas letters for the first time would likely think I was crazy, and to receive a cookbook with a bunch of those letters sprinkled throughout would be a bit much. Make that a lot much—and a lot of me, for sure.

Katie soon called, wondering whether David and I would be interested in becoming involved in the research on Fragile X. Would we?! Oh, boy, would we ever! I'll never forget that first call from Katie Clapp. You know that delicious sensation, Megan, that you get when you take your first bite of a crisp, fragrant, perfect apple? You know right away whether this apple is good. That's the sense I got from that first telephone conversation with

Katie. Something way down inside me began shouting, "YESsssssss! You go there, do that, girl."

Going there and doing that was, of course, what Katie and Mike were already up to, big time. In 1992, when they got the diagnosis of Fragile X on both of their children, Andy and Laura, who were then three and one, they simply said, "Well, no, this is not OK with us. We have to do something to fix it." Both Harvard educated, and with Mike being an MD and Katie having a master's in computer science, they were not about to say, "Well, gee, what a shame. Poor us, but we'll just have to live with it." Oh, no. That was not their style and would not be their approach. Thank God. They swung into action.

Katie and Mike and Kathy May heard about each other through Dr. Randi Hagerman, who was then doing clinical work with Fragile X kids at the University of Colorado. Kathy and John May's son, Sam, was then three and had just been diagnosed with Fragile X. They felt an immediate bond and a collective, urgent need to "do something" to help their kids, and others.

Katie and Mike soon learned that there was very little research being done on Fragile X—so little that it was laughable. Except that this was no laughing matter. This was their kids, their lives, their hopes, their dreams, their world. Surely something could be done.

That first year, 1994, FRAXA raised $39,000. That was enough to partially fund the salaries of two research assistants in two labs, those of Ted

Jack Busby (L) with Katie Clapp and Mike Tranfaglia, FRAXA Gala, 2005

Brown at the New York Institute for Basic Research in Developmental Disabilities, and Jude Samulski at the University of North Carolina. It was a start. It was enough to raise the hopes of parents and grandparents and dear friends that something, at least, was being done, was being tried.

ROBERT BUSBY WITH ELEANOR CLIFT, FRAXA GALA, 1999

I could say that the rest is history, but history continues to be made each day in many labs around the globe, and "the rest" hasn't happened yet. The rest will be the discovery of a treatment and—one day—the cure.

In each of the last six years, FRAXA has funded more than one million dollars in grants. So, we're keeping on keeping on.

And you know what, Megan? I have this wonderful sense, now, of being part—in however tiny a way—of a process of turning those proverbial lemons into that proverbial lemonade. The research is exploding now. It's coming. It's moving and moving toward answers about why that one gene turns off and what can turn it back on. I'll admit that so far, the things that turn the gene back on are toxic substances that we can't give to our kids, but researchers will find a way. I just know it and that's what brings joy to my life.

MARY BETH BUSBY WITH DR. DUANE ALEXANDER, DIRECTOR, NICHD, AT THE FRAXA GALA, 1999

Some of the really exciting research now seems to be involving glutamate receptors. Glutamate is the chief substance the brain uses to ex-

FRAGILE X RESEARCHERS (L TO R): DR. PAUL HAGERMAN, DONNA BROWN, DR. VICKI SUDHALTER, DR. RANDI HAGERMAN, MARY BETH, AND DR. TED BROWN AT THE FIRST FRAXA GALA IN NEW YORK, 1998

cite activity between nerve cells. Somehow, the balance can get out of whack between the depressing (long-term depression) of these receptors and the uptake of these receptors. What they're trying to find is a way to strike the right balance so that Fragile X kids can learn. We'll all just have to stay tuned to the research news and hope that FRAXA can continue to fund the promising proposals, the results of which might lead to further breakthroughs.

For all those years, since learning about Fragile X in 1982 until becoming involved in the process of helping to fund research that can lead to a cure in 1994, I felt that Fragile X was a curse. And that's putting it mildly. Now—and I know this is so hard for you to imagine at this point in your life—I've come full circle to the point where I honestly feel that inheriting the Fragile X gene was a strange and fascinating gift. I won't say it was a wonderful gift and all in all, I'd rather the boys had gotten other gifts and gone to Yale. Yet, Fragile X has defined my life, given me a sense that yes, I can make a difference.

So can you make a difference, dear Megan. So, you go, girl.

And tell me. How did you first hear about FRAXA?

Love,

MBBB

PS. "The greatest thing in the world is not so much where we are, but in what direction we are moving." (Oliver Wendell Holmes) ✉

Dear Mary Beth,

The founding of FRAXA and how it all fell into place is very inspiring. Joy truly can come from tribulation and make us better people as a result. Tribulation produces perseverance; perseverance, character; and character, hope. And hope does not disappoint.

FRAXA has maintained that hope. I first found out about FRAXA from my Aunt Daphne, who I believe found FRAXA on the Internet at www.fraxa.org. As you may remember, Daphne is my mother's twin sister. She shared one of the newsletters with me and I became very interested in the cause. It showed me that there was hope and a hard-working group of people who wanted to make a difference. I remember reading about the first Mary Higgins Clark FRAXA Gala. I believe it was in New York in 1998. I read about it on the listserv and about the beautiful song that was sung by one of the guests. I even had my sister-in-law, who is quite musical, find the song and play it on the piano for me. I knew that I wanted to be part of that group, and I remember telling John that someday we were going to go to one of those galas. He just smiled.

During the following year I had many phone conversations with Mike Tranfaglia and Katie Clapp. If I remember correctly, this was the same time we were all gearing up to contact our congressmen and senators for the first ever Fragile X bill. Before the 1999 gala that you chaired in DC, Katie asked me to be a member of the board of directors. I, of course, was thrilled. Being a part of a group that is going to try to solve a problem that affects not only my own children, but also over one hundred thousand others was definitely something I was interested in!

I attended your gala with my mother, her twin sister, and her younger sister, who are all carriers of the Fragile X gene, as well as my three cousins and my two sisters. In fact all of us who were there have the Fragile X gene except for two! We had such a lovely evening. I remember meeting you, and a researcher from Rome who was working on demethylating the gene in his laboratory. He said he could do it, but it couldn't be done in humans yet, only in a test tube. Imagine, and you can, as a mother of two affected children and hearing all these possibilities, I was ecstatic! All of us girls had such a fun weekend together. Seeing Hillary Clinton on the videotape that evening was thrilling. The first lady of the United States could say Fragile X! I think she even applauded FRAXA! What an accomplishment for all of you who worked so hard to put together an exceptional fund-raiser. I remember re-

MEGAN MASSEY WITH HER FAMILY (L TO R) HEIDI WILKE (OLDEST SISTER), KRISTY DOOLING (MIDDLE SISTER), SUSIE CHARLTON (AUNT), DAPHNE FLETCHER (AUNT AND TWIN SISTER OF MEGAN'S MOTHER). MEGAN, LISA GRAHAM KEEGAN (COUSIN), DIANE HAMSA (MOTHER), AND ANNE SOUDER (COUSIN)

turning home and telling John what a fabulous time we all had. It was so inspiring that it made me want to do one myself. After seeing all the enthusiasm I showed for FRAXA, John was more interested then ever to try to attend a gala. I desperately wanted him to come in 2000, but knew I would sure miss the great girls' weekend!

John and I met Kathy May in 2000 at the Fragile X gala in New York. It was at the newly remodeled Russian Tea Room. We had the pleasure of sitting with Kathy and got to visit just briefly. I find it interesting how we, "the carriers" seem to hit it off. As if we knew each other forever. One of the first FRAXA researchers I ever got to know, Bill Greenough, told me he notices how driven and enthusiastic carriers are and he thought it would be interesting to look into that some day. I guess Kathy left FRAXA to pursue other endeavors, but she certainly had an impact on the beginnings of FRAXA's history.

Well, it will be interesting to watch the progress that is being made. You be sure to record it. Maybe you and David should be our official historians. I'm out here in the sticks, busy keeping my little X-men in line. I will be here to help and do all I can!

Take care and we hope to see you soon.

Love,

Megan, John, and the boys ✉

Roger Mudd with Mary Higgins Clark,
FRAXA Gala, 2005, Washington, DC

(L to R) Senator Chuck Hagel, Senator John Edwards, and Roger Mudd,
FRAXA Gala 2005, Washington, DC

8

Lobbying

Dear Megan,

Your account of having read about that first FRAXA Gala at the Essex House in New York and the wonderful singer makes me know in my heart that Frank Patterson will live on in the memories of so many people. He was the singer, and we were all blown away by the clarity of his glorious voice. I'll confess that I had never heard of him before that evening, though I had been told that he was a great favorite of Mary Higgins Clark and that she had made his performance for the gala possible. Soon thereafter, I began to hear him sing on PBS shows, and David bought one of his CDs, which to this day we enjoy hearing. I don't know if you've heard this, but Frank Patterson died tragically of a sudden heart attack, just about a year after that dinner. What a loss for the music world and for his many friends and admirers.

Also, I want to let you know that although Kathy May, who founded FRAXA along with Katie Clapp and Mike Tranfaglia, no longer serves on FRAXA's board, her heart is very much with us. She is truly doing the Lord's work with the Association for Retarded Citizens (ARC) of Northern Virginia. I couldn't admire her more, and she and John May have done an extraordinary job with their son, Sam, who has Fragile X. He's a neat young man. Kathy is always available as an advisor for Jack—and me too.

And now, Megan, let me offer big congratulations on all the spectacular work you're doing for FRAXA. You and your mom are quite a team. You don't seem to want to toot your horn, but David told me of your recent contacts with yet more people who have written letters supportive of our cause, and I have to tell you that you should win a prize of some sort for the most productive lobbying efforts. Right *on*!! Once we find the cure for Fragile X and once Jack and Jacob are grown up to the point where they don't require such constant attention, you have a whole new career in store for you. I don't know whether it will be as a lobbyist, but there's no question that this particular work will hone skills that you never knew you had. Those skills will lead to something even more fun down the line. One thing always leads to another. Always has. Trust me.

I wonder if you do think of all this lobbying activity as fun? I don't, really, but it has to be done. First it was our Fragile X Research Act of 1999, and it was visiting congressional offices to meet with health staffers—most of whom, I must say, have always been receptive. I have to admit that each time I would hear of another senator or House member who had signed on to our bill, I would get a rush. Then in 2000, it was the effort of the Coalition for Children's Health, of which both FRAXA and the National Fragile X Foundation became a part, to lobby through the passage of the Children's Health Act of 2000—into which, as you know, our little Fragile X bill was folded. We spent the next year trying to get the money appropriated to fund what was mandated in that bill. And, as you know, the three Fragile X research centers that were called for are up and running. So, your tax dollars are indeed paying off.

Were it not for the fact that I know that lobbying Congress is the way to get money for the National Institutes of Health (NIH) to fund major research toward a cure for our children, I'd never go to the Hill. Not my scene. For the most part, I'm more than content to leave the lobbying to David, who really does enjoy it. He likes going to the Hill, I think partly because it gives him the opportunity to revisit the days of his youth, back in the '50s, when he worked there as a committee counsel for Senator Mike Monroney of Oklahoma, on what was then the Interstate and Foreign Commerce Committee. That experience led to his career as a trade lawyer. See what I mean about lobbying expertise leading to something else? For David, it's now coming full circle. Having had the career as a trade lawyer, now—in his retirement years—he's become a lobbyist again. This time, it's for no pay; but he says the payback he gets, in having the sense that he's helping FRAXA to contribute to getting major research funded, is rich indeed.

I honestly don't know of anyone who has enjoyed a "retirement" career as much as David is enjoying his. He also enjoys dinner, however, and I've got to run to the supermarket this very little red hot minute, or Papa Bear will have no porridge this evening.

But before I go on to the supermarket, let me tell you again how much I appreciate your efforts, and those of your entire extended family, on behalf of FRAXA and the legislative agenda. David thanks you too, and sends love.

Love from me too,
MBBB

PS. I always remember a quote attributed to the late Nancy Hanks who was the chairman of the National Endowment for the Arts. She said something to the effect that the art of lobbying comes with recognizing when you've cut your best deal and then taking it.

Dear Mary Beth,

It was exciting for me to be able to contact friends and family about the Fragile X bill. Actually, it was therapeutic. It gave me the opportunity to tell others about my children and their handicap. At the same time, there was something they could do to help. It was a rewarding project.

I remember the day after your DC gala. We were all briefed by David and sent out to speak to our representatives about Fragile X. My mother was with me, and she is so charming. She suggested we ask Senator Chuck Hagel to cosponsor the bill and he agreed on the spot. I thought, hey, this is easy. All you have to do is ask! I guess it doesn't always work that way, but we were sure fortunate in Nebraska to get each one of our representatives on board

Megan Massey with Senator Chuck Hagel

to support Fragile X research. I remember Steve Irizarry (on Hagel's staff) saying he got more letters on Fragile X that summer than on Medicare.

Just as FRAXA's motto, the Margaret Mead quote, says, "Never doubt that a small group of thoughtful, committed citizens can change the world. Indeed, it's the only thing that ever has."

I am anxious to see where this all leads. I know there is much more in store for all of us.

It is a joy to be corresponding with you. Your friendship is a blessing. Please tell David hello.

Love,

Megan 🖂

9

Making New Friends

Dearest Megan,

Attending the International Fragile X Foundation's conferences is always an exciting time for David and me, and we were thrilled that you and your mom were at the one in Los Angeles. Gosh, that seems now like such a long time ago. It was great for us to be among over five hundred parents, researchers, and health professionals, all there to learn about the latest research on everything from fixing the gene to fixing the school programs of the kids. I'm sure you found, as I did, that there was something for everyone, even the Fragile X kids and siblings. There was child care for the kids, a workshop for siblings, grandparents, and everyone else in between. For me, of course, the researchers' presentations were the best. David asks me why I enjoy sitting there listening to things I can't possibly understand, and I have no real answer. It's just exciting to me to hear what I can't understand. And not all that unusual either. Being a little symptomatic as a carrier, I have always not understood a lot of things, but that never stopped me from wanting to hear them—except math. I never wanted to hear anything to do with math.

I still remember that on one of the days during that conference, the organizers planned—as the cultural event of the week—a trip to the J. Paul Getty Museum. I don't think you and your mom took that trip, did you? When we arrived, some of us went right to the orientation movie. I was sitting with Mary Bernardis, a lovely lady from Montana, and her young adult daughter, Amy, who has Fragile X. At the beginning of the movie, they were showing some of the treasures of the museum, one of which was a sculpture of a nude woman. Amy exclaimed, "Look, Mom. *She's* not perfect either!" I loved that. Mary told me that she's always saying to Amy that nobody's perfect. It occurred to me that this lovely young girl is more perfect than she knows. Being a girl, with that other "good" X chromosome, she's quite high functioning. She can even drive a car—something that for my boys would be totally out of the question.

But back to the conferences. The National Fragile X Foundation does a superb job of putting them together and keeping them moving on schedule. This takes massive planning on the part of Robby Miller, the foundation's terrific executive director, the foundation's board, and a dedicated group of parents in each city where the conference is held. So, do plan to be at all of them, okay? I can promise you that you will never be disappointed. Besides, you will always make new acquaintances who will quickly become fast friends. You need to have a bunch of Fragile X friends who are your own age. As flattered as I am to think that you might benefit to some extent from my experience as a fellow mother of two Fragile X sons, the fact is that my experience is such ancient history that a lot of it isn't relevant to your situation today.

Another bonus to meeting other Fragile X parents is that you can maintain a relationship via E-mail. You can literally exchange daily notes on everything from IEP issues to potty training. Gosh, it takes my breath away to think that I might have had that kind of support from a peer group in those "hurricane years." Since I didn't know that Robert and Jack had Fragile X, I sure didn't know anyone else who had an affected child. Looking back, I can think of kids who most likely did have it, but who knew? So, count your blessings, Megan, in that regard.

Count your blessings, period, okay? Bad as it is, it sure could be worse. Fragile X is not fatal. No one ever dies of it. We all just live with it, which is difficult but doable.

Love to you,
MBBB

PS. "The greatest use of life is to spend it for something that outlasts it." (William James, 1842–1910)

Dear Mary Beth,

My first International Fragile X conference, the one in L.A., was a great experience for me. As you know, my mother attended as well and we learned so much. It was a life-changing experience, just as you said. I met people

"FACES OF FRAGILE X"

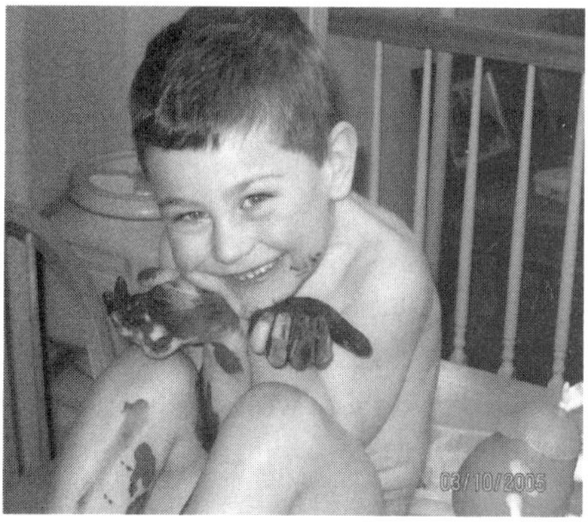

Cody, son of Ryan and Kelly Randels (see chapter 24)

Taylor, son of Jeffrey and Debbie Stevenson, chair of FRAXA's board of directors

Alec Souder, age 14, cousin of Jack and Jacob Massey

Sam (L), son of John and Kathy May, a founder of FRAXA, with his camp counselor, Simon Candy

who live in Denver who have children with Fragile X. Denver is only three hours from where I live. In fact, one of the mothers was in Debbie Stevenson's video that she produced for her FRAXA fund-raiser. I felt as if I met celebrities.

I would encourage every family who is affected in any way to attend a conference. As the boys reach different stages in their lives, I can see how it would be helpful to go and gain insight for what I might have to handle next. There are so many presentations to choose from. I almost needed a committee to have representation at each workshop I wanted to hear. It is truly an extraordinary event to have so many experts and families gathered together to learn and discover new ways to help those with Fragile X. There is not a doubt in my mind that everyone who attends will take some invaluable knowledge home.

I must admit that by the end of the week, I had hit sensory overload. Now I know how my children must feel. I did maintain my self-control without any behavioral outbursts! My brain could not hold any more information. Saying good-bye to friendships made during the week was sad, yet comforting. I knew there were many other people in the world dealing with similar or worse struggles in their homes. I had friends I could call on for support, ones who have been there.

A friend told me once that if we all gathered together and put our problems in a basket, we would much rather draw our own problems back out. There always seem to be others dealing with situations worse than mine. Maybe it's my sunny outlook again, but I don't think so. The problems we are dealt are ones that we can handle. We all seem to forge ahead and do the best we can.

Love,

Megan ✉

10

Robert's Birthday: Trauma Time

Dear Megan,

Today is Robert's thirty-ninth birthday. Now isn't it miraculous that I could have a thirty-nine-year-old child, and there's not a gray hair on my head? God is good. So is Clairol. So is my hairdresser, Johanna. Both Robert and Jack have a fair amount of gray in their hair, so mine is getting harder to explain by the day. Ah, well.

Robert's birthday has always been difficult for him. DB says it's because he had a traumatic birth, with the cord wrapped around his shoulder and causing oxygen deprivation, and that somehow in his subconscious he knows that March 1 was a *really* hard day for him, from the beginning. I'll admit that this theory has always seemed a bit far-fetched. But who knows?

I remember that when he was about four or five, he was in school at the DC Society for Crippled Children, which took any kind of a kid who couldn't function in a normal classroom setting. The school just labeled them all as cerebral-palsied, which even the staff admitted was a throwaway term. That particular March 1, I took a birthday cake and ice cream and punch for his class. The teacher said we should surprise him and that I should come in bearing the cake with the lighted candles while they sang "Happy Birthday." Right. Way to go. Except that it was the wrong way to go. Robert doesn't respond at all well to surprises, even as he reaches the age of thirty-nine. When I walked in, he totally lost it and screamed and cried and ran up to me, pulling at my skirt, almost making me drop the cake. At that stage, I probably would have been more upset over dropping the cake than upsetting my child. I didn't relish the thought of Mr. Frosting all over Mr. Floor at the DC Society for Crippled Children. I did, however, learn a lesson myself that day: surprises and Robert don't mix.

There have been years when on Robert's birthday, I have allowed myself to fall into a funk. I never called it a depression, but that's what it was. I think we call it a situational depression. Whether I was dwelling on the contrast between the kind of birthday party we were having and the kind we would be having if he was normal, or whether I was just so exhausted after the birthday party, with twelve or fifteen or twenty hyperactive kids running all over the house, I was always a basket case by the evening of March 1. I was really ready for my bourbon and soda, big time. Ah yes, those were the days, the Bourbon Days. It was amazing how much easier it was to get through the evening after a Big Bourbon. Nowadays, after a Big Bourbon, I'm afraid I'd head straight to bed and forget about getting dinner on the table.

Oh, poor you, Megan! I'm probably freaking you out, because I know you have Jacob's birthday coming up in a few weeks. Knowing you, though, you're so well organized and emotionally centered that you'll get through it with the greatest of ease. Gosh, you'll likely even enjoy it. I wish I could say that I had enjoyed even one of my boys' parties, but I didn't. Of course, I have to say that for you to have your wonderful family's support is a huge help. I never had that—not because my parents weren't supportive of me or my boys, because they really were in those earlier years. But they simply didn't live close enough to participate in events like birthday parties. You're far better situated, with your parents at least in the same state.

We called Robert first thing this morning, to sing "Happy Birthday." Even that is something of a risk, as he hasn't always liked hearing "Happy Birthday" or seeing candles. He sounded really "up" today, though, and he's looking forward to hosting his group home for dinner at Bandanas, one of our favorite Ada restaurants. He wanted a heart-shaped cake, so that's the order.

This year, for the first time, we didn't send him a big package of clothes for his birthday. When we were there in Ada last week, even he agreed that he has too many clothes and "things." Even with the new chest of drawers we got him this past year, there simply isn't space in his room for one more sock or one more coffee mug. Let alone another shirt. I mean, we're talking shirt city. My spies tell me that on occasion, he's been known literally to throw away perfectly good clothes, which of course is outrageous. But I can understand it because there is simply no place for them. The very fact that he would do that should tell us that all these "things" we give him are not a very important part of his life.

Instead of sending clothes, this year we decided to outfit a computer for the group home, and let that be his birthday gift. They have a computer tower down there, but they need a monitor, keyboard, and mouse. We think that's a great thing for these kids. There may be others in the group home who will do better with it than Robert does, and of course we'll have to find an instructor to work with them. We think it's worth a try, though. We've tried to sell this to Robert as a really exciting thing, with modest success.

There's sort of a dichotomy working within these kids when it comes to "things." On the one hand, most of them end up living in circumstances where there's very little personal space. On the other hand, their families—because they are living away from home—compensate for their guilt by giving them more "things" than they need. The idea of simply giving our kids a check for their birthday doesn't cut it, in that money means so little to them.

Megan, honey, if my boys were the ages of your boys, I would start right now on a massive training program to teach them that occasions like birthdays are not about things. What's needed is simply a recognition, and even a celebration, of a milestone. That recognition, however, need not consist of material gifts. I know that's a taller order than any of us can fill, and I think a lot of it has to do with the guilt we feel because they don't have the normal kinds of celebrations. Their celebrations, if they happen, happen only because we and their caregivers make them happen. But I hope you'll at least think of this when you plan Jack's and Jacob's next birthdays. Trust me, the day will come—as it has for us—when there literally isn't the space available to house that thoughtfully purchased and given birthday gift.

We've always had the same problem with Christmas. Years ago, I simply wrote notes to friends, who had become accustomed to giving my boys gifts, and said that it had gotten to be too much. We gradually had come to realize that the focus of the holiday season had become gifts, rather than the Christmas celebration and joy of being together with family and friends. I have to say that both the boys and our friends were great about it, and this has made a felicitous change in our holiday season. This was about the same time that we started drawing gifts within our nuclear family—including Hopie and Alison and theirs. That means that each of the thirteen people draws one name for a gift to give. Of course, Hopie and Alison and I end up buying all four or five gifts for us and our kids to give, but that's a lot better than purchasing and sending—or wrapping, if they're coming here—thirteen gifts. I know there are families who would no more dream of cutting down to this extent than the man in the moon, and that's fine. I think, though, that especially for our kids, the simpler we can keep holidays, the better. Even visually, all of these packages can be too much extra stuff going on. I usually end up putting about six packages under the tree for each boy—whereas it used to be about twenty—and I pretty much get them things I think they need. It's hard when they're too old for toys but can't read books or enjoy good wine or the latest gadget or appreciate money. Subscriptions to *TV Guide* are a traditional favorite with Jack and Robert. Videotapes seem to be a hit, too, though who knows if they ever watch them?

On Robert's birthday, I often remember the time when I took him shopping at Sears. He must have been about twelve or so. I don't even remember whether it was before or after he went to McCall's Chapel School in Ada. But I took just him, without Jack, shopping at Sears, which used to be on Wisconsin Avenue. They had a hot dog stand on the top floor, and part of the drill was always to have a hot dog for lunch. We bought some clothes for Robert, had our hot dog—more likely in reverse order—and had a nice time together. No scenes, no getting lost from one another, no panic when it came time to step on the escalator. Everything went perfectly. I don't remember what I bought him, but I think it was some clothes and a ball of some sort. When we got back in the car and were fastening our seatbelts, Robert said, "Thank you, Momma. Thank you for Sears." I'm sure I didn't cry then, but I always cry now when I remember that simple expression of gratitude from my Robert for such a simple outing together.

You know as well as I that expressions of gratitude come few and far between from our boys. It's not that they think about it and then don't do it. It's just that they don't think far enough beyond themselves even to have the notion of gratitude.

Not surprisingly, Megan, it's now after supper (four-bean chili), and we just called Robert to see how his birthday party went. He said it was "fantastic." Can't ask for more than that. "Fantastic" is as good as it gets.

I guess I have to say that, overall, these kids are pretty happy as long as their basic needs and desires are met—and as long as they keep taking their antidepressants! If they need them, that is.

Robert has, just this year, begun writing us letters. I know perfectly well that this is the fine influence of Josie Christian, his personal trainer, who spends about ten hours a week with him. They go to the East Central University gym to work out, or they go for walks in Wintersmith Park, or they go to the library, where he checks out books and writes us letters. David and I are amused that instead of signing his letters with "Love, Robbt (the way he spells Robert)" he signs them, "Like, Robbt." It's that holding back of affection and displays of emotion that goes along with autistic behaviors. For us, though, the triumph is that now he likes to write us letters. And I like, "Like, Robbt."

You know what? As I think about Robert's birthday, and all that having these two dear, sweet boys means, I'm struck by the fact that what made this particular day truly wonderful for me was long conversations on the phone with Diane, Ellen, E. J., Jane, and Peyton. They are such dear and special friends and hearing about their lives and their activities truly keeps me sane. I don't think I even mentioned to them that it was Robert's birthday. After all, how on earth could they begin to understand the fact that I dread my own child's birthday and simply "get through it." I know you have this special bond with your girlfriends too, especially with Sue, Helen, and Joni. As much as I cherish you and Katie and Mary Jane and the marvelous group of young Fragile X moms in the Maryland Fragile X Resource Group and *all* of my FRAXA friends, and as unique as our bond is, we all need to have local "civilian" friends who operate in the "normal" world. We have to straddle both worlds. It's enough to make you feel downright schizophrenic, isn't it?

When I think of the contrast between how I'm feeling about myself now and my total lack of self-esteem thirty years ago, I know that I'm blessed indeed. And now it's my responsibility to give back. Somehow.

Do have a great day, Megan girl, and if I don't talk with you before Jacob's birthday, just get through it and know that they get easier. And better.

And now, as Jack would say, it's bedtime for all us Bonzos.

Lots of love to you and John and the boys,

MBBB

PS. "Wherever you are it is your own friends who make your world."
(William James, 1842–1910)
Well, Megan, maybe our friends don't entirely make our world, but they sure do enhance it—right? ✉

Dear Mary Beth,

I am right there with you on not liking kids' birthday parties. It's because I have never been very good at it. And neither have my kids. I am not a great organizer and I don't know many of the games the kids like to play. I should have hired a birthday planner, but I don't think they have any with a special-needs endorsement. My kids wouldn't play games for long anyway. Outdoor games always worked better. But, with April and December birthdays it could be below zero outside.

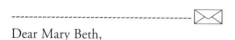

We often had trouble rounding up kids to come to the parties. I must say all of my friends' kids were more than happy to show up. I bet their moms made them or gave them no choice. Actually, Jacob had many more options than Jack. He is just more social and could actually name all of his buddies that he wanted to invite. He has a bunch of them! Jack, on the other hand, always named adults. They were usually family, friends, and his teachers. And you know what, I just had them over, all of them. One of Jack's biggest birthday parties included four couples that we often do things with as well as two of his teachers.

It seemed that no matter what the kids receive, they hold it up in the air and say, "Yes!" They may not even know what it is, but if it can go above their head, they do it. It's probably in a movie they watch. One of my good friends, Sue, gave me excellent advice. She told her kids they could have parties every other year and on the off years they could take a friend to dinner or go see a movie. I don't think I ever officially adopted that plan, but I sure wished I had in the midst of the bedlam at the birthday party.

Both boys always love to watch the other one open his gifts. We often had to physically restrain one so he wouldn't tear all the wrapping paper off the other one's present. They also enjoy watching each other suffer through the thank-you notes their mother insists they complete. I remember Jacob telling Jack one night that he could not watch television until his thank-you notes were done. I wonder where he ever heard such a thing? That sounds like it is straight out of the mouth of a mother. Jacob just wanted to have control of the remote.

These notes were another painful event. The boys could think of maybe two sentences to write and they were very brief. Grammar and spelling were incorrect. The attention span was a big issue too. They were always thrilled to know we didn't require them to write us one.

John's parents, affectionately known as Boppe and Bucko, are always the first on the list along with their Aunt Sandy. They are fabulous and very supportive of our family. They have attended more of their birthdays than anyone. In fact, I bet they have perfect attendance. If you can believe this, they just came to a birthday party for Jacob and he didn't show up! He was at a basketball game with his friends and didn't want to come home. John tells me the game was in double overtime. I guess you can't walk out of those. Now who else can get away with that? His grandparents said, "Oh that's fine. Be sure and let him open his gifts." Wow, that is unconditional love.

The family birthday is really the way to go. You don't have to worry about bizarre behavior offending anyone, or explaining why Jack just disappeared upstairs. He could stand the commotion for about fifteen minutes and then he was out of there. We were also not allowed to sing. Jack and Jacob don't know how good they have it. The members of John's family are beautiful singers. Sandy could have been a professional. You would get chills listening to her sing "Happy Birthday." I'll have her do it for you sometime. She usually attends the FRAXA Galas.

Well, speaking of birthdays, I have the birthday mess to clean up. It was a party with two shifts. First the guests came, then the honoree showed up after the guests went home. Jake opened his presents and now he is crashed in his bed. I just might pick up some of the "things" we gave him and save them for next year. He'll never notice.

Much love,

Megan ✉

11

All That Autizzing

Dear Megan,

My friend, Ted Brown, who is the director of the New York State Institute for Basic Research in Developmental Disabilities, sent me a fascinating article by a Stanford group that appeared in the November 1, 2001 issue of the *American Journal of Medical Genetics*. The article[1] cites contradictory findings as to whether some carriers of the Fragile X premutation are symptomatic for the syndrome. In a study of 85 women with the premutation, there didn't seem to be a relationship between the number of CGG repeats they had and their scores on an IQ test. But women with 100 repeats and higher seemed to be more prone to depression. Despite the low number of participants with those higher CGG repeats, the study's findings suggest that those females display some clinical manifestations of Fragile X. Previous studies[2] had suggested higher levels of social anxiety among women with the premutation; but the Stanford study doesn't address any manifestations besides depression.

I don't know about you, Megan, but far from being indignant at the suggestion that some carriers may be symptomatic, I sort of glommed onto it—though I'm afraid this study doesn't explain why I've always been such a klutz at math. I can't even balance my checkbook. Hopeless, hapless, helpless. Also, to be honest, I've felt for years that I had some autistic tendencies; but I never had the nerve to say so, even to myself—to whom I love talking more than to anybody.

1 Johnston C, Eliez S, Dyer-Friedman J, Hessl D, Glaser B, Taylor A, Reiss A, "Neurobehavioral phenotype in carriers of the fragile X permutation. AmJ Med Genet.2001 Nov 1; 103(4):314-9.

2 Hagerman and Sobesky, 1989; Borghgraef et al., 1990; Hagerman et al., 1992; Lachiewicz, 1992; Freund et al., 1993.

For one thing, there must have been a reason for my parents' referring to me repeatedly and often as "our strange child." They did it in a kind of bemused way. They didn't ridicule me and they were always more than loving and supportive, but clearly, they thought I was a bit of an oddity.

The first time I remember noticing that I was regarded as a little strange is actually one of my earliest memories. I hear other people talk about memories from as far back as when they were two or three, but I remember very little until I was five or six. Maybe this is a happy thing, in that nothing traumatic happened to me as a tiny child. Anyway, this particular incident probably occurred when I was seven or eight. I was walking home from school, talking to myself as usual. Maybe I was having an animated conversation with an imaginary companion, I don't know. What I remember is that I walked by a house where two people were sitting on the front porch, and they looked at me and then at each other as if to say, "Whoa. This child is a real nut case." I remember thinking to myself, "Hmmm. I wonder if maybe everybody else doesn't talk aloud to herself." From then on, I tried to be more careful about it, but the tendency exists to this day.

I remember being at the Safeway one day, pushing my grocery cart along and saying, right out loud, "Now, let's see. We had chicken last night, so how about . . ." I then saw someone looking at me the same way as those folks on that long ago and far away front porch.

Then there was the stuff I used to eat. As a child, probably up until I was ten or so, I used to eat soap. Loved the taste. Loved it almost as much as I loved the taste of Jergens Lotion, which I used to drink. Loved the stuff. Talk about a drinking problem! I just loved that taste. Yikes! Are you throwing up yet? It's a miracle that I lived to tell the tale—right, Megan? No wonder my parents called me their strange child. Nowadays, I think we call this disorder "pica"—though my parents would never have had the occasion to hear this term. "Strange" was good enough for them.

Then there was the business of picking up items and smelling them. My parents used to tease me because whenever I picked up a phonograph record, for instance, I would smell it before putting it on the record player. I would smell the mustard when I opened the jar. Ditto the grape jelly, the peanut butter, the bar of soap—which of course I was looking forward to tasting. You name it, I smelled it. I was particularly sad when the cosmetic companies stopped putting fragrance in makeup and lotions. I had always bought those things according to how much I liked the fragrance. Period. Never mind what the product did to or for my skin. If I liked the smell, I liked the product. It practically ruined my whole life when they started putting things like makeup in packages encased in plastic so you can't open it to smell it until you've bought it and brought it home. Rats! As you can tell, I tend to buy drugstore cosmetics. I can assure you, though, that whenever I do shop for cosmetics in a department store, I would never dream of even considering buying something I hadn't smelled. Even "fragrance-free" cosmetics tend to smell like something. Oh, how I miss stuff that used to smell like powder—at least the way powder used to smell to me when it had a smell. Is this tragedy in my life right up there with having two Fragile X kids, or what?

Then there's the business of screwing on lids and caps so tightly that I can barely—and sometimes can't—get them open the next time I want to use whatever is in the container. I always know I have no one to blame but myself. This is truly obsessive-compulsive behavior, right? Oh, yes, and there's my extreme reluctance to throw away an empty bottle or jar or box without first putting the top back on. I still have problems with the whole recycling bit, because (at least in the District of Columbia) you are supposed to put the empty bottles and jars in a separate bag for recycling and put the lids and caps in with the regular trash. This gives me a conflictive pang of anxiety, because it's just not right to send these things on to their reward in an incomplete state. Not OK. Well, at least I'm not as bad as Robert, who's been known to take—as requested—a big load of dirty laundry down to the laundry room and then (not as requested) fold all the dirty laundry and neatly stack it on top of the washing machine to be washed. OK, now that's the real thing, in terms of a genuine obsessive-compulsive disorder. I'm just a wannabe OCD type.

Now, I'm not saying that I think I'm really autistic. I don't think so. I do think, however, that I have certain autistic tendencies in some minor regards. Maybe no one has ever noticed them, but I'm convinced that my parents did notice and acknowledge—at least to each other—that they had a strange child. If I heard them call me that once, I heard them call me that a thousand times—enough times, for sure, for it to sink in.

There is no question that I'm a person who loves being alone—another autistic tendency. Maybe part of it is because when I'm alone in the house, I can talk to myself and solve all my problems. My idea of heaven is a day when I don't have to go any farther than the health club down the block on Connecticut Avenue. As much as I love staying home alone, you'd think I'd be better organized. But here I go again with this autism stuff. I spend a lot of time spinning my wheels, acting organized without being organized.

Speaking of spinning wheels, the last time DB and I took a car trip, we had gotten—as always—a recorded book to listen to in the car. This time it was *To Kill a Mockingbird*, and oh! It's marvelous. When we stopped and switched places because it was my turn to drive, DB said, "Do you mind if we turn the book off and I read the *New York Times* for a while?" I said, "Well, yeah, I sort of do, because then I won't have anything to listen to while I'm driving." He said, "Well, you could autiz." I said, "But autizzing is no fun unless I'm by myself. I can't autiz with you sitting here." After we finished laughing about my autizzing, we ended up compromising by having him read the *Times* aloud to me as I drove. DB may have created a new verb there, what do you think? Shall we call *Webster's* and register it for the next edition?

I was talking with a young Fragile X mom the other day about being symptomatic, as carrier moms. She said that one way she's symptomatic is her tendency to multitask. Immediately, I knew what she meant. You like to talk on the phone while you pay bills. You like to listen to the radio while you're folding laundry. You like to have the TV on while you're cooking dinner. Gee, you might think, on the one hand, this must mean that you get a lot more accomplished. Wrong. You cope, you deal with it all, and you keep several balls in the air, so what's the problem? The problem is that you don't *really* focus, you don't make the best use of your time, and you don't accomplish the task in the shortest possible time.

As to your Jack's tendency to withdraw into his own little world, I don't know what to tell you. I simply let my boys do it, hoping it might help them to better organize their thoughts. Or was that my excuse for allowing myself to withdraw into my little world while they were in theirs? I even used to let my Jack ride in the backseat of the car by himself, with me driving, because he seemed to enjoy sitting there in his own little reverie. The experts today, of course, would insist that the child ride in the backseat for safety considerations, but they well might discourage letting the child talk away to himself, and they're probably right. Nowadays, our Jack chooses to ride up front with me—though I can't say he's outgrown his backseat reveries. Except that now we call it autizzing. I simply say, "Jack, stop autizzing;" and he knows precisely what I mean.

You probably should read more child-rearing books than I did, and I'll bet you already have. I didn't read a lot of child-rearing books because I found them too depressing. If it was a book geared to normal kids, it was depressing because my boys were never anywhere near reaching any of the milestones. If it was a book about handicapped kids, it never seemed to fit. Of course, this was eons before the discovery of Fragile X.

Just remember that whatever mistakes you make with Jack and Jacob have nothing to do with your devotion and dedication as a mother. We just do what we feel is right and then hope for the best.

And always and ever, dear Megan, do remember each and every day that John fell in love with you the way you were then, and you're still the same wonderful, adorable Megan—autizzing and all, all the way, all the time.

Lotsa love, always,
MBBB

PS. "I was never less alone than when by myself." (Edward Gibbon, 1737–1794, *Memoirs of My Life and Writings*) ✉

Dear Mary Beth,

I have never been tested to see if I am indeed fully affected or just a carrier. Dr. Randi Hagerman tells me I'm just a carrier. I must have really dazzled her with my brilliance that day! It would be interesting to know. I've just never taken the time to do it. After all, we know the boys didn't get this syndrome from their dad.

Even though we don't know my repeats, I use my X chromosome for an excuse whenever needed. I have told people before that we know my genetic flaw. It is a great way to explain away all my unwanted hang-ups.

Reading about your "autizzing" made me laugh. I multitask all the time. I can talk on the phone, pay bills, and check E-mail all at once. I am often working on three or four projects throughout the day at home. I do draw the line when I'm driving the car. I cut it back to one or two tasks at a time when I'm behind the wheel.

John will sometimes ask me what I am thinking about when I appear deep in thought. I tell him he doesn't want to know. He wouldn't believe it. There would not be enough time in the day to tell him. I can get more topics flowing through my mind than anyone can imagine. I can cover the boys' needs—past, present and future—along with all the chores for the day, a few vacations I want to take with John, and then throw in a conversation or two I need to have with a teacher or therapist.

There is always the menu for dinner and numerous phone calls to make. Last time John asked me what I was thinking about, I laughed. He said, "OK, give me the top fifty." He really does know I struggle with my brain working overtime. Sometimes I wish I could turn it off. And other times my brain feels like it's blank and no synapses are connecting.

Oh my, someone may commit me if they read this. A padded cell might not be too bad if I'm feeling depleted in my quiet time. For now, I focus most of my energy on the boys. Their autizzing is always worse when they are together. They can get each other into headlocks, bite their own hands, and seem to enjoy it. It's very strange, but very Fragile X. No, I don't do that.

Well Mary Beth, thank you for sharing all of your experiences with me. I have always been curious about how you survived raising two Fragile X boys so graciously. I guess you're not done yet. That thought may make your brain hurt!

Speaking of brains, mine seems to be slowing down to about third gear. It is late and I have to get up early for work.

I do love my job at the Oregon Trail Eye Surgical Center. This is my first year there. I work two days a week, Tuesdays and Wednesdays. The perfect job. Work two, take five off. John says I live the life he dreams of, so I sure don't want to let him down. Actually, we start pretty early, around 5:45 a.m. That works well for me as I am a morning person. We are usually done at the clinic by noon or shortly after. It just depends on how many patients are scheduled. The center does mostly cataract surgeries. We have a few other procedures every now and then, but for the most part it is cataracts. The gals I work with are fabulous. Sue is one of them. She is an RN too. In fact, she hired me. We all have so much fun together. We have been told that we need to keep down the chatter on some days. We are all good friends, and usually just see each other at work. We love to share our lives and family stories with one another. A lot can happen in five days if we haven't had the chance to visit. I guess we must remember work is not social hour. Darn. Everyone knows the tasks that need to be accomplished and we work as a team. Our patients are generally older. I must be careful here. What is old? OK, most of them have raised their kids and have a few grandchildren. They are so dear. Oh sure, we have a grumpy one every now and then, but if you just treat them with loving kindness they usually come around. I think I have told you I am a registered nurse. I have always felt the desire to keep my license current. I love my profession. It has been enjoyable for me to work over the last sixteen years. It provides a little break from the routine and allows me to focus on my training as a nurse. But since we start so early the nighttime hours dwindle quickly. So, it is off to bed now for me. It's bedtime for Bonzo. I think I heard that from you.

I will try and write you again soon.

Love,

Megan 🖂

12

Guilt Trips and Valentines

Dear Mary Beth,

I am just heading to town. Jacob has a basketball game. He plays on the seventh grade C team. He is by far at the bottom of the talent list. He actually has good skills, but is so easily distracted with all the activity on the court. I don't need to expand on that issue. You know.

Jacob did score two baskets last week. After his second basket, his coach threw his arms in the air and stomped his feet on the floor. I think the coach knew what an accomplishment that was for Jacob! Jacob ran down the court celebrating, with his hands in the air. I guess we need to talk with him about keeping his head in the game.

Jack, on the other hand, is a student manager for the eighth grade basketball team. He takes his clipboard and wears a whistle to all the games. He is a true nerd. When I drop him off at practice all the other players yell, "Hey, Jack! What's up?" The kids really do enjoy him. They give him "five" and always greet him happily and lovingly. I'm so grateful for their ability to accept him.

At a basketball game that John and I did not attend, Jack had an opportunity to call a play. The eighth grade assistant coach happens to be a family friend. She has stayed with the boys when we travel. Her name is Amy Blehm. Amy made sure Jack had a great experience and she truly understood the situation. In the town of Alliance, Nebraska, we, the Scottsbluff Bearcats were ahead by thirty points. Amy called a time-out and let Jack call the play. All the players huddled around him and watched as he drew line after line all over his clipboard. He was speaking at a fast rate, and I'm pretty sure no one understood what he said. But what they had to know was they were making a difference for Jack. He must have felt so proud and important. One thing that is so interesting to me about these kids is their confidence. I'm sure Jack believed he was making perfect sense, and was handing out valuable and much needed information for the next play. I'm so sorry I missed it, but I'm pretty confident that I appreciate this story a lot more after the fact. Watching it "live" was probably more than I could handle. You know how anxiety provoking that can be! I would have had my head in my hands thinking, "What is he doing?" or I may have jumped out of the bleachers and put him back in his seat. He often would sit in the head coach's chair anyway. And that coach never seemed to care. I would have loved to see the faces on the players in that huddle. I guess they were learning about acceptance, compassion, and diversity.

Well, for a person who is just heading to town, I sure had a lot of information to share. Finally, I wanted to tell you that John and I will be off next week for a long weekend of skiing and fun with friends. I feel awfully guilty about not taking the boys, because they love skiing as much as we do. But we decided we need this one for ourselves, so we're going to be a bit selfish. Wish us luck on pulling this off without tears and cries of protest.

Take care.

Megan

Dearest Megan,

Now, listen here. Do not, repeat *not* feel guilty about leaving the boys and going off on a ski trip over Valentine's Day. I mean, Valentine's Day is not Christmas Day. It's not Thanksgiving Day. It's not even a legal holiday, for heaven's sake. So, just pack your little suitcase and get outta there and have a grand time with John on the ski slopes. Just try not to break a leg, OK?

Surely you've long since known that feeling guilty is the story of our lives. I've been sitting here today feeling guilty as all get out. I received in the mail a nice letter and a sort of self-help inspirational book from the wonderful and caring social worker at the retirement center where my parents lived for several years before they died. This is the second in a series of books to help people deal with their grief. I sat down and read the whole thing, and now I feel like such a fraud because I just don't feel the grief that I know I'm supposed to feel over Mother's death. I will admit that I've yet to get out her old letters to David and me that she used to write every Tuesday and every Friday at 7:30 a.m. I suspect that I won't really deal with her death until I go back and read them.

Mother's letters were wonderful, because they told us what she and Daddy had for dinner the night before, who was at sewing club the day before that, what tablecloth and napkins she was going to use for her church circle's luncheon the next week, and what—in detail—she would serve. Reading her letters, I could visualize their day-to-day existence, and both David and I thrived on the minutiae of their domestic routine.

What, of course, she never said was anything truly meaningful to me. She never said how she really felt about the things that mattered most. Looking back, I realize that my mother was probably clinically depressed for many years before she was widowed and diagnosed and treated. People of her generation simply didn't deal with such things, not unless they became an emergency. Her depression was never an emergency. It was just there.

I didn't learn until fairly recently that depression among Fragile X carriers is not uncommon. I hardly need to tell you that having children with Fragile X is enough right there to send a mother into a state of depression, big time. I gather, though, that it's more than that. Maybe we have lower levels of serotonin, or something. I have been so fortunate to have dodged that bullet, so far. I honestly don't know why I tend to have a rather sunny outlook. I guess, though, that when I don't know whether to laugh or cry, I usually laugh.

Perhaps I've always tended toward cheerfulness because when I was a child, my parents made our home a pleasant place to be. We were sort of an Ozzie and Harriet family—except that Harriet was fat. Indeed, that was the only problem I remember having as a child: a fat mother. People would come up to me at church, chuck me under the chin, and say, "Now, Mary Beth, I hope you're not going to grow up to be fat like your mother." I would think to myself, "Fat chance of that." That's why I've always watched my weight like a hawk—getting on the scale every morning. David's happy for me to watch my weight, but he sure wishes I'd stay away from watching his. Not than I'm likely to, not after forty years.

I'll never know whether my mother was depressed because she was fat or fat because she was depressed, and as a child, I wasn't even aware of what depression was.

Far "outweighing" (ha!) the fat issue, I must say, was one priceless gift my parents gave me. It was the sense that their marriage, their relationship with each other, was far and away more important to both of them than my brother and I or anything else in the whole wide world. That was a given, and it was fine with me. It didn't make me feel any less loved. Always clear was their love for my brother and me. It was simply a matter of everyone having a place. That was also true of extended family and friends, none of whom ever made it into their magic circle. Outsiders need not have applied. Those other people—family and friends—may have been admired, enjoyed, liked, and appreciated, but there it stopped. Except for each other and Jesus Christ, I don't think either of them ever truly adored anybody. And I don't mean for any of this to sound critical of them. I admired their relationship. Gosh, they were nice people. And they were good, dutiful, devoted, devout, caring, and loving parents. I couldn't have asked for more as a child. It was a good childhood.

I guess the downside of that closeness between my parents was that when my daddy died, Mother's life, as she saw it, was over. From that time on, she just—as she herself said to me—marked time until she could join him. She even rejected lifelong friends who lived in the same retirement center. It was as if the only relationship worth having was the one she had with my father.

Megan, your relationship with your own mother is so different from the one I had with mine that I'm not sure you can even understand how I could have so loved this woman I was never close to. All I can say is that I hope you spend a little time each day savoring your special closeness with your mom. For her to have taken the Fragile X ball and run with it the way she has is truly in another stratosphere altogether. Just the fact that she was the first person you called after the diagnosis and that she said, without your even having the chance to ask, that she'd get herself tested right away is special beyond comprehension to some of us in the Fragile X community. I am not, believe me, the only one whose family has not been able to deal with Fragile X. I will never know how my mother would have handled it, had she and my father been told. I would like to think they would have dealt with it in a supportive manner, but, hey, I don't know. What I do know is that you need to cherish your terrific mom with your life. She's a keeper.

I tell you all this because I don't want you ever to look back with any regrets about your relationship with your mother, as I do. I fault myself for not having told my parents about Fragile X in 1982 when I first learned about it. If I had, all might have been different. I say "might," because I don't know. At least, though, I wouldn't have built up that wall of secrecy between my mother and me, and between my father and me, that rendered our relationship dishonest. I hated that. From that time until they died, I simply didn't tell them about the single most important thing in my life, which was Fragile X. That was not a sin of commission, but one of omission. When I told them about what I was doing and what was going on with me, I just happened to leave out another very important thing, which was the work that David and I were doing with FRAXA, to promote research. I didn't lie to them. I just didn't tell them the truth about my life. I regret that. I don't know how they would have reacted or to what extent they would have wanted to be part of it. Chances are that my mother would have pretty much ignored it all—in other words, not dealt with it—and that my father would have become fascinated with the research and wanted copies of everything I got. With his lawyerly precision, he would have absorbed it all with great interest. But I'll never know, and it's a lose-lose situation all the way around.

By the time we learned about Fragile X in 1982, my parents were already seventy-two years old. That's not really old, of course (and it's getting younger all the time), but they felt old by then, and they wanted to be treated as "old." But your mom, Megan, seems so young and vital and energetic, and I love hearing how much involved she is in your life. That's another reason for you not to feel the slightest guilt about leaving the boys over Valentine's Day. Your mom, after all, will be there with them. I hate to tell you, but they won't miss you that much. So, just go and enjoy, OK? Bring them some of those candy hearts, or Valentine teddy bears, or something.

And, for heaven's sake, Megan, do *not* feel guilty about lying to the boys about the fact that you're going skiing. I don't think you really have to tell them it's a business trip in order for them not to fall apart when you walk out

Jack Massey with his grandmother, Diane Hamsa

the door. Just because you took them on a ski trip last year and they had a good time on the baby slopes doesn't mean they couldn't bear it for you to go this year without them. But what do I know about your situation? And that's not to say that I don't approve of lying to kids when the situation dictates it. I sure did enough of that. Still do, as a matter of fact.

Lying, when you have boys like ours, becomes a way of life. I giggle as I say this, because I think and hope that everyone who knows me would say that I am, if nothing else, an honest woman. I can't even lie to telemarketers. You have to determine, though, when the lie is indicated, when it saves our boys' little egos, and when it's the fair thing to do. My modus operandi with lying is to omit telling the truth beforehand, but to tell the truth afterward. For instance, I didn't tell the boys about the true nature of the trip David and I took, just this last year, to attend his grandsons' graduations, Christian's and Patrick's. While we were on the trip, however, I sent them postcards saying that we had gone to Christian's graduation in Newport and Patrick's in New Hampshire. By the time they got those postcards, I knew we'd be back home and the graduations would be history. Bottom line is that they need to know what you do, generally, but they don't need too many details––especially things like how much fun you had on the ski slopes. Sort of like my mother, right? Right.

Shall I leave it on this note, or shall I tell you again what a terrific mom you are, what a great dad John is, and that Jack and Jacob—in their own special ways that you cannot now even imagine—will do you proud? Now, that's the fact, Megan girl. I promise. Swear to God. And that's no lie.

Much love,
MBBB

PS. "No man has a good enough memory to make a successful liar."
(Abraham Lincoln, 1809–1865) 🖂

13

Family History

Dear Mary Beth,

While we're talking about family, I think you might be interested to know a bit about mine.

I'm sure my family history has some interesting characters. Don't we all? But there is some information I would like to share with you.

My great-great-grandfather was Senator Gilbert Monell Hitchcock. This was on my mother's side. This must be where I got my middle name. Megan Monell Massey. Actually the middle name came from his mother, Anne Monell. Gilbert's father, Phineas W. Hitchcock, a Republican from Nebraska, was appointed by President Abraham Lincoln as the marshal of the territory from 1861 to 1864. In 1871 the state legislature elected Hitchcock to serve in the U.S. Senate for a term of six years.

Gilbert Hitchcock was born in Omaha. Gilbert was a lawyer and established the *Evening Herald* in Omaha in 1885. He was elected to the Fifty-eighth Congress, defeated in the Fifty-ninth, and elected to the Sixtieth and Sixty-first. Senator Hitchcock led the fight for the League of Nations, which was defeated in the Senate. He actually received a letter from Woodrow Wilson, which my mother has, that says, "You did everything that was possible to do to secure its passage." Gilbert Monell Hitchcock died in his Washington, DC, home at 2125 Kalorama. Does that address sound familiar? It can't be far from you.

My great-grandfather was Henry Doorly, who married Gilbert Hitchcock's daughter. He worked in the family newspaper business in Omaha and ran the Omaha *World Herald* for fifty-eight years. I never met Henry Doorly, or "Dodo" as my mother called him. He died three months before I was born. He left a legacy in Omaha: the Henry Doorly Zoo. It is one of

MEGAN'S PARENTS, DIANE AND BILL HAMSA

the greatest zoos in the Midwest. Our family is very proud to be a part of it.

My mother tells me some wonderful stories about Dodo and his wife, Nona (Margaret Hitchcock). It always seems like I heard those stories often as a child when I couldn't have cared less, and now that I am interested, I can't remember any at all!

My Fragile X gene has been traced to my grandmother, who was Katherine Doorly. She was Margaret and Dodo's daughter. That is all we know. We called Katherine "Bami." It was a nickname resulting from a grandchild's speech impairment. I believe she wanted to be "Grammy." If Bami was alive today, I know she would be leading the pack to find a cure for Fragile X syndrome. She has left many legacies to do her good work.

My father's side of the family has some interesting heritage as well. I will need to get with him sometime and have him write it down!

Have a good weekend.

Megan

Dear Megan,

This is fascinating. Such a rich heritage you have, and such a special part of Nebraska's history. And your very own zoo!! My, your boys must have loved growing up knowing about that—or did they care? Our boys grew up with the National Zoo, which didn't have nearly the cache of a family zoo.

When next you're here, we'll have to walk over to 2125 Kalorama Road to see your great-great-grandfather Hitchcock's house. I know someone who lives in the next block, and it's right by the French Embassy, no more than a ten-minute walk from where we live. We can also stop by Woodrow Wilson's house, right on our street, which is now a museum. You have lots of connections here within a few blocks.

—MBBB ✉

Dear Mary Beth,

I'm sure I've told my kids about the Omaha zoo connection, but they're not impressed with that stuff. They don't get it. Our family is a zoo. Zoo enough. So, it works quite nicely.

Bye for now.

Megan

PS. "Accidents will occur in the best regulated families." (Charles Dickens, *David Copperfield*) ✉

MEGAN WITH HER SISTERS (L TO R): KRISTY DOOLING, MEGAN, AND HEIDI WILKE

14

So, What Is "Least Restrictive," Really?

Megan, dear,

I'm so sorry that you and John had such an unhappy experience with the Individual Education Plan (IEP)[1] meeting at Jack's school. As you surely know far better than I, being in that stage of your kids' lives, the reactions of the various participants of those meetings can be all over the lot. I'm truly sympathetic—if not empathetic. I have to admit that I'm also sympathetic with the school staff members who likely look forward to IEP meetings about as much as they look forward to their next collective root canal. Just the preparation of all that paperwork must be formidable. Even though—unlike in the '60s and '70s—the forms are computerized and the staff can sort of fill in the blanks, it's still preparation time away from something else. And you know what? I think that how those meetings go can depend an awful lot on what kind of a day the participants are having. I can only assume that at least a couple of the folks around that table were not in a great place at that moment. Bottom line, you'd all rather have been shopping at Wal-Mart.

Chances are that Jack Massey's teacher—even though hopes were so high, both on her part and yours, at the beginning of the year—is simply not the right teacher for him. Listen, personality clashes happen between teachers and kids all the time, and for our kids, it takes a teacher with that

1 An IP is the Individual Plan developed for each adult who receives services from the state. The employment agency or residential facility must hold an IP meeting once a year to assess progress and set future goals. An IEP is the Individual Education Plan that is required by the government for each child in the public school system who receives special education services. This lasts until the child reaches the aged of twenty-two. Both plans are formulated by the administrators of the program in which the child or adult is enrolled, with input from the parents and, in some cases, advocates and other professionals.

extra little indefinable "something" that they all can't have. Would that they could, but we're talking reality here. And you have to keep remembering that she wasn't trained as a special ed teacher.

For me to suggest that I don't empathize is simply to say that I haven't walked in your shoes. Sure, we had IEP meetings for both of our boys, but they were never about the same subject matter as yours are, because they were never about inclusion. Forgive me, but if you'll recount our conversation of yesterday, a fair amount of the problem you had with the meeting was over the issue of inclusion.

Now, sweet girl, I know full well that I am so old that I'm out of step with the current generation of parents, and that your generation feels very strongly that their children—no matter how handicapped—should be educated in the public schools with whatever additional aides or helpers those children need in order to function properly in that setting. OK, I know that's how you feel, so we're just going to have to agree to disagree on that point, and I hope you know how very much I love and adore you and John, and that at least you'll hear me and let me give you a bit of American history.

In 1975 Congress passed PL 94-142, the Education for All Handicapped Children Act, which mandated that the public school systems shall educate all handicapped children in "the least restrictive environment." Now, look at that term, "least restrictive," because that's the term that David and I—and thousands of other parents in the 1970s—went to court over.

In the decade after that law passed, public school systems throughout the country began attempting to develop programs for handicapped children within the public schools. It was slow and heavy going, certainly in the District of Columbia. What we were saying was that for our child, at that time, a private school for handicapped children was truly less restrictive than putting our child in a regular public school. Jack, when he was twelve, did receive funding at the Kennedy Institute in Washington. It was a wonderful little school, run by the Sisters of Mercy. It was a great environment for him. The sisters were loving, but tough. To this day, when Jack is in one of his little autistic reveries, I'll sometimes hear him say, "Jonathan, you'd better say your prayers!" This is what the sisters would tell a student who was caught misbehaving. Jack still remembers that when caught in the wrong place or doing the wrong thing, there are and will be consequences. I'm sure that Ellen Atwell's Montessori school and the Sisters of Mercy teaching methods aren't the only game in town, but I do feel that their influence has given Jack a sense of order and a sense of security when that order is missing.

Now, again, you likely feel that a small Catholic school for only handicapped kids is about as restrictive as any place could be. But I don't think so. I believe that Jack 's capacity to be a leader among his peers in that setting has come in handy in the years since. I don't mean that he was class president or anything. They didn't even have things like that. But he wasn't left sitting on the sidelines. I believe that in the intervening years, the behaviors he learned there have made him better able to cope in the world around him. I believe the time he spent at two other "special" schools, the Ivymount School in Rockville, Maryland, and later at Maplebrook, a boarding school, helped to *un*-restrict his future possibilities.

I know that what I'm about to say to you will put me, now and forever, into the category of an old crone who doesn't understand the way things are today and surely doesn't know what's good for your child. Indeed, you may think that I didn't know what was best for my own children either, judging from the way we went about getting special education services for them. I can't argue. I'm just telling you that things were different then, and from what I can tell, I'm not sure they're a whole heck of a lot better now.

I can't help wondering whether Jack Massey's teacher—I forget her name—might actually like Jack, and that because she likes him, she'd like to see him get the education he deserves in a setting where he can thrive. Now, it could truly be a personality clash, as I suggested before, but I can't help wondering.

I also can't help wondering if perhaps it's ever occurred to you that a "free and public education in the least restrictive environment" can, but must not always, mean in a public school setting with "normal" children?

Could it be possible that a "free and public" education could indeed mean the public school system funding tuition for your Jack to attend a private school for similarly handicapped children?

Just think for a moment whether it's possible that "least restrictive" may not necessarily refer only to a large public school where there are a zillion distractions for kids like Jack. But a small, private setting with a teacher who is specially qualified to employ special education methods to teach special children could actually be *less* restrictive to his development.

Has it ever occurred to you that just possibly Jack could, in a small, private placement, be a real leader among his peers, and not just a token leader like we've heard about on TV?

At the risk of appearing to put myself—in your mind, anyway, and your mind is all I have in my mind here—in a corner other than Jack's, I still have to ask you this: has it ever occurred to you that the other children in the classroom in which Jack is "included" are not being well served by the distractions inherent in a situation where the teacher is having to focus more than a fair amount of her time, attention, and energy on Jack? Is this fair to the other kids? Is it fair to their parents, who pay taxes just like you do? Is it fair to Jack, who—and trust me on this—will be resented if this situation continues? And when I say, "this situation," I mean the notion of his teacher being unhappy and frustrated with having Jack in her class, and Jack's continuing to act out whenever he's not getting one on one.

Honey, I know it feels good to have your Jack and Jacob attend the public school "just like everybody else." I remember that it felt good to me for the three years we went that route. Sort of good, anyway. I also know that my boys were not "included." They were there, but they were not included. You can't legislate, mandate, or administrate inclusion. Inclusion is a thing of the mind and heart. It's also a matter, for the includer, of what works. If it doesn't "work" to have Jack and Jacob on the soccer team, they—the "includees"—may be there, but they won't be truly included. Gosh, I'd give my life if that weren't the case, but it is. The includers really do want that team to win. A lot. Especially at that age and with parents who are so focused on their kids' winning.

Thirty years later, Jack Busby still remembers the names of his three teachers in the public school: Mrs. McKay, Mr. Jackson, and Mrs. Martin. They were all outstanding as teachers and truly cared for their special classrooms. They did their best, but they could not make the normal kids include the handicapped kids. That, I'm convinced, has to come from home, from dinner table conversations about inclusion. Unless I'm mistaken, most dinner table conversations—to the extent they occur at all—tend to focus on homework, who did well at soccer practice, who did well on the math test—not on which handicapped child did you speak to in the lunchroom today. That's human nature, Megan, and I'm not saying that this is bad. I'm saying that's the way it is.

Later on, when those same bright and competitive children gain more maturity, some—though certainly not all—of them will have a whole different attitude about inclusion. I think of our young friend, Charlie Demmon, the loving and generous son of wonderful former neighbors of ours. Charlie is just four years older than our Jack. When Charlie was in his twenties, he had a job at the White House and his later-to-be wife, Barb, was working in a congressional office. Charlie arranged for Jack to be a member of Barb's staff's softball team. I would take Jack down and drop him at their games, and Charlie would bring him home. While Jack didn't score many points, he did hit in a run now and then. The point is that it didn't seem to detract much from the team to include him. By that age, those wonderful guys and girls could see that it didn't really hurt anything to have him there in the outfield. They were ready, in their own lives, to embrace that sort of inclusion. But, Megan, I would bet my life that when they were your Jack's age, there is no way that those same young people could have dealt with including either of our Jacks on their team with that kind of acceptance.

Let me tell you just one more story about inclusion. Just this morning, as a matter of fact, the guest preacher at the Washington National Cathedral was a distinguished Methodist minister from Maine, Dr. David Glusker. The theme of his sermon was grace and how it's illustrated to us in unexpected ways. He spoke about a high school basketball game when his son was on the team. They had won their first seven games of the season and this eighth game was against the only other, so-far undefeated, team in the league. The game went so well that by the second half, his son's team was thirty points ahead. Then the coach of the other team did something he had yet to do all season. He put Petey in. Just watching him run onto the court, one could tell that Petey was a young man with some kind of handicap. Reverend Glusker said he wasn't sure what it was, but, naturally, I thought of Fragile X. Petey had been on the bench for the entire season, and now the coach was putting him in. The other members of the team could hardly believe it.

Petey wasn't really in the game because by the time he got down the court to where the action was, the action was shifting back to the other end. This went on for several plays until finally, somehow, someone threw the ball to Petey. He stopped. The members of his team stopped. The members of the other team, the team that was thirty points ahead, stopped. Then the referees stopped. They all waited. The gymnasium became still. At last, Petey threw the ball up into the air. It didn't go anywhere near the basket. Back the players went to the other end. Once again, Petey ended up with the ball. The same thing happened, but this time nobody grabbed the ball when Petey threw it and missed. It came back to Petey to throw again. Which he did. He missed again. And again. And again. And again. Finally, on the seventh try, Petey made a basket.

Reverend Glusker didn't say that the stadium erupted in cheers, though maybe it did. He did say that the members of both teams, as well as the referees, exhibited a special grace that was felt by every single person in that gym. He also mentioned that he had been a coach for another kids' basketball team and that there was a rule that a handicapped teammate must be allowed to play for at least one quarter of the game. If that rule applied here, then the coach had been in violation all season for not letting Petey play before. He decided to put Petey in only in the one game when they were thirty points behind and it didn't really matter.

I would love to think that there are plenty of bright, competitive, decent, thoughtful kids out there who are so full of grace that they would welcome the Peteys—and the Roberts and the Jacks and the Jacobs—of this world to play on their teams, no matter what the win/loss consequences. I would love to think that. But I don't.

Now, I know that saying all this not only puts me in the last century—which, after all, is when all of these kinds of occurrences took place for the Busbys. It also makes me sound like I think it's OK to remove our kids from the mainstream, that it's OK not to make the other kids and the teachers and coaches of those other kids have to deal with them, that I think it can actually be restrictive for normal kids and their teachers to have to cope with handicapped kids, and that I think it's quite OK to put our kids in another school all together. And you know what? That's exactly what I do think.

I think you will serve Jack Massey well if you and John will take another look at this. Jacob may be a different story, at least for a while; after all, he's always been able to cope with social situations better than Jack can. But I fear that for him, too, the time will come when a special school might be in his interest.

Having said all that, I realize that, still, I'm probably not going to change your current thinking. Not today, anyway.

But I love you a lot, and you *do* know that, OK?

MBBB

PS. "Educating is not the filling of a pail but the lighting of a fire." (William Butler Yeats, 1865–1939)
And oh, Megan, don't we all wish for all of our children those rare and gifted teachers who can light that fire? ✉

Dear Mary Beth,

You know what I like about you? I always know where you stand, and there is no question that you are telling me exactly what you think. You do it very gracefully.

John and I go back and forth about where we want Jack to be in the educational system. At first, I wanted him to get all the extra help he would qualify for, even if it took him out of the classroom. Then I began to notice that he was always in the special education room. This was not always a place for good behavioral modeling or a positive learning environment. Sometimes it could get a little too relaxed in there. Teachers do make an incredible difference.

One of the best teachers Jack ever had was Mr. Wright. He taught fifth grade. You've got to love that name, don't you? He was perfect for Jack. Having a male teacher was a definite strength. The female teachers tend to fall in love with Jack and not push him. We were so impressed with Mr. Wright's ability to interact with our son and make modifications for him. Because of this, we pulled Jack out of his special education classes so he could be a part of this great classroom experience. There was a sweet young girl in there, Carrie, who took Jack under her wing and made sure he got all the assignments and stayed on task. She is still his friend today. She told her mother that she would like to have a child like Jack some day. She must be crazy.

I didn't want Jack to be working on basic math skills and reading first grade books all day long. I thought he should experience the thrill of a science experiment or looking at a map, or possibly go on a field trip. He loves to ride a bus. Something new has to sink in and stimulate his brain.

Certainly being with his peers is helpful, isn't it?

Then there is the other side of the coin. Does he even get it? Are we wasting his time and that of his classmates? Would the anxiety of leaving the school building to go on a field trip take all the fun out of it? I wish Jack had an opinion about the matter, but he wouldn't even understand my question.

You have certainly given me things to think about. I love having him part of the school experience. It helps build social skills and offers the opportunity to make friendships.

WRESTLER JACOB MASSEY

Home schooling has always been out of the question for me. I would be in jail for murder.

I agree with you that inclusion is a thing of the mind and heart, and it is a matter, for the includer, of what works. When you find the right includer, you never want to let that person go. It is sad even for normal kids to learn that not all adults or teachers are good influences.

Your Petey story sure hit home. I have often thought my kids would never be able to participate in any school event. But you are right, Jack and Jacob do make me proud. It is just on a different level. For example, my friend's child was singing a solo at the middle school choir concert. My friend was worried about her making all the right notes. I'm worried about whether or not Jack will be able to stand in one place for the entire concert without being a distraction, picking his nose, or hollering "Hi, Mom" in between songs. My, how our perspectives must change when we have special-needs kids.

As far as sports go, I don't think I could have handled it anyway—Fragile X or no Fragile X. So many parents are living their lives through their kids. It is nauseating. I'd like them to try my shoes on for one day and they would quickly change their attitudes. They complain when their child doesn't play, or if the team loses a game. It's usually a "coaching problem." If they are victorious, all is well. If not, it's because they practice too much or not enough. They should use this game plan instead of that one. This child plays because he is the coach's kid, this one doesn't because the coach doesn't like the parents.

True or false, they are all missing it, according to me. Jack and Jacob do have such different needs. Jacob is my social one, but some day all of his peers will pass him up too. I see glimpses of it now.

I get one child in order in school and then it is time to get going on the other. It is truly a full-time job just to keep the schools on track. We have been fortunate, so far.

You know I will keep you posted.

Love,

Megan ✉

15

Let's Party

Dear Megan,

First of all, I apologize—profusely and all over the place—for the delay in getting back to you. The boys' vacation sidetracked me, as it always does. When they're home, I spend all of my time either in line at the Safeway or standing at the kitchen counter. One of the fun things we did during this vacation was what we do every Labor Day, which is to host a potluck supper. They're great fun, and all I have to do, besides getting all the equipment organized and the wine and liquor and soft drinks, etc., etc., is to coordinate what people are bringing. The main thing is to insist that every person calls to tell me what he or she is bringing, so that we don't end up with seven chocolate cakes and no salad. It truly is a fun kind of party to have. Maybe they give a lot of them in Nebraska nowadays, but they don't in Washington. At least, I don't hear much about them. The super Maryland Fragile X Resource Group has had some of them, and the one we were able to attend was great fun.

You know, Megan, I think that one reason I've entertained at home so much over the years is because of our boys' handicaps. I have tended to give our big parties over holiday weekends because we wanted to be with friends. On the other hand, we didn't feel comfortable taking our boys to friends' homes, for the most part, and our boys didn't have friends who invited them to do things. In other words, our boys' social life was our social life, and vice versa. That's not the best plan, and the older they get, the more I realize it's not the best plan. It's simply the way it was. We had to make a social life for them, and having friends over was the logical way to make it happen. Our friends, who have been coming to our parties for years and have watched our boys grow up, are so dear about standing here in our living room listening to Robert talk about some trip his group home is going on next April or about his personal trainer's college courses. If, however, they hadn't known these boys for years and years, they would be freaked out or turned off by the experience. Bottom line: you need some friends who like coming to your house, enjoy your other friends whom they can usually count on seeing there, and accept your boys for who and what they are. In other words, you need friends for the long haul. And the bottom line of the bottom line is what David Busby has always said: "If you want to gain social acceptance in Washington, hang a lamb chop out the window." If you feed them, they will come.

We can all, of course, just have a cocktail party and invite all of our friends. That would work fine for Jack and Jake, because they could mingle among the guests and feel very much part of the party. I'll tell you, though, who it won't work so well for, and that's your friends. Besides the fact that inviting someone for cocktails doesn't begin to pay back a dinner you've had at their house, I think people like to be fed—as in sitting down with a plate of food and visiting with friends while eating that food. If your invitation is only for cocktails, people will come, but they won't look forward to it the way they will if they know they won't have to go home afterward and scrounge for leftovers or ice cream. Too, there's something traditional about having practically the same party for the same people with the same basic menu

Jack Busby with Diane and John Rehm at one of his family's parties

year after year. It's these traditions that are precious and priceless to our boys, and will be to yours.

As you surely know with your own boys, our kids like tradition. Indeed, we've always joked that if we try something new and it works, it's an instant "Old Family Tradition." We've also joked that when we have a big party, Robert will talk of nothing else for days beforehand. Then, when party time comes, he will often simply disappear upstairs to watch TV most of the evening. Then, the next day, he'll go on and on as if he had been the life of the party. The point is that he loves the idea of the party, of the friends coming, of family coming, of an occasion. When the occasion arrives, however, it's often simply too much. Except when we're actually eating dinner. Then he's a player. The good thing about having the party here is that when it gets to be too much, he simply opts out—which is kind of hard to do away from home, at someone else's house.

For a couple of years, during the week between Christmas and New Year's, we tried taking the boys, plus Hopie and Alison and their kids, down to the Homestead, a wonderful resort in Virginia. They have so many great things for families to do that we thought there would be something for everyone. Wrong. "Everyone" is not our boys. We discovered that they do better right here at home, with other people—whether family or friends—coming here to see us. This was a rather painful, and decidedly expensive, lesson to learn: it's easier to walk on home turf.

Not that you asked, but one of the biggest mistakes I see women (and not just young women) make is going with the notion that they can't have a party until the new sofa—or wallpaper, or whatever—arrives. Do not pass go with that idea. If I had postponed doing a party for all the "things" I was waiting for, we'd still be planning our first party, forty-odd years later. OK? No one is going to really look at the existing sofa, trust me. And if they do, they'll just think, "Gee, that off-white sofa of Megan and John's wasn't any more kid-proof than mine was." Maybe you can bill the party as a "farewell-to-our-old-sofa" or "sofa-send-off" party. Either make a joke of it or ignore it, but *don't* delay the party for a stupid sofa. Life is quite literally too short to let your social schedule revolve around what things you have ready for prime time. Oh, and if you do have a white sofa, next time choose a darker color.

I know one of the reasons we're all reluctant to entertain at home is our concern about the boys' behavior. Just getting a babysitter for the whole afternoon and evening goes a long way toward solving that one. After all, if you were going out, you'd have a babysitter come in, right? So this should be the same thing. You can't take care of the boys while preparing for and having a party. That's asking a bit much of even good multitaskers. In the best of all worlds, you could get the babysitter to take the boys to McDonald's for supper, which would solve the problem of feeding them their dinner and get them out of the house for that crucial hour before your guests start arriving.

I'll never forget the time Jack Busby, who was about seven, opened the door to our friends and neighbors Hugh and Ann Sidey—stark naked. That is, Jack was stark naked, not the Sideys. Oh, yikes! It was wonderful, as you might imagine. They were great about it and we all just laughed it off, but I'm sure we all still remember it. That's the kind of thing a two-year-old—not a seven-year-old— might do and get away with, but of course that's what makes our little guys their unique little selves, right? Ah, yes.

By and large, I think Robert and Jack have turned out to be reasonably socially acceptable—as long as people understand their limitations. They're not really a problem at a stand-up party—partly, I guess, because they're not prone to standing up for just too long a time at one stretch. They'll mingle around for a short time, then find the nearest TV set if we're at someone else's house, or disappear upstairs here at home. At a sit-down dinner, it's far more difficult. I'm never comfortable putting them by anyone except David or me or a really close, extended-family friend because they simply can't hold up their end of a conversation. For the dinner partner, it quickly gets to be a conversational case of empties, which is pretty unfair. So for us, a buffet supper works best. The boys don't need to be too much a part of it until dinnertime. Then they'll fix a plate and find someone they know well to sit with, and then they'll disappear before dessert. They almost never sit through dessert, which is fine. They don't need dessert. Plus, they know that if they sit through dessert, they'll probably be asked to help with the dishes. About some things, they're plenty swift.

Knowing you, you'll always be able to figure out what works best for you and John and Jack and Jacob, and you know what? That'll be just the right party for you. This means that you'll have fun doing it. And if the hostess has fun, the guests have fun.

So, Cheers! And love,

MBBB

PS. "Thousands of candles can be lighted from a single candle, and the life of the candle will not be shortened. Happiness never decreases by being shared." (Buddha, 563–483 BC)

PPS. Here, just for fun (my own fun, I suspect, more than yours), are two of my old tried-and-true recipes.

You can make the guacamole early that day, or even the day before. The grits can be made at least two, or even three, days ahead of time. The point is that if you do all the things ahead of time that can be done ahead of time, it won't kill you and you can enjoy your party.

GUACAMOLE

3 ripe avocados[1]
Juice of 1 lime (if it's not a juicy one, use 2)
1 heaping teaspoon Lawry's garlic salt
1/4 teaspoon Tabasco sauce
1 can (3 1/2 ounces) chopped green chiles (I like the El Paso brand)
Chopped onions—enough to almost equal the volume of avocado
2 or 3 Italian plum tomatoes[2]
Cilantro, finely snipped—about a half cup

Chop and mash the avocados with a potato masher. Add the lime juice, garlic salt, Tabasco, and chiles. Stir this, then add the onions and tomatoes.

Put 1 or 2 of the avocado pits in the bowl to keep the guacamole from turning dark. Cover with plastic wrap and refrigerate until serving time.

Serve with Frito Scoops, or whatever chips you like. We especially like the Frito-guacamole marriage. Keep in mind that some tortilla chips are too fragile for a dip this thick.

MY MOTHER'S CHEESE GRITS

My mother made these as far back as I can remember. They are great to serve at a buffet supper or brunch—especially around the Christmas or Easter holidays. They are even better when served with ham and black-eyed peas.

1 The avocados I like best are the California Calavo Hass variety. They are the dark green, bumpy ones. The ones I really don't like are the larger, shiny, lighter green ones. Frankly, if they are the only ones you can get, I wouldn't bother making the guacamole. They are simply too bland. If I bring home hard avocados, it usually takes two to three days for them to ripen. They're supposed to be ripe when the stem moves easily and when the flesh feels soft, but still firm—which sounds like a contradiction in terms. You get the hang of it quickly, though. I always get an extra one because, once in a while, you get one that's all black inside.

2 These are mainly for color and to add another texture. If you can't find decent ones, leave them out.

6 cups water
1 1/4 teaspoon salt
1 1/2 cups quick (not instant) grits
1/2 (scant) teaspoon garlic powder
1 1/2 sticks of butter, cut into chunks
12 ounces Velveeta cheese, cut into 1-inch cubes
3 eggs—put them in a 2-cup measuring cup and add enough milk to fill the cup to 1 1/4 cup. Stir with a fork.
8 ounces grated sharp cheddar cheese, to use later for topping

Preheat the oven to 350 degrees. Butter a 9-inch-by-13-inch Pyrex baking dish. Set aside.

The trick to this recipe is to have your butter and cheese cut up and your eggs and milk mixed and set aside before boiling the water. Once that water is boiling, you can't stop to cut or mix anything.

Bring the water to a rolling boil. This is important in order to keep the grits from being lumpy. Add the salt, then gradually stir in the grits with a wooden spoon. Cook for two or three minutes, stirring constantly. If it starts boiling over, just lift the pan off the burner for a second or two. Or you can turn it down a bit, but you don't want it on low at this point.

When the grits are cooked, turn the heat down to low, then immediately add the garlic powder, butter, and cheese, stirring constantly. When the butter and cheese have melted, slowly and gradually add the eggs and milk mixture, still stirring constantly. You may not need all of the mixture. You just have to judge when the grits seem cooked, and then stop adding the liquid. It's sort of like cooking scrambled eggs. There's a fine line between cooked and overcooked.

If the phone rings while you're doing this, just let it ring. You can't leave it, even for a few seconds, until the grits are safely in the Pyrex dish.

As soon as you decide the grits are cooked, immediately pour the grits into the Pyrex dish, cover them with aluminum foil, and bake them in the oven for 30 minutes. Remove the foil and spread the grated cheddar cheese over the top. Heat uncovered for another 15 or 20 minutes, until bubbly.

This can all be done a day or two ahead. The dish can be covered with foil and refrigerated until you're ready to reheat it for serv-

ing. When you're ready to reheat, take the dish out of the fridge a couple of hours before you want to serve it. Then follow the directions above for heating the grits in the oven.
Serves 15 (unless the Busby boys are part of the party, in which case it will serve more like 8). ✉

Dear Mary Beth,

You describe my boys to a tee when you talk about entertaining in your home with Robert and Jack. I have always farmed out the kids in order to clean the house and prepare for friends to come over. However, I must admit I like the philosophy of just picking up the big chunks before everyone comes over and then clean when they leave.

We have done quite a bit of entertaining in our home and after reading your letter I know why. It never really occurred to me, but it does stress John and me to take the kids to other people's homes or parties. We have to watch them like hawks and there is always a problem, usually with Jack. He doesn't mean to cause trouble. He just gets overstimulated so easily and that is not a pretty sight.

I remember one party in particular. It was the Rotary Christmas party at the Scottsbluff Country Club. The boys were maybe five and four years of age. Santa Claus attends the event and brings each of the children a present. All the Rotarians are there with their spouses and families. Jack and Jacob were scared to death of Santa Claus and didn't even want to enter the dining room. After much encouragement we settled in for dinner. Jack's fear quickly subsided when Santa brought him a plastic sword. Just picture Jack running through all the tables at the country club swinging his sword and yelling. He was enjoying himself at that point, but needless to say, we weren't. I think that was our last appearance at the Christmas party with the children. This all occurred before we knew our kids had Fragile X. I must have thought they had something after that evening. It was a disaster.

I remember seeing a lot of my friends' daughters in beautiful party dresses, the little boys in pants and sweaters. My boys hated wearing sweaters, or anything tight on their bodies. The other children seemed to behave so nicely. The good thing was everyone loved our boys and all their enthusiasm and energy. Oh boy, don't they put that nicely. For many months after that evening Jack and Jacob feared going out to the club. Even if we just wanted to eat in the grill room, they were convinced Santa would be there. If it happens once in their world, they think it will always be that way. We could call it a Family Tradition. One that had to be broken immediately!

One year, we took the boys to Disney World when the Society for Neuroscience convention was in Orlando. I actually spent a day with Katie Clapp at the convention.

Our trip was a surprise for the boys. Since their reading and understanding of geography was so poor, they didn't have a clue about our destination. When we finally arrived in Atlanta to change planes and fly to Orlando, we told the boys where we were going. We should have known that surprises were not good for our fraggles. Jack burst into tears and begged us to send him back to Scottsbluff. He wanted to stay with Boppe and Bucko. When we finally got settled into our room at the Wilderness Lodge at Disney, Jack seemed a little calmer. The next morning he refused to get up and get dressed. When we started to head out the door (we would never have left him), I said, "You will get pretty hungry while we are gone." Jack replied, "I'll just get room service." Jack finally agreed to come and we did have a fun day. The Buzz Lightyear ride was the highlight. They had no interest in anything else. Maybe Blizzard Beach, but it was pretty cold for swimming.

Another story that comes to mind is the day Jack had a friend over to play. That was an event that took weeks to plan. It was just as hard to find that friend as it was to set up a time to come. After weeks of planning, seriously, and it was weeks, the day finally arrived. Guess what? Jack totally ignored him. We had activities and all kinds of games to play. I found Jack upstairs watching TV and his friend was outside in the yard. Upon questioning Jack he said, "Mom, I just want to be alone." Ugh. Fortunately his friend didn't notice, but needless to say we didn't do that anymore.

I never intended this letter to be so long. I guess my memory bank just kicked in when you mentioned kids and entertaining. Those situations are improving, but it is always easier to entertain at home. Jacob is my social butterfly; he loves to mingle with the guests. I'll never forget the evening United States Senator Chuck Hagel came to our home. We rehearsed and rehearsed with Jacob on the correct way to address the senator, look him in the eye and say hello. When the senator arrived in the driveway, Jacob hollered, "Hey, Hagel!" We did receive a note from the senator a few weeks later telling us to let Jacob know "Hagel" said hello. It was another humbling moment with the children.

I just reread this letter, as it has been sitting on my desk awhile. I think I better plan another party. I have recipes from you that I can use. Or better yet, I'll have it catered. That is my best solution. And the greatest thing is when my friends ask if I made it, I always answer, "Oh, yes!" And they quickly, teasingly, and lovingly respond, "Liar!" They know me too well. I will keep those recipes in my recipe box and they'll be used someday. Maybe I'll send them to my sisters. They can make them for me when I go to visit.

Thanks again for all of your love and support.

Megan ✉

16

Your Tax Dollars at Work

Dear Megan,

Now, didn't I tell you how easy it is and how your congressman works for *you*, and *you* have the power to help him/her stay in office or not—depending upon how effective you think he/she is on your issues? As Tip O'Neill said, "All politics is local." And you, Megan girl, are big-time local to your congressman—a fact he's not likely to forget, even if perhaps you do. So, I'm not the least bit surprised—nor can I understand why you are—that both Congressman Douglas Bereuter and Congressman Tom Osborne signed on to the joint resolution promoted by our dear friend Congressman Wes Watkins of Oklahoma and Katie and Mike's congressman, William Delahunt of Massachusetts, declaring October 5 Fragile X Research Awareness Day. Needless to say, it didn't hurt matters that John's uncle works for Congressman Bereuter. The only thing better than having a friend in a high place is having an uncle with access to that high place. When you stop and think about it, though, this resolution should be a no-brainer for anyone in Congress. I mean, what's not to like here? It's not as if we're asking for money. Except that really, in our clever little way, we are.

As much money as FRAXA has been able to raise over the years to put into dozens of different research grants, the hard fact is that the really big money spent on research is now and ever shall be spent by the U.S. government, through the National Institutes of Health (NIH) and the Centers for Disease Control and Prevention (CDC). So, what we have to do and have had to do from the start, is to convince those with their fingers on the purse strings out there in Bethesda and Atlanta that Fragile X should be a priority of theirs, as it is of ours.

Our relationship with the National Institute for Child Health and

David and Mary Beth Busby with Congressman Wes Watkins (FRAXA's Republican champion in the U.S. House of Representatives, far right) and his wife, Lou Watkins

Human Development, one of the twenty-seven institutes of the NIH, goes back to 1994, the year FRAXA began. Or, perhaps, I should say that it really began in 1955—which, of course, is before NICHD was even founded (that occurred in 1960). Minor detail, but never mind.

I say 1955 because that was the year David came to Washington to work on the staff of the U.S. Senate Interstate and Foreign Commerce Committee. One of the women on Senator Monroney's staff, Jo Nobles, was the Senator's personal secretary. Jo was from Idabel, Oklahoma, even farther southeast than Ada, where David was from, so they had that bond. When Senator Monroney left Congress, Jo worked for Senator Harold Hughes, then for Senator Dale Bumpers of Arkansas until he retired from the Senate in 1996. Jo was, and still is, tough, smart, and has good, kind instincts. One of my favorite stories about Jo, who was the keeper of Senator Bumper's personal finances, is when he came to her one day and said, "Jo, I need some spending money." She answered, "Senator, I gave you fifty dollars last week. What did you do with it?" Nothing gets by Jo.

Knowing that Senator Bumpers was on the HELP committee, the Senate's Committee on Health, Education, Labor, and Pensions, David went to Jo and asked her how she would suggest proceeding if we wanted to form a relationship with the NIH. Jo said that, for starters, we should meet with Mary Ann Chaffee, Senator Bumpers's staff member who dealt with medical issues. Jo invited us, along with Mary Ann, to have lunch in the Senate cafeteria. It was the week before Christmas, when Congress had adjourned, but most of the staff was still around.

I'll never forget that lunch, because Mary Ann Chaffee got up out of a sick-with-the-flu bed to come to it. She had nothing but ginger ale for lunch, and I remember thinking that this woman is a real hero. My first instinct was correct, because she got right on our case. She said that the first thing we needed to do was to meet with George Gaines, Legislative Liaison Officer in the office of the director of the NICHD. Mary Ann (who, I have to tell you, has become one of my dear and special friends) not only arranged the meeting for early in 1995, but she also went out to Bethesda with David and me. George Gaines is a marvelous person. He didn't skip a beat. He immediately arranged a meeting with Dr. Felix de la Cruz, then the chief of the mental retardation branch of NICHD. We urged Katie Clapp to come down for that one, as we figured we needed her to talk the talk, which David and I couldn't (and still can't) begin to do. We also needed Katie to work her special brand of charm to make our case on why Fragile X research

FRAXA Co-founder Katie Clapp with Congressman Bill Delahunt of Massachusetts

can lead to a portal for other diseases. That meeting went well, eventually leading to a conference of researchers in 1998.

Katie came down for a later meeting with the extraordinary Dr. Duane Alexander, director of NICHD, during which we discussed the possibility of having FRAXA cofund some grants with NICHD. We were impressed with his extensive knowledge of Fragile X, his recognition of the importance of the research, and his can-do attitude when it came to making things happen. Besides, he's a very nice man.

Katie also developed a working relationship with the National Institute of Mental Health (NIMH), and both the NICHD and the NIMH contributed, along with FRAXA, to the first conference of Fragile X researchers at the Banbury Center at the Cold Spring Harbor Lab on Long Island. Those conferences have become annual events, and we are most grateful because there is always the sense there that important exchanges are taking place among the researchers. I remember at the first one, in 2000, I asked one of our major researchers if he ever leaves a conference feeling that it was sort of a waste of time. He answered, "Often, but never a Banbury conference."

Also at that first Banbury conference, I had the honor of having dinner one night with Dr. James Watson, who codiscovered the structure of DNA in 1953 and who had been sufficiently impressed with a meeting with Katie Clapp and FRAXA'S board chair, Debbie Stevenson, that he joined FRAXA's board of scientific advisors. Dr. Watson has famously said:

> I became very excited when the Fragile X gene was discovered in 1991. It was the first major human triumph of the Human Genome Project. The impact upon affected families rivals that of Down Syndrome. Unlike Down Syndrome, with Fragile X there is just one functional protein missing. So we must entice key young scientists now working on nerve cells to focus on Fragile X. It has to be a simpler disease to understand and eventually conquer.

Dr. Watson also not so famously said something memorable to me at that dinner. I mentioned having noticed the tennis courts on the grounds––that entire campus, by the way, is gorgeous—and asked him if he played tennis. He said yes, he played every day. "In fact," he added, "When I die, I want to be playing tennis. *And* it has to be singles." Do you love that, Megan?

The bottom line is that the NIH funding on Fragile X research has gone from less than 1 million in 1994 to 19.8 million in 2004.

Recounting all of this, starting with the political process and my pride in your work with your members of Congress, Megan, brings home ever more clearly the fact that, working together, and not much caring who gets credit, there is no limit to what we parents of fraggles can achieve. So, you keep on goin', girl!

Love,
MBBB

PS. "Government is the enemy—until you need a friend."
(William Cohen, former Republican senator from Maine and former secretary of defense for President Bill Clinton) ✉

Dear Mary Beth,

I can't take much credit for all of the Nebraska representatives in Washington signing on to the resolution. Sure, I called on them out there in Washington, DC. But I believe that in the great state of Nebraska, the *people* elect outstanding congressmen and senators. They do listen and respond. It must be the kind of citizens Nebraska attracts. I think we are mostly Republican—a red state.

I do love you and David, despite your political affiliation.

Have a great day. Got to run!

Love,
Megan ✉

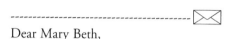

17

Guardian Angels and Messenger Angels

Dear Megan,

Jack lost his job today. He's been working in a deli for three weeks, and I'm afraid we knew it was going to be a no go from the beginning. They had him washing dishes from 8:00 a.m. until 2:00 p.m.. He was too easily distracted and had trouble staying "on task." Today, they told him not to come back. Task maybe not completed, but over.

David and I feel so guilty about this because we knew, in our heart of hearts, that he wasn't going to do well at this job. Having been a busboy and a food runner for fourteen years, Jack was accustomed to being "on task" when there was a task and "resting" between tasks. Most of all, the Callahan family, for whom he worked all those years, was incredibly forgiving.

I know, Megan, that hearing about this job stuff is probably a bit distressing and depressing to you, as at your stage, you just want to get your Jack and Jacob grown up and semi-independent. Hearing from me that "it's never over" is not exactly the message you want to get, is it? How I wish we could reach the stage where both of our boys are totally stable and maybe, indeed, we still will. I'm not giving up yet. I'm afraid, though, that during all those years Jack worked for the Callahans, who were better to Jack than he had any right to expect—and more forgiving of his faults—we allowed ourselves to nestle in a little cocoon of job security that was literally unreal. Now things are getting very real.

When Jack began working for the Callahans at La Fonda, we had a driver, a kind and gentle man named James Cooper, who took him back and forth from our home. After a couple of years of that, I began walking him the mile or so over to the restaurant and then picking him up and walking him home, training him to take the route with the fewest dangerous streets to cross. Then after a few weeks of that routine, I would walk him halfway, then a quarter of the way, until finally he went both ways on his own. At the time, I didn't realize just what a triumph that was for him, to have that measure of independence. I do remember, however, standing at my bedroom window where I could see about halfway down the block, watching—with tears in my eyes—my baby start out to work on his first day of going it alone. They were tears of joy, pride, relief, and anxiety over what might go wrong. But mostly, they were tears of pleasure, shared with Jack in his joy of feeling on his own.

Going along with that independence, of course, came Jack's notion that he should stop in at the 7-Eleven across from La Fonda to get a Coke on his way to work. They came to know him well, which was neat—except that sometimes he would dillydally around there until he was late for work. The Callahans would always call when he was late, and when he was late arriving home, I wouldn't hesitate to call them to see what time he had left.

There was also a flower shop across from La Fonda. After Jack developed a huge crush on Bessie, one of the waitresses, he would stop over there on the way to or from work to buy Bessie a single rose. He would also write her notes, extolling her beauty and goodness. The fact that Bessie was married, with a child, was simply an obstacle—not one to be overcome, but essentially overlooked. In short, it was not a problem for Jack. Bessie, slight of build with lustrous dark hair and a pretty face, truly was a sweet girl, and I'm sure the Callahans told her to be sweet to Jack, without in any way encouraging him.

Bessie eventually left La Fonda to take another job. While you might think this would have been a devastating loss for Jack, it really wasn't. I suppose that one of the silver linings for Fragile X kids, and especially for those with autistic tendencies, is that they suffer from neither the highs nor the lows that we have. A loss lasts for a few days and not much more. This extends even to dealing with a death. Of course, I tend to overdramatize things to the point where a lost job, or a lost love, constitutes a death of sorts. But that's my problem, not Jack's.

Jack's best years at La Fonda were when the Callahans' son, Danny, came back from the army and became the assistant manager. He was given the Jack portfolio, and he managed Jack rather like a tough but benevolent and all-forgiving drill sergeant. That may sound like a contradiction in terms, but I think this is exactly what our kids need. They need someone who understands and works within their limitations, while being tough as a boot. I don't know about your boys, but my boys love rules. I think that whether

JACK BUSBY (R) WITH HIS BOSS, DANNY CALLAHAN, AT THE SPECIAL OLYMPICS

in school at an early age, or in the workplace, understanding those rules evolves into a work ethic.

The Callahans' good nature continued to thrive after Jack moved to the Wellspring Ministries group home in Fairfax, Virginia, in late 1995, when he was thirty. Then he began commuting from Fairfax to work. He would take a bus to the Pentagon, taking the Blue Line on the Metro to Gallery Place, then switching to the Red Line to Dupont Circle, from which he would then walk the five blocks to La Fonda. The good news is that this opened up a whole new world for Jack. The bad news, as I'm sure you can imagine, involved the myriad opportunities for dawdling, shopping, and stops at Starbucks. But the Callahans continued to nurture Jack in his job. It was sort of, "Let Jack be Jack." None of us appreciated our great good fortune in that relationship. We go all the way back to the 1970s with the Callahans, when their son, Jon, who is also mentally challenged, was in school with Jack. Jon has gotten himself to work on the Metro, in two or three different jobs, for years. So our two families have always been on the same page.

The one day of the week when Jack always made it a point to get to work on time was Wednesday, when beer was delivered in the morning. His job was to put the beer away. Danny took the time and trouble to teach Jack where each brand of beer should go and how to keep count of how many of each brand they had. I was told that Jack was meticulous about this, once he learned the drill. That's the great thing about our boys as employees. Once they learn the drill and are convinced that the drill is necessary, it's a done deal. Even should circumstances change and the drill becomes no longer necessary, it's difficult for them to unlearn the drill. They simply do it, do it consistently, and do it right.

It was inevitable that the Callahans would one day sell the restaurant and move on to enjoy grandparenthood and travel. Still, it was a blow when they sold La Fonda. Danny Callahan bought into a sports bar, The Rock, across the street from the brand new MCI sports arena, now called Verizon Center, in downtown Washington, and he was wonderful to offer Jack a job as a busboy there. That meant a whole new commute, for which Mitchell Thompson, the terrific director of Wellspring, took on the travel training responsibility. Jack quickly got the hang of the new route and all went pretty well for a while—until two things happened. One was that Danny, while remaining an investor in The Rock, left the day-to-day operations to take another job. That left Jack without a tough drill sergeant. He ended up doing a lot of standing around watching the TV sets, which were all over the restaurant—watching sports while eating and drinking is the name of the sports bar game. We're still laughing about Adelina Callahan's story of dropping into The Rock one day and finding Jack standing by himself out in the foyer. She asked him what he was doing out there and he answered, "They told me not to watch TV." He figured that the foyer was the only spot in the whole place where he couldn't watch TV!

The other development at The Rock was that there wasn't enough lunch business to stay open, so management cut the lunch down to only Fridays. That meant that Jack didn't have a place to be on the other four weekdays, which no longer made the job workable. That's what led to the job coach, who didn't really know or understand Jack, and the ill-fated job in the deli and where we are right now.

We shouldn't have let this happen, and we're most anxious for Jack not to feel that he has totally failed, even though he has. On the other hand, we want him to understand that he was indeed fired and that this is what happens when you don't perform your tasks as instructed. If he's ever going to have a job in the workplace, he's got to relearn the work ethic, which I'm afraid we didn't talk about enough with him before he started this job.

Tomorrow, we're meeting with his job coach again, to see where we go from here. I think that he'll go into a workshop program, with the hope of an eventual "enclave" job, where four or five handicapped people work with a coach until they are ready to progress further. Of course, this is exactly what we should have done in the first place before letting him go into a job with absolutely no training in the work ethic for that job. I think the lesson here is that each job, and each boss, is different and must be approached anew. The hope will be that eventually, he'll be able to go on to employment at a competitive job, rather than one connected with a workshop program. But I honestly think—indeed, I know—he's really not up to that and maybe we just thought he was all these years because the wonderful, caring Callahans were so tolerant of his shortcomings.

Mitchell Thompson and I had a long talk today. He and David and I all agree that we do need to make Jack aware that he was fired and not laid off because there wasn't enough to do—which was what Jack told me when I picked him up on Friday to bring him home for the weekend. I noted he had just gotten a haircut and asked when he had time to do that. He said that he had left work an hour early because they said there wasn't anything to do. When he came back from the barber shop to catch his ride home, they told him he was fired.

Now, you might think that this was totally devastating, that it wiped Jack out, that he fell apart like a dollar watch—right? Wrong, Megan. Jack was not devastated, he was not wiped out, he did not fall apart like that dollar watch. From Jack's point of view, it was, "Hey, it didn't work out, OK?"

It's at times like this that I feel I've totally failed. How could I have given Jack the notion that *he* can decide when there's work to be done and that he doesn't have to follow instructions? Aaarrrgggghhhhhh! Will tomorrow be better? I hope so.

In the meantime, we have Jack at home with us for the time being, because the Wellspring program requires residents to be out of the house at a job during the day, and Jack needs a place to be. I'll take him back out to his home for the weekend. We are anxious for him not to feel he's being rewarded for losing his job by spending more time here with David and me. Over dinner tonight, we talked about his getting fired and how he had walked off the job without permission and how that's one sure way to get fired and how he's not going to do that ever again and how he really didn't like washing dishes all that much, though he didn't hate it.

Gosh, it's so hard to instill the work ethic. I'm afraid all we can do is let him learn from his mistakes about what doesn't work and that there are consequences for doing the wrong thing. I think he must have known he would get in trouble for leaving work an hour early, but I don't think he realized he would get fired. I'm afraid that because Jack is such a "neat little kid," even in his thirties, he's been cut too much slack all around. Hopefully, this last week has taught him that now it's big-time grow-up time. And what David and I have to do is to continue to talk and talk and talk with Jack about "the rules."

At times like this, I also need to remind myself of something wonderful I heard at a lecture by the late Carter Brown, the director of the National Gallery. He was talking about how to get children interested in art, and he said that when he deals with children, he doesn't ask himself, "How intelligent is this child?" but rather, "How is this child intelligent?" All of our kids are intelligent in their little ways, Megan, and we just have to remember that, don't we? We have to focus on the ways they can excel and find what will work for them. They can't find it themselves, so we have to do it for them.

My dear friend, Ellen Atwell, reminded me the other day of the time she took Jack for a walk in Georgetown. She wanted to see if he could find his way home, so at each corner she would stop and wait for him to start across the street, to see if he would take the right direction. He would always wait for her to start first, and she couldn't decide whether he really didn't know which way to go or whether he was just being perverse. Finally, in exasperation, she asked, "Jack, what would you do if you were by yourself?" His immediate response was, "I'd take a cab." She decided he was plenty smart—in survival instincts, anyway. Not that he would know if he had enough money for a cab. But, hey, let's not sweat the little things.

Ellen has always been a source of positive behavior reinforcement for our boys. She genuinely likes spending time with them, having known them since they were toddlers, plus having Jack in her extraordinary Holden Montessori Day School for four years. She knows them as well as anyone outside the family, and certainly better than a lot of folks inside the family. So many aspects of her Montessori training have been invaluable, especially to Jack. For instance, she will make a point to notice and comment on the things they do right—rather than only mentioning behavior that needs improving or changing. She might say, "Jack, I like the way you hung up your coat," or "Jack, I like the way you spoke up and told the waiter what you want to order." I've learned a lot from Ellen over the years. Not enough, though. One thing she's always correcting *me* on is when we're together with the boys and she asks one of them a question, I'll answer for him before he has a chance to give her his own answer. Boy, talk about a controlling mommy dearest. I've gotta keep working on this tendency of mine to keep the conversation moving. Ellen will stop and say, "Mary Beth, I asked *him*—not you." And she's right, of course.

On a day like today, when it's all I can do to keep from being down on Jack for having lost his job, I need to remind myself that Jack and Robert are still my little angels. Some angels are messenger angels and some are guardian angels. My boys *need* guardian angels, like Ellen and the Callahans and Mitchell Thompson and the Wellspring staff members, and Robert's wonderful employer, New Horizons Unlimited, and his caretakers at McCall's and his trainer, Josie, to watch over them and keep them safe and help them to develop their strengths; I guess my boys and yours must be messenger angels. Indeed, I know that's what they are. They were sent here to accomplish something important. They can teach us lessons that we couldn't learn from anyone else. But we must listen. Hark! The Herald Angel Sings! We must listen to Robert and Jack and to Jack and Jacob, and to all those special messenger angels, who can teach *us* the most valuable lessons of all.

I'm really giving myself a good talking to here, aren't I, Megan? I'm trying to put my own best face on my child's losing his job, and I'm trying to summon the emotional energy to go back to the employment drawing board, yet again.

Hope your day was better than mine. Now I've got to go get dressed up and go to a party, where I have to play sort of a hostess role. Can't think of anything I'd less like to do. I'd far rather stay home and feel sorry for myself. Guess I'll have to put that off until tomorrow, but I will for sure find time to do that on the morrow. But let's see. Will I find that time before or after meeting with the job coach?

Oh, but before I let you go, I do want to ask if you've received the new FRAXA newsletter yet? We're so pleased, of course, about being able to cofund the Ampakine trial that Dr. Elizabeth Berry-Kravis is doing out in Chicago. Whether this drug turns out to help those patients with learning and memory skills—and I gather there's reason to think it might—it's a start. It won't cure Fragile X, but if it works, it sure could make life a lot nicer and more productive for lots of children and adults with Fragile X. Anyway, be sure to read that piece carefully. Katie does a great job on the newsletter, doesn't she? She and Mike are a dynamite team, because he can explain the science in such a way that even *I* can understand it. Sort of.

Speaking of Katie, I know she's talked to you about taking on a much more active role in FRAXA, and I want you to know how thrilled David and I are. You're a huge asset to the board, and we're all delighted that you want to make this commitment. The thing that, to me, is so marvelous about you young parents is that you seem to be able and willing to manage your kids and everything else in your lives while doing major work in your communities. I honestly can't say I did that when my kids were little. In fact, I can honestly say that I didn't. I was so overwhelmed with my own situation that I couldn't see much beyond it. So, power to you, Megan girl!

Love to all the Masseys,

MBBB

PS. This quote from the Bible is what I need to keep in mind whenever—if ever again—I get to thinking that I've done a pretty good job with my boys: "for all who exalt themselves will be humbled, but all who humble themselves will be exalted." (Luke 18:14)

PPS. "The most authentic messengers may be those whose own experiences validate their message." (Ellen Goodman, from a *Boston Globe* column, August 31, 1996) ✉

Dear Mary Beth,

I am sorry it has taken me so long to respond. You have been such a good letter writer, and I have not. I have been so busy with Jack and Jacob. I may even need to reintroduce myself to John.

Your recent letter about Jack losing his job was a little heartbreaking for me. I am sorry that you had to go through that experience. However, you sure are good at it. I could just picture you and David at the dinner table discussing topics of work ethics and job responsibility with your son. I often tell my friends it will be harder for me to address these simple issues when I'm looking at a mature man with facial hair. Obviously, you are doing it. But are the issues really so simple? Don't you know many adults who haven't mastered these essential skills? Do you think Jack feels bad? Does he really understand the situation? Maybe in his mind it really appears a different way.

I know our kids are exceptional in many areas, like memory. One of my kids appears to be a master at manipulation. Or are they really that confused? Who knows? I could ponder that forever, and what difference would it make? As a parent, I must love them and encourage them. I have to believe in their strengths, and you said it best, we have to find those for them. Gosh, I'm still looking for mine.

There were many parts in your letter that made me laugh out loud. I loved the story of Adelina Callahan finding Jack in the foyer of the restaurant because he was trying not to watch TV. It was such a practical way to solve a problem. I would give him an A plus for effort. Adelina is a guardian angel, isn't she?

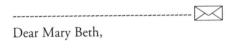

One day our neighbors found my boys waiting at the bus stop. They can be a bit loud. They stand out on the deserted country road and holler, “Here bussy, bussy.” This particular day the bus had come and gone and my boys had missed it. When the neighbors tried to tell them to come along and go to school, Jack tried to convince them that their clock was wrong. Indeed, in his world, there is no way that a schedule can be altered.

I did share some of your letter with John. I told him how you had picked up Jack from work the day he was fired and noticed he got a haircut. John was so impressed. He put his fist in the air and said, “Yes, let’s hear it for haircuts.” He is so good at looking at the bright side of things. He thought it was great use of his time. After all, Jack could have been watching TV.

You mention your dear friend Ellen, who reminds me of the boys’ tutor, Lori Blehm. She was the kindergarten teacher for both boys and has continued to work with them throughout their school years. She always points out their progress, academic growth, and maturity. She is a role model for me.

In our world today, I am convinced that the kindergarten curriculum is all a person needs. Be kind, don’t hit. Wait your turn. Ask permission. Raise your hand if you have a question. (Our kids do that at the dinner table. It gets a little interesting when we are out at a restaurant.) Remember your manners. Greet others when you come into a room. Make eye contact when you speak. No blurting out. Be courteous. Answer your own questions and not others. Does that sound familiar? Explain, demonstrate and encourage.

Lori does so much for the boys’ self-esteem. She instills qualities that they really need to possess. She has been an invaluable resource for us. She attends all their IEP meetings and can communicate to the other teachers what is truly important for the boys to achieve.

Last week Jack brought home a worksheet for homework. It was on common and proper pronouns. Common nouns had to be circled and the proper nouns underlined. Usually his worksheets have instructions to underline verbs. So, Jack, being a little impulsive, underlined all the verbs. Once I read him the instructions, and we started over, it occurred to me the assignment was ridiculous. Who needs it? We certainly didn’t. I couldn’t help but think, I am forty-two years old and have made it through yet another day without knowing the difference between the two types of nouns. How about giving him a worksheet on writing a sentence? Any sentence will do. One with a complete thought would be nice. A sentence that he could read would be even better.

John and I need to focus on the curriculum that will help Jack and

Jacob succeed in life. As time goes on, I don't know if I will be able to find that in our public schools. We need to work on life skills and vocational training. Mastering independent living skills would be beneficial as well. I am pretty sure this is not in a high school curriculum, let alone middle school. We need to find their areas of interest and help them to succeed. All parents do this, but our tasks here are on a totally different scale. We will forge ahead, and just hope for the best.

One last thing, thank you for encouraging me on my FRAXA journey. I know it will be a rewarding experience. David has sure done a super job rallying all the troops for support of the Fragile X cause.

Lots of love,

Megan ✉

18

Necessarily Delayed Gratification

Dearest Megan,

Oh, honey, I'm so sorry about the trip. Bummer. What can I say? To have made all of those plans and arrangements for the boys and to have had all the reservations to go to Las Vegas, and then to have it fall through is indeed a double bummer. Tell the Reinhardts and the Martins not, under any circumstances, to send you a postcard. That would add the proverbial insult to injury, for sure. And just don't ask John whether it's really the golf he's more disappointed about missing, or the vacation time with you—just as he won't ask you whether it's really more the spa days, dinners, and shows you hate missing or the time together with him away from the kids. Let's face it, it's all a big bummer.

I guess what I might say is that this aborted trip of yours reminds me—in of course a different sense—of the European honeymoon David and I had planned to take in 1962. He had made reservations for us to sail over to Europe on the SS *United States*, and we were to spend a week in Paris, then fly home. Does that sound heavenly or what? The day he had to pay for the trip, which was a couple of months before our wedding, he called me in Oklahoma, where I was happily preparing for it all, and he said, "You know what, angel? I really don't have the money to pay for this trip. I spent just about every dime I had on your engagement ring. Now, I can borrow the money from the bank and we can go on our honeymoon, or we can defer the honeymoon until we do have the money. So, what do you think?"

Without missing a beat, I said, "By all means, let's cancel it. Who needs it? And I really don't want us to start off our marriage in debt." Of course, being the daughter of my father, who even paid cash for things like cars and houses, the idea of debt was a no-no. Needless to say, I've learned, over the years to relax and enjoy. Debt, that is.

David promised he'd still take me to Paris on our honeymoon, and he loves telling people that he did just that—five years later. And you know what? In five years, we truly *needed* that trip. By that time, we had the two boys. When we were first married, we didn't need anything except to be together.

So, although I know that, at this point, you really do need that trip, try to believe that it *will* happen. Just not now. Just not in the delicious way you envisioned those days of fun in the sun. But Las Vegas will be there, the sun will still shine, and it will still be fun.

I do have an idea for you. We have some friends who had children about the ages of ours. I remember that when theirs were very young, they had a regular babysitter who came every Thursday afternoon. Elaine would pack her little suitcase, drive downtown, and check into the Madison Hotel. Then she and Mike would have that whole night and the next morning together. They felt that they needed this, their marriage needed this, and that ultimately, it was good for their kids. I have no doubt whatsoever that they were right. And they're still together all these forty-odd years later.

Why don't you and John ask the babysitter you had lined up if she would be interested in making this kind of arrangement with you? You don't really need a "Big Trip." What you need is time alone with John. If you're to be truly honest, I'll bet that much of what you were looking forward to was simply getting away from the boys, away from the routine, the daily battles, and the constant frustration that goes with the Fragile X territory. You can do that in more than one way. You can go to downtown Scottsbluff instead of to Las Vegas. You can go to "Holland" instead of to "Italy." I guess this would be making Las Vegas the equivalent of Italy and good old Scottsbluff is—well, OK, it's Holland. You see, I do remember that wonderful story you told me in your first letter to me.

Surely you know by now that the two biggest problems in marriage revolve around money and sex. I would have a hard time determining which of those is the most important element, because they're both so essential, but I would almost think sex is the most crucial. The late John Anschutz, our dear friend and Episcopal priest, used to say that the center of marriage is the relationship between a man and a woman, and the center of that relationship is sex.

I've never heard of a couple separating because there wasn't enough money. Indeed, I've heard of cases where couples stayed together because there wasn't enough money and they couldn't afford to separate and maintain two households. And some marriages break up because there's enough money for each partner to go his or her own way. But, needless to say, we all know of myriad cases of marriages breaking up over sex. What it all comes down to, ultimately, is two people trying to agree on how to prioritize the allocation of time and resources.

Also needless to say, I only know about my own marriage, but I can say without doubt that if our sex life had ever gone by the boards, the marriage would have gone right with it. It's hard enough to deal with two handicapped children and all that their care entails. Having a wonderful, loving, and fun sexual relationship keeps a couple sort of "other" from the children, keeps that couple "other," indeed, from the rest of the world. But you have to set aside some time for it. If you don't set aside that time and close out the rest of the world, then it gets pushed onto the back burner, where the flame slowly simmers for a while and then gradually flickers out.

Some people can make time and space for each other at home, even with children all over the place. They just lock the door. We've always been able to do that. Pretty much. I'll never forget the time when Jack came pounding on our door, yelling, "Are you guys all right in there?" I guess we'd been a little too noisy. We of course had to open the door and assure him that we were OK before collapsing in laughter. Still, for the most part, we've been pretty successful at simply closing the door and turning on music. When the boys see our door shut and hear classical music playing, they don't go there. I don't know what they really think about what may be going on behind that closed door. And you know what? I can't worry about that too much. Whatever they think is whatever they think.

I also have to say that, for us anyway, it's important to have a particular time each week when we make love, no matter what. Well, all right, I don't mean that exactly. There *are* Saturday mornings when we have a plane to catch, or someone has an appointment, or someone's sick, or whatever. But for the most part, that commitment is pretty sacred. Other times during the week can be catch-as-catch-can, but there needs to be one time that's literally scheduled. If it's not a priority, it gets to be an option, sort of on the order of balancing the checkbook. It's infinitely put-offable, and though you have no intention of letting it slide, it just does. Things like putting meals on the table and doing laundry are not options. Sex is. The problem arises when it's a priority for one-half of a couple, and an option for the other.

So, until that next big trip comes along, just check into a local hotel now and then, OK? And rental movies and room service are delicious options. Trust me. Not as delicious, I'll grant you, as that trip to Las Vegas would have been. But just the ridiculousness of spending a night in a hotel in Scottsbluff will make it fun. And, after all, "fun" is what getting away from the kids is all about.

Speaking of delicious, and speaking of staying at home, since you're not going to get to make the trip, why don't you have one or two favorite couples over for dinner next weekend? Hire a sitter to take care of the boys, and get out your silver.

And if I get to Las Vegas again before you do, I'll play a couple of hands of blackjack for you. You and John will get there.

Much love,
Mary Beth

PS. "Husbands are like fires. They go out when unattended." (Zsa Zsa Gabor) Seems to me, however, that Zsa Zsa "attended" to several husbands, didn't she, Megan? ✉

Dear Mary Beth,

I cannot agree more with your thoughts on quality time with your husband. It is so important to have alone time with them. A time when you don't have children interrupting, running around screaming, or making requests. What makes husbands feel loved? I know it is different for so many people.

I was told about a question that everyone should ask his or her spouse. That sounds kind of scary, but it's not. The question is, "What makes you feel loved?"

1. Words of affirmation
2. Gifts
3. Acts of service
4. Quality time
5. Physical touch

John answered 4 and 5. He wanted them both. I would say 4. After all, the question didn't say you could give two answers. How did he think of that? It must be the lawyer coming out in him.

As a young mother, I was constantly tugged on and felt so smothered all day by the kids. When it was time for bed, touch was the last thing I wanted. Not to mention, I was emotionally and physically exhausted. That was not the norm, but I do have definite memories of feeling that way. As the boys have grown older this has certainly changed.

John and I have always put the kids to bed early, like at 7:30 p.m., just so we would have some time to visit and wind down. I tell my friends, there is a silver lining to having children who are not competent with telling time. In their world if it's dark out, it must be time for bed. Jack used to put his pajamas on at 5:30 in the evening. I never argued with him. I should have tried it. Maybe the good fairy would have cooked supper and put us all to bed.

We have always had a sitter at least one night at week. I have often said, children don't run your life, sitters do. One of my most precious commodities was a babysitter list that had over twenty names of sitters along with phone numbers. Some names were listed as "Ashley's friend who came along to babysit last week." I have been known to call fifteen names, just to try and cover one night out. Missing out on any type of fun is not the name of my game. I guess I was really looking forward to the fun and games in Las Vegas.

We have been very blessed to have many girls available to help with Jack and Jacob. Ones who drive were an extra added bonus. I would tell the sitters if they cleaned up the house, I would compensate them for their efforts with more money. Many of the girls were good at cleanup duties. Some were even smart enough to have the boys help them. The boys knew a song with a catchy tune called, "Clean Up Time." If you started to sing it, they would run around and pick up all their toys.

We had a young sitter, Colleen Eckhart, whom the boys loved. She was only twelve or thirteen years old when she started watching them. She came from a large Catholic home and was experienced with caring for young children. Little did she know, she was getting experience in caring for children with special needs too. As it turned out, Colleen needed more training in the laundry department. I never asked her to do it, but she always washed Jack's special blanket after he had fallen asleep at night.

One evening, Colleen decided to expand her laundry duties. She found our hamper and washed the clothes that were in it. This all sounds well and good, right? Not so. John would often put his suits that were to be taken to the cleaners in a special laundry basket. She found it. John's suit was washed and dried in our Maytag washer and dryer. What a sight! I never mentioned it to her. We just hid that special laundry basket when she would come over.

Colleen even cooked. She loved to make Jell-o salads and chocolate chip cookies. I would often have John drive around a little longer before going home, so all the baking mess would be cleaned up. We often walked into a spotless home with a fresh plate of baked cookies on the counter. Once I found a salad in the refrigerator that she had made. It was a Snickers-apple salad. It had sliced apples, chopped-up Snickers bars, and whipped cream. It was delicious. It may sound terrible to you, but if you want the recipe, I will send it to you.

Holly and Heather Sweeney were our other super sitters. We called them our Fragile X-perts. They were twins who lived up the road. I think I have told you about them before. We brought them to the FRAXA Gala in New York at Tavern on the Green. They were huge Mary Higgins Clark fans. They both had their pictures taken with her.

They began sitting for us when Jacob was a baby. They were maybe twelve years old. Both of them would come. I would usually have Jacob in bed, and they would just play with Jack. I told them to take the kids out of the house if it caught on fire, and that we'd be home in a week. Needless to say, we always returned a few hours later.

Holly and Heather have truly been a special addition to our family. The first five years of our marriage John and I often talked about how much fun it would be to have twin girls. John says Holly and Heather were God's gift to us. They shared in our family vacations. We watched them grow up from little girls to beautiful young women. Neither of them dated much, which worked out well for our family. One of them was always available. Holly and Heather both participated in sports. We would always go watch them compete as if they were our own. We had them come to our house for prom pictures so we could check out their dates. We had heart-to-heart talks about many things.

The girls have very loving parents. We were just extra support. I know the girls shared thoughts with us that they wouldn't tell their own parents. It was so nice to carry on a meaningful conversation with an adolescent. John always offered wise counsel for them. They called John the "Moral Man."

Holly and Heather stayed with the kids when we left town. Their first year of college was here in Scottsbluff at our local community college. We were thrilled to have them another year. Now, Holly is following in her mother's footsteps and is a schoolteacher in Lake Havasu City, Arizona. Rojean Sweeney, their mother, was Jacob's first and second grade teacher. It's a small world in Scottsbluff. Heather is in medical school in Kansas City, Missouri. We are so proud of both of them. We still keep in close contact. We truly feel no amount of money we ever paid them could possibly make up for all the loving kindness they showed our boys.

We took the girls to Las Vegas for their twenty-first birthday. They were crazy about the country-and-western singers Faith Hill and Tim McGraw. We scheduled our trip so we could see them perform at Mandalay Bay. It was so fun. I felt quite old at the concert. I forgot to bring my cigarette lighter to hold in the air! You may not get this, Mary Beth, but at concerts of this kind, people bring cigarette lighters and click them on, so that it makes an impressive flame. It's quite a visual image. But oh, it was terribly loud. Now I know how my kids must feel when they're subjected to too much noise, too much sensory overload.

We sat by the pool, went to the spa, ate dinner in nice restaurants, and took in some shows. We didn't even have to worry about how they would behave at dinner, or review social rules before entering a public place. It was a great weekend. I guess that's part of why I'm disappointed about not going back to Las Vegas next week for our long-planned adult weekend with our buddies.

Thank you for your words of wisdom on intimacy. I will remember those valuable thoughts. John always affectionately refers to me as his girlfriend. He calls me that in front of the boys. Being the concrete thinkers that they are, Jacob went to school and told his teacher, Mrs. Sweeney, that his dad had a girlfriend. That made for an interesting story!

I took your advice and we are having some friends over for dinner next weekend. When the Reinhardts and the Martins return from Las Vegas, they'll give us notes on their trip and I'll give them notes on the party we had.

Our friendship, Mary Beth, is very valuable to me. Thanks for continuing to write and for being one of my guardian/messenger angels. I classify you as both.

Love,

Megan ✉

19

Mother's Day

Dear Megan,

I loved being able to laugh at your telephone report of your Mother's Day—if only because it allowed me to take a break from my everlasting and less than productive focus on my own Mother's Day.

You of course knew that I am likely the person in all the world most able to appreciate both the horror of Jacob's dropping the special Mother's Day German chocolate cake, splat on the living room rug at Uncle Jim's house, and your joy in his wanting to surprise Mommy with something special. I know you ordinarily don't go out of your way to wash the relatives' carpet before you've had a chance to enjoy their hospitality. I know that we Fragile X moms tend to appropriate each and every negative aspect of motherhood for ourselves. We'd like to think that *no* one else on earth has had her kid drop a cake for others to clean up.

Of course, my very first thought was, "Oh, no! Surely not a German chocolate cake, with that sublimely rich frosting with all the butter and sugar and coconut and pecans! What a waste!" And wouldn't you know, Megan, that my first thought would be for the loss of the cake? Yikes, sometimes I do wonder about my priorities.

At least Jacob dropped the cake and didn't "toss" it. I'll never forget the time David took us to a charming little country inn for Mother's Day lunch. Just as we were served the first course, Jack Busby tossed his breakfast cookies, or whatever it was he had last eaten, all over the luncheon table. Needless to say, we made a hasty retreat from the charming little country inn and never went back. Ah, yes, that was one of my more memorable Mother's Days.

Come to think of it, Mother's Day has always been one of my least favorite occasions on the calendar. At the end of the day, it always seems that I have spent the day doing for and trying to please my child (Jack, as Robert is always in Oklahoma in May), running all over the place picking him up, taking him where he wants to go, in order for him to participate in being with us for the day. I guess my idea of a perfect Mother's Day would be to spend it in bed, reading the Sunday newspapers, and receiving calls from independent, adult children who want me to know they're thinking of me. In my dreams, and in my next life, this will be my Mother's Day.

This year, because David had knee surgery just a week ago, I thought that it would be a quiet, stay-at-home weekend, but no such luck. Saturday happened to be the last day of bowling for Jack's Saturday bowling league's season, and I knew he would want me to be there for the presentation of awards. Thank God, I did get there just as his team received theirs. I didn't stay for the luncheon, as I needed to get back to do lunch for DB. Then I dashed out to Germantown, Maryland, to attend the monthly meeting of the Maryland Fragile X Parents' Resource Group, a group I'm crazy about and love to be with at every chance. From there, I dashed back home to get both David and me dressed to go to the annual spring dinner dance for Jack's workshop program. You can imagine how much David needed to go to a dinner dance five days after surgery. We stayed for the dinner, but left just as the dancing started, which of course was the part of the evening Jack most wanted to enjoy. We left him there with his buddies to dance the night away, while we came crawling home to bed.

Jack called first thing this morning, hinting that he would love to spend the day with us. I knew this would happen, Megan. How could it not? I told him to go ahead to his church and to come right home afterward and I would be there to get him. Since David and I had told the Rehms we would join them and another dear friend for lunch, I scarcely had time to get David's surgical wound dressed, etc., etc., etc., and get out to Fairfax to Jack's house. By the time I waited for Jack to gather his stuff together to spend the night with us, get back, and get David's shoes on, we were late for lunch. I kept thinking, "Why, oh why are we doing this?"

I guess I know now why we did this. At the end of lunch, David pulled out and started to read the Mother's Day letter he had written to me on May 7, 1966. He began to cry before he had read the first sentence. Diane took it and was able to read it aloud. I don't know how she got through it either, but she's a pro. That Mother's Day in 1966 marked the worst spring of our lives, the spring when we learned that Robert was mentally retarded and that Jack might be as well. David had written me the dearest, sweetest letter, of which I now have no memory whatsoever. It goes to show that I have repressed all of that year, even the dear, sweet part of it. David had found the letter a couple of weeks ago, when the law firm moved offices up one floor and there was an old safe that had a packet of David's ancient history in it—including my birth certificate, my confirmation certificate, and who knows what else. When we got home from lunch, he asked me if I wanted to see the rest of the stuff in that packet and I said no, thanks, I've cried enough for one Mother's Day.

On the way home from lunch, we dropped Jack at the Hair Cuttery at Dupont Circle, and he just now walked in the house with a buzz cut. Not my favorite look for him, but you know what, Megan? I am so happy that he was able to get it cut by himself and walk back home by himself, that I can only rejoice in even this small measure of independence for him. As we both know, so many of the kids that our kids know will never achieve a milestone even as small as this one. So, this has not been a bad Mother's Day. Not on the scale of things. Indeed, I could and certainly should think of it as one of the better ones. After all, hearing that precious letter from David Busby confirmed in yet another of the myriad ways he has let me know over the forty years of our marriage just how very much he loves me and why I love him with my life. What a Mother's Day gift I received from him, one I'll cherish always.

And neither was yours a bad day, I'll bet—not unless Jake decided to try delivering dinner. And remember, we only have to get through one Mother's Day a year.

Much love,
MBBB

PS. "A fella that doesn't have any tears doesn't have any heart." (Hubert H. Humphrey)
Here is David's 1966 letter to me. He told me that he especially wants me to send this to you. Bear in mind that at that time he wrote this, Robert was called "David."

> A Mother's day greeting to Mary Beth:
> You stand strong in the center of the world, surrounded by Jack and David and me.
> To each of us you are all the kindness, all the love and all the fun there is.
> Without you none of us would have a friend or a reason to be.
> With you each of us has someone to please and tease, to skip and cuddle with, to kill tigers and leopards and lions for.

Only you're funny—most girls cry when they're not needed by their men. You cry because you are!
Funny or not—you're the center of our world and all the fun there is in life.
We love you XXXXXX,
Jack and David and David

PS. And here's a little Mother's Day present for you, Megan: "Yesterday is history, tomorrow is mystery, today is a gift. That is why it is called the present." (Eleanor Roosevelt,1884–1962)

Mary Beth,

What a beautiful letter David wrote you back in 1966, and you got to enjoy it again many years later. I cherish all those gooey letters I get from John. It doesn't happen frequently, but when it does, you can bet it goes in my special drawer. They are great to read when my spirits are down.

JOHN MASSEY WITH HIS SONS, JACOB (L) AND JACK

We don't do a lot of celebrating around here on Mother's Day. John says with tongue in cheek that every day is Mother's Day! Don't you love it? I do love sending my mother the perfect Hallmark card. She usually gets more than one. A serious one and a funny one.

All of my friends and I agree that Mother's Day is just a day where we may expect too much and end up cooking and cleaning anyway. Who invented that holiday? I bet it was a card company.

John prefers that we ignore Father's Day too. Maybe every day is Father's Day?

The truth is John and I say every day is Christmas at our house. We have so much to be thankful for and feel we our truly blessed. I have said this before and I will say it again. I wouldn't give up this journey for anything. Psalm 139:14 reminds me to continually praise Him.

I will praise you for I am fearfully and wonderfully made.
Marvelous are Your works,
And that my soul knows very well.
(Psalm 139:14)

Our children are beautiful to Him and He calls them His own. What more could we ask?

Happy Every Day, Mary Beth!

Love,

Megan ✉

20

What I Woulda, Coulda, Shoulda Said

Dear Mary Beth,

I was writing a letter of recommendation the other day for Heather. You remember Heather. She is one of the twin girls who babysat for our boys. They were like our adopted daughters. We loved them and still do. I started to sob when I was finished writing her letter. She holds such a special place in our hearts. Maybe those tears came from a deep place in my heart that still mourns for a child who would be achieving goals like hers. Or maybe it was just my time of the month to cry. I am pretty sure that no one will ever write something like that about my children. Actually, that is OK with me. I do know Jack and Jacob have touched many people's lives in their own special way.

A pastor once gave a sermon about Jack and his experience at a grade school track meet. Jack was on his way to being the second to last to cross the finish line. There was a young boy behind him, Michael, with cerebral palsy using Canadian crutches. Jack stopped and saw that Michael was quite a ways behind him. He stopped and went back to run with his friend. Actually, Jack had to walk. We were all yelling for him to run until we realized what he was doing. Winning a race meant nothing to Jack, but helping others was important. Even though in worldly matters their accomplishments may be few, Fragile X kids' hearts are genuine. I know they plant seeds in other hearts that we do not even imagine. I have seen it happen.

This winter, Jack was a manager for the eighth grade basketball team. The coach was very intense and would yell. I visited with the coach before the season started so he would be fully prepared for circumstances that could arise with Jack. But you know, Mary Beth, no one can be prepared for what our kids may do, including us. There were games when I would sit in the stands and just want to die, watching Jack and his antics. For starters, he would sit in the coach's chair. He would get in the middle of the huddles during time-outs with his clipboard in hand. He loved leading the team in their cheers before the huddle would break.

Sometimes he would extend his arm into the middle of the huddle before the coach was through giving instructions as if to say, "That's enough, lets play ball." The coach would calmly touch Jack's arm and put it back at his side.

The coach would finish talking to the team and then look at Jack to go ahead. "One, two, three defense" was his favorite phrase. One time he went and showered with the team! I guess sitting on the bench can be physically exhausting. During one game, the assistant coach called a time-out and let Jack send in the play. He apparently drew on his clipboard and talked away. I did not see it happen. The players had to have been laughing.

At the completion of the season, Jack received two medals along with the A and B team players. The coach told John how much he enjoyed having Jack as part of the team. He said Jack really helped him keep it all in perspective. I think the coach really enjoyed him. For whatever reason, he was much calmer when Jack was around.

Jack was thrilled with his awards. But isn't it interesting, Mary Beth, that when I asked him whether he wanted to be a manager or a basketball player, he said, "Oh, I want to be a player." Well, I can guarantee you that will *never* be an option for him in our schools. Oh sure, you say there is Special Olympics and that is true. We have tried that venue. We competed in the equine division, as we have horses. It was a great experience, but he had to drive three hundred miles across Nebraska to the show. Jack competed in swimming and he also tried track. In our community most of the Special Olympians are over thirty years old. This bothered me, however, I don't think Jack noticed. I guess I need to learn once again that this is not about me.

I told a friend the other day I sometimes wonder how I would have responded to different situations if my kids were not handicapped. Would I be one of those parents who simply don't get it? Would I be wrapped up in winning, concerned about whether or not my child will get the lead in the play, angry because he got Bs on his report card instead of As? Would I complain that my boy was on the B-team squad when I knew he was A-squad material? I hope not, but God may have known I would not have handled it well.

I usually get my daily dose of humble pie. You can have all of that you want on the South Beach Diet.

I'll write again soon, hopefully on a better day.

Love, Megan ✉

Dear Megan,

Oh, Megan, honey, I know, I know, I know. I really do know. It's so hard. It's also not fair. Your last letter made me cry. That clearly was a bad day. We moms of fraggles don't get to have anything as luxurious or benign as bad hair days. With us, those days escalate right on up into bad life days.

I think that perhaps our "bad" days tend to be those days when we have too much time to sit. Like your taking the time to sit down and write the letter of recommendation for Heather was also taking the time to reflect not only on Heather and what she's meant to your family, but also on the child you didn't have and how different your life might have been. But I think our better days, actually, are the days when we are at the basketball game, are working things out with the coach and other players, are—in other words––dealing with our boys' lives, rather than sitting at home thinking about them. You're probably laughing to yourself as you read this, thinking, "Well, for a woman who feels that way, she sure spends a lot of time sitting at home writing letters to me." And you would be correct. At the very least, I need to get my rear end down to the gym more. Lifting weights lifts my spirits.

How I love the image of Jack giving up his lead in the race to help his friend. That's what it and we should be all about. I well remember that our Jack had no sense of urgency when he swam in Special Olympics. He knew he needed to get to the other end of the pool, but he couldn't focus on the idea that he needed to get there before the guy in the next lane did. And you know what? He didn't need to. I needed him to, but I had to remind myself that his needs were what we were dealing with, not mine.

It's so strange, the way the tiniest thing will trigger the biggest thing. For you, that tiny thing was writing a letter of recommendation for Heather, an outstanding young woman with endless possibilities before her. For me, at your age and stage, it was often a simple printed invitation to a friend's son's or daughter's graduation. I simply made it a policy not to attend the graduations of my friends' kids. I knew I couldn't handle it. No way. Simply receiving the invitation would send me into a decline, so why risk attending the event itself? Don't need this. And more important, neither did our friends or their graduating kids need this. Didn't go there.

One thing I did risk doing—because I couldn't figure out an excuse not to, even though I suspected disaster—was to accompany a very dear friend and her daughter on an all-day expedition to shop for the daughter's wedding dress. I can remember sitting in an elegant dress shop, watching this precious daughter of my friend try on wedding gowns, and thinking, "I don't think I can get through another moment of this without screaming, "It's not fair!" I would have given my life for a daughter who was about to be married—and who then, of course, would give me grandchildren, who would of course be "perfect," and who then would adore me and give me great joy and companionship in my old age. Right. Clearly, it's those children and grandchildren we don't have who are "perfect." Somehow, I got through that shopping day, when the going did indeed get very tough, without spoiling it for everyone. Somehow.

You know what might be helpful and useful? And I wish I had thought of doing this myself earlier. Why don't we both, you and I, sit down and write letters—you to Jack and/or Jacob, and I to Robert and/or Jack—on a couple of the occasions of those special milestone events in their lives that are of course only going to happen in our dreams. They didn't and won't happen, but might have been. Let's simply get it all down, get it out, and get it over with—so as to get over it and move on. This may sound nuts, but it might be therapeutic. OK, I'll go first.

Dearest Robert,

In my excitement over your graduation tomorrow, I want not to forget to let you know how profoundly happy and proud you have made your dad and me. I know that you are to receive a special award tomorrow, and that is marvelous, because it will serve as recognition of the many years of hard work on your part that have made this award so richly deserved by you. You simply decided, quite on your own, to use each hour of each day to the fullest. I honestly don't know how or why I could have had such an extraordinary son. All I know, all I can tell you, is that my cup runneth over with pride and joy.

Tomorrow's commencement is just that: a beginning. For you, it will be the beginning of endless possibilities, endless accomplishments, and—I so hope—of endless joy and service to whatever community you decide will be yours.

Congratulations, Robert, and so much love,

Momma

OK, Megan, I've decided to have some real fun with this, and here goes. This one is far more likely to be what I *would* have written—or felt like writing:

Robert, dear,

Dad and I so look forward to your graduation tomorrow, and we'll get there early in order to get a front-row seat. I want to be situated for the best photo op, as you walk across that stage. Besides, mothers of graduates tend to be so foolish, when it comes to wearing those ridiculous big hats, and I simply won't risk having my view spoiled by some idiot woman in a straw hat out to here. So look for us down front.

And now, sweetheart, I can't bear to think that you're still—after all these years—feeling less than successful because you didn't get into Yale. Honestly, love, if your Dad and I have told you once, we've told you a zillion times that he didn't really like Yale even when he was there, and it meant nothing to him to have or not have a son accepted there. The fact that all our friends kept asking us, for approximately two years, if you were applying to Yale should not have caused us to suggest to you that this should be a priority. We were wrong and you were right: Common Community College has been just the best choice in every way, and it's a vastly underrated school—just as Yale is so overrated. Besides, having you nearby has simplified our lives immeasurably, saving us from marathon trips back and forth to wherever. Yes, it's truly been perfect, dearest one.

And of course Dad and I are thrilled at the prospect of having you back home with us until you decide what you're going to do next. It will be a piece of cake to move my computer out of your room and down to that wee cubby off the pantry. I never could imagine what that bit of space was supposed to be, and now I know. Voilà! It will be my office, now that your room will once again be your room.

And, love, I hope you know how we look forward to meeting Sandra's parents at graduation. I promise to be an angel. And I truly do regret what I said about Sandra's choice of dress for church last Sunday. I felt wretched about it afterward, and of course I'm a silly goose to let things like fishnet stockings get to me. God would not have been amused—either with Sandra's outfit or my behavior toward that outfit. Twenty lashes, OK?

So, just know, Robert, that we are just proud as punch and pleased as bees and looking forward to celebrating this joyous occasion with you.

Love you, angel,

Momma

And now, another might have been:

Dear Jack,
In the last-minute preparations for your and Sarah's wedding tomorrow, I don't want to forget one important thing. And, after all, as the mother of the groom, I have only a fraction of the responsibilities being shouldered by Isabelle. So, I do have the luxury of sitting here at my desk, where you so often find me, thinking of my many blessings.

No blessing to be counted today rings truer, sounds sweeter, or feels more fulfilling than this wonderful sense that you and Sarah are embarking together upon a voyage of unimaginable joy and promise. Some young couples seem to have a lot going for them. You seem to have "it all" going for you.

Do know that Dad and I (and, yes, this is a promise) are going to stay out of your way for a while. So don't expect to hear a lot from us. We feel that it's of utmost importance for you and Sarah to have some space and some breathing room in this early, delicious stage of your marriage. But know also, Jack, how truly happy we are and how good we feel that you and Sarah found each other and have each other. If we had conducted a worldwide search, we truly would have picked Sarah for you. That's how happy we are tonight, and expect to be tomorrow, that you found her and that you love her. We love her too, and we think she has exquisite taste in men! And you be sure to tell her that.
So much love to you both,
Mom

Or, it could, and likely would, go more like this:

Dear Jack,
Here I am at the hairdresser, getting all gorgeous for your wedding tomorrow, and since I'm sitting down for the first time all week, I'll write you just a tiny note to let you know how happy Dad and I are for you and Sarah.

Wasn't the rehearsal yesterday a riot? You know what they say—if the rehearsal is a mess, the performance itself is bound to be perfect. So this means a perfect wedding, right? Who could have known that Sarah's dog would insist upon coming to the rehearsal? All I can say is that I'm glad it wasn't our church. I would have hated to deal with the carpet problem after Poochy-Poo got too excited. But I guess Sarah and Isabelle will manage to work out something with the sexton about getting carpet cleaners in. I do hope you were pleased with your old Momma for not saying a single word, not one. And who could have known that one of the bridesmaids would show up in shorts? What can that child have been thinking? But Jack, honey, those things aren't too important, and the ceremony itself will be the very essence of decorum. And I know that you'll make sure that Eddie gets to the church on time and that he will keep his voice down if he gets tickled again this evening the way he did at the rehearsal. It was sort of cute and funny then, of course, but I shouldn't think it would do for the wedding. But not to worry, love. All will be perfection, I'm sure.

And I'm assuming that someone has been rehearsing those precious nieces of Sarah's for their roles as flower girls. The rehearsal was a bit rough. I mean, it was cute the way Sissy dropped the rose petals and then Laurie came along behind her and picked them all up. But being too cute can totally detract from the bride and groom and the solemnity of the occasion, don't you think? But of course, you're not thinking about any of this kind of thing now. I must say, though, it still mystifies me that people love having wee tiny children in weddings, as they can hardly be expected to perform as grownups. They're *not* grownups. They're wee tiny children. And Jack, dear, do you think everyone will "get" the idea behind having Sarah's ring bearers dressed up like midget train engineers? I mean, I do get it—how they will be the train bearers, as they'll arrange her train as she goes back up the aisle with you at the close of the ceremony, and of course it was a novel idea to dress the "train" bearers as engineers. It simply seems a bit of a jarring note, somehow, having them dressed in that ticking fabric with the bandanas and the hats and all. But of course, I'd never breathe a word of such sentiments to Sarah. And neither should you, precious one. We shall all simply love everything and everyone—certainly for this evening. All will be perfection, I'm sure.

And oh, darling, I hope you can encourage Sarah to forgive and forget my frightful slip at the bridesmaids' luncheon, when I called her Anna. I still cannot believe my unthinking idiocy. I *promise* that I have long since come to grips with the fact that just because Anna's parents were our dearest friends, there was no reason on earth that you and she should have been right for each other. Mothers are so silly that way. And where can my poor mind have escaped to, when I made that unfortunate toast? Heavenly days, I wasn't even *thinking* Anna, so how on earth—oh, well, my love. Knowing your diplomatic skills,, surely you can make it all right with Sarah. Isabelle, of course, may be another matter. I'll never forget the look on her face. One can only hope that, given the amount of champagne Isabelle had already had (has Sarah ever suggested a "problem"?), that perhaps my little "Anna" slip might sort of "blend," if you will, into everything else that was said at that luncheon. I will say that some of the toasts the bridesmaids made were right on the border between tasteless and vulgar. But then, darling, you and I both know that your old Momma is an old pain in the you-know-what. And by this evening, all will be perfection, I'm sure.

Oops. Gotta close this laptop down now, as Daisy's ready to do my nails. I'm having her use a pale peachy shade to match my dress. Can't help wondering if Isabelle will still be wearing those scarlet nails of last evening's rehearsal dinner. Who knows? She told me her dress for the wedding is deep violet. You don't suppose she would have deep violet nails, do you? Come to think of it, perhaps the scarlet would be the better choice. But my, my, they do stand out. Not my idea of mother-of-the-bride understatement. But then, how silly of me to have even noticed. All will be perfection, I'm sure.

Oh, and I promise most especially to love Sarah's dress. No matter how much I hate it, I will love it. All will be perfection, I'm sure.

And I do so love you, dear Jack, my own perfection,

Momma

So there, Megan. I feel so good having given myself the luxury of writing these ridiculous letters. Robert and Jack would never in the world have been as perfect as the first letters to them would suggest. And even I would not have been as silly as the second ones would make me out. I might have had those thoughts, but I'd never have acted them out. What fun, though, to imagine I might have.

Of course, the day will come when you will, if you should bother to keep this letter, look at this and say (while tearing it up into little bitty pieces), "My God, was she crazy?" And of course, you and I both know that the answer to that is a resounding "YESSSsssss!" Just a little crazy, that's me.

Now, you get crazy and go, girl, and write your letters to Jack and Jacob. It will make your day. Promise.

Much love,

MBBB

PS. "Vision is the art of seeing things invisible." (Jonathan Swift) ✉

Dear Mary Beth,

I cannot even begin to write those "woulda, coulda, make-believe" letters to my boys. I did enjoy reading yours. They were quite entertaining. I don't know why I can't write them. It seems so out of touch with reality. No, this does not mean I think you're crazy. There is no doubt it was therapeutic for you, but I just can't go there.

I agree that the more time we have to sit around, the more likely we are to begin dwelling on things that are not part of our lives and never will be. When I hear friends talk about their kids dating and exploring what relationships are all about, I can't even imagine what that must be like.

On the other side of the coin, I am grateful I won't have to deal with many of the adolescent issues. Oh sure, I know I'm not free and clear of any disaster, but my kids will be much more sheltered than others. Especially, Jack. Jacob is much more social and may be in more awkward situations. He is a rule follower and a parent pleaser, and he seems to bail out of uncomfortable situations quickly.

What would make it all better is to find a treatment for all these children. As each day passes, I feel FRAXA is getting closer, but my boys are also getting older. I honestly believe some day we will have more options. I wonder how it will work? Will they take the medicine and all of a sudden understand? Will I need to send them back to school so they can learn again?

Won't these be nice problems to have? As much as I love all the people I have met in this organization, nothing would bring me greater joy than to have FRAXA "close up shop" and have the treatment or the cure. The journey continues to be an exciting one.

Sorry I couldn't get those letters off to you. If anything ever comes to me, I'll do it. But don't hold your breath.

Take care Mary Beth, and I'll see you at the gala.

Love,

Megan

21

Residential Placement: The World's Most Agonizing Decision

Dear Megan,

Part of me wishes you hadn't told me about the baby steps you and John are taking toward a residential placement for Jack. It brings back so many memories—most of them painful. That being said, though, I do think you're doing the right thing to take a look at what's out there.

Back in the 60s and 70s, there were, I suspect, more private day programs for our kids than there are today. Because of the political climate now, however, I gather that with some terrific exceptions, there are not too many choices between going the public school route and the residential placement route.

I suppose that, at this point, it would be so much easier to be one of the many Fragile X parents who look upon their children as "gifts from God, perfect in His sight, so why not in ours?" Those parents don't want to consider sending their children to a residential facility, because they don't want their children treated any differently from normal children in any way whatsoever. They want them to go right on through the public school system and get that graduation certificate—whatever that may or not mean in terms of achievement. Don't misunderstand me. My admiration for these parents is boundless. I'm truly in awe of their ability to see their children as perfect, not in need of any "fixing." I really envy these people, just as I envy people with normal children. But I am incapable of having this mind-set. I do want them "fixed."

The first thing you have to realize about the process of finding a residential placement for your Jack is that *no one* but you and John can know what's right for Jack. You just have to hope and pray that all who know you will understand how traumatic this is and that what you need is support for you and for the process. You will learn, in the next months, that you will have a newfound realization that to pass judgment on someone else's decision is unwise, unhelpful, and uninformed. Rather than passing judgment, your family and friends need to trust your judgment. And you know what? People who can't trust your judgment are people you just can't worry about—even if some of those people are family. If anyone asks you, "How can you do that?" just answer with, "How can you ask me that question?"

Maybe it's because David and I are pretty inner-directed as a couple, but I don't remember telling anyone of our decision about Robert until we had made it. I guess that nowadays, no couple would make such a life-altering decision without a few counseling sessions, but we have always pretty much just counseled each other. I can remember David saying that if we were British, no one would think a thing about our sending our son off to school. We used to have some friends at the British embassy who sent their son back to England to boarding school. I think he was about eight at the time. David mentioned to our friend that in America, we don't even have boarding schools for normal children that age. He answered, "Well, we don't believe in entrusting anything as important as raising children to parents. We believe in leaving it to the pros." I'll admit that recalling that statement gave us heart when we decided the time had come to look to the pros.

Robert Busby, age13, 1977

We were fortunate because McCall's Chapel School, the wonderful residential facility where Robert has been since he was twelve, happened to be right there in Ada, Oklahoma, where David grew up and where his mother, Hope—called "Ma" by all the grandchildren— and his brother Phil, and Phil's family lived. Ironically, David's dad, Orel Busby, was the lawyer who incorporated McCall's when it was founded in 1954—long before I was even in the family. He died when Robert was two years old, not knowing that his grandson would one day be a resident there. We were fortunate, also, because from the time Robert was a tiny little boy, he has loved Ada.

He always seemed to do well there. So, when the time came to consider a residential placement, we naturally gravitated toward McCall's. The reason we allowed ourselves to send Robert so far away was that we did have his precious Ma and his beloved Uncle Phil and Phil's wife, Carolyn, right there in Ada. Ma died in 1986, at the age of ninety-one, and her death was a terrible loss for Robert—more so than we realized. Phil, bless his sainted heart, still takes Robert to church, and then out for lunch every Sunday. I thank God for lots of things, but right up there at the top of the list is Phil Busby. Without him, we never could have gotten through those first years of having Robert so far away from home.

Home. It's an interesting word, isn't it? What is home? Where is home? I remember a few years ago, when we were down in Oklahoma for a weekend at Blackrock, our little cabin near Ada, we had Robert and a few other people out for dinner, as we always do. When Uncle Phil got up to leave, Robert got his things and went to put them in Uncle Phil's car. He knew that Phil would drop him at Oakcrest, his group home on the McCall's campus, on his way back into Ada. I said, "Robert, honey, wouldn't you like to spend the night with us here at Blackrock?" He said, "No, I've got to get on home."

After they left, David and I said to each other, almost in unison, "Did you hear him call his group home *home*?" That, believe me, was a happy evening for us. Just hearing him call it "home" was blissful music to our ears.

Robert drives me crazy the way he talks to perfect strangers about things they couldn't possibly know or care anything about. But one thing I love hearing him say, to supermarket clerks and anyone else who is his captive audience for a minute or two, is, "I'm from Ada, Oklahoma." McCall's, for him, has truly become home. It's taken a long, long time for that to evolve. A long time and a lot of heartache. For it truly is a heartache, both for the parents and the child, to make that transition from one home to another.

So you and John are beginning to talk about the notion of a residential placement for Jack. And you know what? It's kind of like moving to a different house. Once you start even thinking and talking about it, you're sort of in the mode to go forward. So, methinks you're partway there already, and the decision is the hardest part.

No, scratch that. The hardest part is the day you leave him at the school, or the camp, for the first time. There is nothing, nothing, nothing harder than that. It's just the worst, that's all. For me to say otherwise would be the biggest, fattest lie I've ever told.

I will never, ever forget the day I left Robert at McCall's for the first time. He was twelve. We had presented McCall's to him as a summer camp experience, as it was June when I took him down there. This was actually true, because we considered it to be a trial run to see if we all felt it was the right place for him to be. I was told that it might be best to take him into the big central rec room, where kids would be watching TV, and to leave from there. I'll never forget that he was sitting on the floor, watching TV, when I decided I'd better leave before I fell apart. I got down on the floor with him and tried to get him to say good-bye. He wouldn't say good-bye. I tried to get him to give me a hug. He wouldn't give me a hug. Or couldn't. He just sat there staring at the TV, ignoring me but knowing full well that I was there, that I was about to leave. I kissed his cheek and told him I'd see him soon (knowing it would be six weeks), and barely made it to the car before the weeping started. Driving back to Oklahoma City to my parents' home, it was a sunny, hot Oklahoma day, but I sure needed windshield wipers for my eyes. Not a happy day. Not a happy memory.

Sometimes I try to crawl inside Robert's skin, to imagine how he must feel about something. When I think of leaving him at McCall's that first time, I can only imagine him having a sense of abandonment, a sense of wondering when he would see his momma and daddy again, a nonexistent sense of how long six weeks would be. Would it have seemed to him more like six days or six months? What was it like for him? I didn't really want to know at that point. I just wanted to be strong. In that situation, for both Robert and me, being strong was really being tough. Could he tough it out? Could I?

I've long been fascinated by the difference between toughness and strength. I suppose my sense of it is that someone who is merely tough simply bulls on through a situation, getting through the barrier between that situation and the desired outcome. Somehow. True strength, however, is that almost indefinable quality of being able to summon up grace under pressure, grace that gives one the sense that the course—while perhaps rocky, while certainly unpopular with some of the principals—is the right one, at least for that time and in that situation.

I can assure you, sweet Megan, that in that dreadful first six weeks during the summer of '76, I was tough as a boot. But strong? Oh, no. Not yet. On almost any given day, I would have hopped a plane and gone back to get Robert, to bring him back home to Washington to make our family whole again. And but for the grace and strength of David Busby, I would have. I would like to think that over the course of the intervening years, my toughness has been at least partially burnished into a strength of sorts, but the distinction is clearly in the eye of the beholder

There were plenty of those Oh-dear-God-I-can't-stand-this moments that summer. One I remember was one night as I was preparing dinner. Jack was setting the table. I looked at the table and saw that he had set four places. I said, "Jack, there are only three of us tonight. Why did you set four places?" He looked at the table and said, "Oh, that's right. Robert's not eating." A simple enough statement. A simple enough happening. But I nearly lost it, with everything rushing in at once: things like wondering—and desperately wanting to know—had Robert had a decent dinner at McCall's? Had he missed us while having that dinner? Did he cry at night––as I did? Could my toughness hold out for the entire six weeks?

The thing that saved my sanity was writing letters to Robert every day. Yes, Megan, I did say every day. Admittedly, that was totally obsessive on my part, but it was the only way I could deal with my guilt. Most of the letters were short, and they told him things like what I got at the Safeway and which checkout person I had and that Daddy was at work and that Aunt Sally said to tell him hello—that sort of thing. I rarely mentioned Jack. I never mentioned anything fun we had done or were going to do. As far as poor Robert was concerned, his mom spent all day every day doing laundry, making the bed, and going to the supermarket. But I wrote about those things every day. I must have kept up that everyday letter writing for about three years. Then it went to maybe three times a week, then to two, and then to pretty much one letter a week. Sometimes I write more, but he no longer expects it. He really loves postcards—maybe even more than letters. He also loves receiving photos in the mail. Sometimes I'll run across an envelope of old photos (if I would make myself open about seventeen different drawers in this house, I would run across a zillion of them), and I'll send some of them to Robert. Of course, I'm careful not to send any that show us having any fun without him.

Jack Busby, graduating from Maplebrook, 1988, with nanny Irene Denault

One thing we've learned that works well is to give Robert a certain date when we will next be in Ada to see him before he leaves home to return to McCall's. He doesn't care how far in the future it is. It can be three months from now. He just wants the date. Then he can focus on that date and that gives him a sense of security.

The first week back at McCall's after being home on vacation is always difficult for Robert. When the boys are home, we simply plan everything around them and we don't try to do other things. So naturally, Robert in particular gets the idea that if he were home all the time, it would be just one great big party with him as the honored guest. Then he goes back to McCall's and zap! Back to normal. Not so much fun. Chores. Work. Getting up early. Yuck! Not fun at all. So, I always make an extra effort to get letters to him that first week. Indeed, sometimes I even send him a letter while he's still here—so that he'll get it within a day or two of returning. Once he caught me doing this. He saw me addressing a letter to him and asked, "What's this?" I simply told him that I was sending him a letter to Ada, where he would be in a couple of days, so that I could remind him of a few things he needed to do. He said, "Oh."

In thinking about the course you'll be taking before even thinking about writing letters to your Jack, I agonize for and with you and John and the hoops you'll have to jump through, and all at a time when you feel least like jumping, period. It's truly unfair that in addition to putting your dear, precious child and yourselves through the world's most traumatic experience, you and John will also have to deal with people like lawyers and school system administrators; but you do have to do just that.

With Robert, we didn't have to go that route, as we simply decided to send him to McCall's, and we were prepared to pay for that. We had reluctantly come to the conclusion that because Robert required so much of our attention, we were beginning to neglect Jack, plus Jack's asthma was barely manageable at that point, making his health fragile and worrisome. We wondered if, with Robert away at school, Jack might blossom into new stages of development and an improved state of health. We felt that we owed Jack that chance, and it was true that Jack did blossom, partly because he adored being an only child.

I'll never forget that on one of Robert's first visits home to Washington from McCall's, we were all sitting at the kitchen table having dinner, and Jack pointed to Robert and asked, "Now when did you say he's leaving?" I was furious with Jack, and after dinner I took him aside and explained what he already jolly well knew: this was not an OK way to treat his brother. I stopped just short of saying to him, "And furthermore, buster, you'd better watch it or *you'll* get sent to boarding school too."

With Jack's schooling, our decision was a different matter. Within a few months of Robert's entry to McCall's, we decided to sell our house in Potomac, Maryland, where Jack had been attending a public school for three years, and move back into Washington. For one thing, with Robert gone, the house seemed even bigger and sillier to maintain. We no longer needed or wanted that kind of house and we were truly missing the convenience of being in town.

We felt strongly that the District of Columbia school system had nothing to offer Jack, who by then was twelve. The Kennedy Institute, at that time, was just right for him. We thought we had a case for getting the District to fund his tuition, but as a lawyer, David wasn't silly enough to think he could handle it. We hired a lawyer who specialized in these sorts of cases, and I'm so glad we did. He was able to get our case brought up in a timely fashion and we did get the funding for Jack to attend Kennedy. Even if we had lost, we would have just paid the tuition, but only kids funded by the District were eligible to ride the school bus, and Jack was obsessed with the idea of riding the school bus. He adored it.

After Jack had been at Kennedy for three years, we decided that, for lots of reasons—the chief one being his asthma—we would look around for a boarding school in a different climate. I got the *Directory for Exceptional Children* from Porter Sargent Publishers, and went through it, section by section, culling thirty schools that I wrote to asking for information. Out of those, I narrowed it down to eight, which I visited—all the way from Connecticut to Arizona and New Mexico.

You know how you feel when you first arrive at a new place and it just feels *right*? When even though you've never been there before, you feel that somehow you're home? That's the way I felt in 1980 when we first drove onto the grounds of Maplebrook School in Amenia, New York.

Maplebrook's policy is to always have a potential student come for a week, during the school session, to see how it works. Jack's trial week was in February, and there was snow on the ground. David and I were blown away by the sheer beauty of Duchess County, New York, and the drive up there was a joy. Except that we were all scared to death. Jack had been very excited about going to try out Maplebrook. We presented it to him that he was trying them out, just for a week, not the other way around—even though we knew that with an IQ of fifty-five, he was not quite up to their academic standards. Seventy to eighty was more what they dealt with, as a rule, and although we were able to get a wonderful psychologist (Barbara Mullins, the only one I've ever liked) to squeeze every last, remotely possible point out of Jack's tests, we knew it was going to be dicey.

As we neared Amenia, winding through the foothills of the Berkshire Mountains, Jack became quieter and quieter. So did I. Was this a mistake? Would a week here be such a disaster that we could never get him to go anywhere else again? Would it traumatize my baby? Would he love it, only to have Maplebrook say that he wasn't up to their program and they couldn't accept him? Oh, dear God, please, no. Don't let my baby be rejected there, the way he had been rejected from Cub Scouts at the public school in Maryland, the way he had always been the kid no one wanted on the basketball team, the way he and the other special ed kids had been segregated in the lunchroom. Please, no.

On about the third night at Maplebrook for his tryout week, Jack called us. After listing all the fun things he had been doing and mentioning several of the kids by name, he said, "I want to go to school here next year." My heart leapt and dropped at the same time. What did this mean?

What it meant was that the headmaster at Maplebrook, Lon Adams, after testing Jack, had seen potential that had not come through on his previous tests. He was convinced that Jack would indeed fit into, and would benefit from, their program. He called me the next morning and said that they weren't absolutely sure it would work, but that they were sure enough that they wanted to give it a try, at least for the six-week summer session. Then, if it didn't work, we could just treat it as a summer camp experience for Jack and that would be that. A good plan.

Lon Adams ran the place like a fine New England boarding school. He enforced a dress code and required a certain degree of formality of behavior at meals. Everything ran pretty much on time, rules were rules and everybody knew what they were and what happened when they weren't obeyed, and it just worked. It worked because the staff, from Lon and Judy Adams on down—and especially the wonderful housemother, Aunt Ruth Bodner, loved the kids, encouraged each and every one to be the best he or she could be, and focused a lot of attention on the kids having fun.

Bottom line is that Jack spent five great years there at Maplebrook. The fact is that he truly wasn't up to their academic standards, but they accommodated his limitations. Chances are there were times when they regretted having accepted him—especially during the several times they had to take him to the local hospital for an asthma attack—but no one ever, ever suggested his leaving. They probably knew I was so fragile I'd fall apart like a dollar watch. My take on it is that I can't imagine where else he could have gotten such a positive experience. He learned—the hard way, of course—that he has to pay attention to the signs that an asthma attack is coming. He learned to share space. He learned to travel alone—with, of course, monumental backup both at the Maplebrook end and on the home front. He learned that sometimes things just have to be the way they have to be.

And speaking of positive experiences, Megan, for David and me, knowing that both boys were being lovingly cared for, it was heaven. It was a delicious five-year honeymoon. I look back on those five years with such joy and pleasure—what can I tell you? Except that if, *if* you and John should eventually begin even to consider going the residential route for Jack, there are lots of things and people to consider. And please, honey babe, you and John let two of those people be yourselves. All I can tell you is that those five years gave us a life, plus the renewed strength to accept—and really to welcome—Jack's coming back home to live after he graduated from Maplebrook.

After Maplebrook, Jack got a job as a busboy at La Fonda, and we settled into the routine of having him home again. It was a pleasant little routine, and when we traveled, we found a young person to stay with him. It worked out. It worked out for ten years, until he moved to one of the Wellspring Ministries group homes in Fairfax, Virginia. Jack himself, about three years before he moved, began saying to us, "Why don't you find me a group home?" If he hadn't done that, I'm not sure we would have made the effort, as complacent as we had become with our situation right here in our cozy home. But gosh, Megan, what a mistake that would have been. I don't think there's anything sadder than a mentally retarded adult left alone after the deaths of both parents. At that point, it truly is difficult for them to make the transition to group home living. So, Jack did us a favor by urging us, from time to time, to find him the right place. Wellspring turned out to be that right place.

Wellspring Ministries has four group homes in Fairfax—two for boys and two for girls. Ed Guinan, the executive director, and Mitchell Thompson, the program director, are saints. This was what we wanted: saints to be guardians to our little messenger angels. I thank God for guiding us to Wellspring.

Jack moved into his group home early in December of 1995. You cannot imagine how excited he was. I remember that when we drove him out there on a Sunday afternoon, he was downright giddy, and once we got there and got his bed made, he could scarcely wait for us to get out of there and leave him in his new space. That was a great day for the Busbys.

As you might imagine, that euphoria didn't last. It was December. It was cold. It got dark early. It was dark well before Jack got home from his job as a busboy at La Fonda. He missed being able to watch as much TV as he wanted to watch. He missed going to the Cathedral every Sunday. He liked the guys "some of the time, but not all the time," to put it in his words. It was rainy in paradise. The saving grace was that Christmas was around the corner, and he would be back home with us for the holidays—to which we all looked forward.

The holidays were wonderful as usual, and Jack was still expressing general—if not effusive—enthusiasm for group home living. Then the holidays ended. And then the worst happened.

On Jack's first day back at work, he took the Metro, and then the bus home. It was dark, it was cold, it was raining, and he missed his bus stop. Realizing he had missed it, he didn't know what to do, so he just got off at the next one. He had never before been in that place, a couple of miles from his regular stop, and he was confused. He started across the street, which might have been OK except that traffic had a green light and Jack had the red. This was Braddock Road in Fairfax, a busy street where the speed limit was forty-five. My hands, Megan, are literally freezing as I write this to you.

Looking back, of *course* I should have realized that having only done the commute for three weeks before Christmas, and having been at home for ten days over Christmas, we needed to go back to the drawing board on the travel training. Of *course* it should have been a no-brainer. Of *course*.

The call came from Inova Fairfax Hospital, where Jack had been taken in an ambulance. Why he was not hurt badly, Megan, I will never know. He was skinned from head to toe and he had a bad cut on his leg, which ended up taking months and months to heal. But he was okay. I can only think that God still needed him here for a messenger angel.

After Jack's accident, he was home with us for several weeks. After a few days, he was able to go back to work, but I walked with him—partially because he was afraid to cross the streets and partly because we had a couple of big snowstorms and I was unsure that oncoming cars could stop. Jack had sort of lost his confidence in his own ability to function independently. When he first moved to Wellspring, I think he had this notion of moving on, moving upward, and moving out into the world. Then the accident occurred, and I could just see the bewilderment, the uncertainty, and almost the defeat on his face. David and I were of course so grateful that his injuries were minor that I'm afraid we didn't sufficiently focus on what was going on within Jack.

After Jack returned to Wellspring, he gradually adapted to the routine. Now, after eight years of group home living, and even after these many years at McCall's for Robert, I'm afraid that if we were to ask either of them if they'd rather stay in their group homes or move back home with us, they might both say they'd rather come back to us. But surely you know, Megan, that there is no way that question is going to be asked. We learned a long time ago that we don't offer our boys either/or choices unless we're prepared to do either/or. And we're not going there. Of course, part of the reason they love being at home is that when they are home, which is often, we focus on them and plan all activities around them. So, of course they have a great time. It wouldn't occur to them that our home is not and cannot be their home—not for the long haul. And the long haul is what we've got to think about.

So, there you have my thoughts on the residential placement question––at least from my experience and from within my very limited frame of reference. What you have to keep reminding yourself, if and when you go down this route, is that no one else can crawl inside the walls of your home and know what's right for your family. Needless to say, Sweet Megan, I will support you to the skies in whatever decision you and John make.

Much love, always,
Mary Beth

PS. "Don't worry about opposition. Remember, a kite rises against the wind, not with the wind." (Hamilton Wright Mabie)
And this quote, Megan, was on a card your marvelous mother, Diane Hamsa, sent me after that National Fragile X Foundation's International Conference in L.A. It had a wonderful photo of a kite on it, and I loved the quote and her note so much that I've kept it all this time.
PPS. Or maybe you like this one better: "When you come to a fork in the road, take it." (Yogi Berra)

Dear Mary Beth,

Your letter regarding residential placement really hits home this week. It is something I never thought I would need to do. I always felt my children would be able to get all the education they needed right here in Scottsbluff. Wrong again.

So much of what Jack needs to grow and mature can only be obtained by living away from home. No school program can teach the living skills, the independence, or adequately instill life acquisition skills. Our school has some vocational training classes, but Jack needs to learn basic communication skills first, social skills would be good too. Not to mention, possibly a third grade vocabulary? I'm really shooting for the moon on this list.

Oh my, you said it first: "Residential placement: the world's most agonizing decision." There is one helpful situation in my family. My sister Kristy has already done it. She has a son who is deaf and attends the St Joseph Institute for the Deaf in St. Louis, Missouri. The rest of the family lives in Omaha. Robby, her son, has adjusted beautifully. He absolutely loves it. He often writes home and asks if he can stay at school for the weekend. They keep them so busy. The school calendar is just nine months, and he is at home in the summer.

When he first went to school he wrote Kristy and told her he wrote "I miss my Mom" in soap on the shower door. He said he could see it every morning when he showered. One day the cleaning staff must have wiped it away. He noticed immediately and Kristy was the first to hear about it.

I read the comment from your friends at the British embassy to John. "We don't believe in entrusting anything as important as raising children to parents. We believe in leaving it to the pros." John has asked me to write that on our shower with soap so he can read it every morning!

We both know it would be the best thing for Jack. We would love to have him here with us, but I guarantee you we would see little growth with that route. The urgency of sending him off at a younger age has also been addressed. When do you suppose a person is more amenable to following directions and instructions, age fifteen or nineteen? When do you suppose he would be more developmentally prepared? Jack needs to be engaged in other activities while he is still ready, willing, and able.

I often have to remind myself that this decision is not about me. We have looked at the Stewart Home School in Frankfort, Kentucky, which may be a perfect fit for him. The school has been in business for 111 years. It is a community dedicated to the care of special people. The setting is a Kentucky landmark, now on the National Register of Historic Places. It sits on a seven-hundred-acre bluegrass estate and provides breathtaking views for residents. They have their own rooms in residential buildings. Many refer to it as their "home away from home." I think it would be a true opportunity for Jack. He could have the chance to be a leader, to participate in sports, and have a curriculum that is tailored to his needs. Yes, it would be the least restrictive environment. I sometimes think I wouldn't feel comfortable there, but I know he sure would. Don't get me wrong, it's a great place, but not having the same needs he does, it would not be a fair comparison. OK, I have some of his needs, some days more than others.

The campus has an equestrian center, ball field, a football field, a track, gymnasium, fishing ponds, and more. The residents participate in so many activities. The school even provides a trip abroad or a traveling adventure across the United States. Each year is a new experience. The academics are very life-skills oriented, like learning to balance a checkbook and making correct change. John would say I could use the checkbook class. Regardless, Jack is the one we need to look out for.

Unlike you and David, I have talked to almost all my friends about our option of sending Jack to a residential program. Surprised? I guess I talk too much. My parents told me that constantly when I was a child. I am so blessed to have so many supportive friends. They all know Jack fairly well and can also see the many benefits of this decision. I have talked at length with my sister Kristy. As she says, "I'm preaching to the choir." She did bring it to my attention that we have tried everything we know how to do for the last fifteen years and maybe we should let someone else try for a while. I think she is right.

Another good reason to send Jack to boarding school now is to truly make his transition from middle school to high school count! Transitions are hard for any child, especially a Fragile X child. To move him into a new environment and allow him to stay there through his high school years would be much easier than the alternative. We hope that he will be able to come back to Scottsbluff and live independently or with some assistance. Hopefully he can learn a vocation during his time there and be employable upon his return. Do you think I have wishful thinking? Or maybe I have my blinders on? We call them "big red blinders" in the great state of Nebraska.

My friends who are sending their kids off to college say it is the same thing, only Jack goes a little earlier. Yes, I can agree to that, but Jack in no way has the maturity or the understanding of this decision. He has very little concept of time, and will just have to figure it out when he gets there. Jack knows we are considering another option for him. He can relate to Robby being at his school, but that is about the extent of the comprehension. He knows we are going to visit the Stewart Home School in June. Seeking reassurance, he continually tells me that we are just going to look and then we will come home. "Yes," I say, "that is right,"—thinking to myself, "That is the case for this trip, but next time, you will stay."

He does continue to surprise us with the things he says. He probably knows more then we realize. He announced at breakfast the other morning that he was going to move into his own apartment! I asked him where that would be and he responded, "Kentucky!" Wow, we were shocked. Jacob immediately asked if he would have a locker. (Our table conversations are ones I should record. They are quite entertaining in the aftermath, but when you're in the thick of it, it can get quite interesting.) Jacob is quite proud of his school locker and the fact that he can work his combination lock on his own.

I haven't even begun to explain it all to Jacob. I'm worried he will think he is next, and he may be. Actually, with Jack gone, I think Jacob will thrive and will be able to do quite well in our high school. Who knows? That is what I have to believe for now. I can't imagine not having any children in my home. Wait, yes I can. It would be peaceful, relaxing, and fun for about a week. Then I am pretty sure I'd be very sad.

I have had so many signs and so many reassurances these last few months that we are doing the right thing. For instance, my parents winter in Naples, Florida, and they just happen to know the Stewarts who run the Stewart Home School. Is that a coincidence? I don't think so. John and I visited the school in January, and the staff gave me two names of families to call for references. One was Jane Jones, whom I met seven years ago at a Fragile X conference in Colorado Springs. Small world? Not entirely. She just sent her sixteen-year-old son, who has Fragile X, to the school last November. He loves it and hasn't asked to come home once. The other woman I called I did not know, but when she described her son, it paralleled Jack's issues perfectly. One of my sisters was flying home from a vacation and picked up a *New Yorker* magazine on the plane. Inside was an advertisement for the Stewart Home School. She said that was her sign that the school was right for Jack. On my trip home from Florida in February I did the same thing. Only my magazine opened to an article on the benefits of boarding schools. I have prayed for answers and signs that we are following the right path. I put this all together and think I have a flashing billboard sign saying, "Just do it!"

We continue to have many humbling experiences with Jack that reinforce to me he needs to go! I told John the other day, after taking Jack to bowling and being embarrassed about his behavior in the car, that I was beginning to see the writing on the wall. He asked me what it said. I told him: Stewart Home School. Jack needs an opportunity to grow in ways that we cannot provide. For example, he would love to have friends. There is just no one around here quite like Jack. Oh sure, everyone loves him and is good to him, but he has no one to confide in or to call his friend. When asked who his friends are he usually names adults, relatives, or teachers and therapists. He is always wanting to have someone spend the night, but can never think of anyone to invite. It could break my heart if I let it, but that is just the truth, a fact of life for Jack.

I attended a Christian women's luncheon a few weeks ago. I really did not want to go but had been invited by a friend numerous times, and it was time to accept. The speaker talked about the importance of invitations. Invitations make people feel accepted and offer them opportunities they may never have had. All I could think of was the great opportunities and invitations Jack would get at the Stewart Home School. I think he will have friends there. The kids are more like him. When I returned home, I told John I should write all of these experiences and sayings down in a book. I would like to be able to refer to it when I question our decision. John jokingly said, "Name the book *The Road to the Stewart Home School.*"

The icing on the cake was our transitional meeting with the high school. Jack should be moving on to Scottsbluff High School in the fall for his ninth grade year. Suffice it to say, that day reinforced my decision to move on with our plan.

I heard a statement from a woman who was retiring after thirty years of employment in the public school system. She said, "Throughout our lives, we grow only by letting go—letting go of persons, of places, of things, of states of life. Whether it's going off to college, or moving to a new city, or retiring from a job—all new beginnings begin with good-byes."

It must be our time to let Jack go.

Lots of love to you and David,

Love,

Megan ✉

22

Right and Wrong Behavior

Dearest Megan,

I truly am grateful for your phone call. How could you have known that yesterday was one of those days that threaten to send me straight on round the bend?

I so appreciate your support in dealing with our current situation with our Jack, and we are indeed going to take him to a therapist this weekend. We have to watch, though, to be sure he doesn't consider this to be a reward for bad behavior. This is the same therapist with whom he was in Group for a couple of years, and he loved going to the sessions. It was sort of a big social event for him. Peter, the therapist, finally decided that Jack really didn't need to be there, that he didn't seem to have any serious emotional problems, and he didn't have much to contribute, so he eased Jack out of the group. Of course, Peter wasn't counting on this latest thing, and neither were we, certainly.

There are numerous things about this disaster that make me feel guilty. I keep asking myself how many jobs Jack is going to have to lose before David and I exercise a little more judgment in expressing our reservations. Now he's in a marvelous workshop program in Virginia called ServiceSource. Its objective is to place the handicapped in jobs in the community, and there is also a workshop program for those more suited to this. When they decided to try Jack out at what they call an "enclave" position (where a few handicapped employees work with a supervisor) at the Air and Space Museum, we thought this was just terrific. What a nice place to work, right? Wrong. If we had had any sense at all, we would have realized that stocking the shelves in the gift shop, with all those people coming in and out, all those items, all that noise and activity, would be a disaster for a young man with an inability to focus. Talk about sensory overload! Anyway, after a few weeks of this, Jack got fired for rummaging through the backpacks of co-workers!! He said he was just looking for his sunglasses, and—as far as I've been able to determine—he didn't take anything. His boss was quite correct, though, to fire him on the spot. So now, he'll be back in the workshop until something else comes along.

David and I have been able to talk of nothing else this week, and it will be interesting to see what the therapist says. We've been told it may simply be adolescent behavior, pushing the envelope kind of thing. Then in our worst moments, we ask each other if there may be a kleptomania gene, and could Jack have gotten that along with the Fragile X gene? Poor baby. But of course we can't say "poor baby" to him. This is not poor baby time. This is the time to be tough and serious.

Oh, it's so hard to instill the precepts of right and wrong in these kids, as you well know. I feel like a bit of a fraud, in that people have sort of patted David and me on the back for having raised what seem to be two pretty nice boys, despite their severe limitations. They are indeed sweet boys and I know they try, for the most part, to do what's right. Every once in a while, though, I get brought up very short—Thwock!!— by a happening, and then I realize all over again that no one can ever rest on one's laurels. That laurel wreath, in one fell swoop, can become the proverbial prickly crown of thorns, and, boy, do those thorns hurt!

I will admit that, far more often than I should have, I've sort of gone along thinking that even with their limitations, our boys are really pretty nice young men and never do anything to hurt anyone and don't cause anyone any major distress. Then something will occur and I realize that of course I've been lax, been less than watchful, and been less than attentive to what is going on in their lives. It's just so hard to have a heart-to-heart conversation with either of them, because they so rarely have anything to say. That's so often the case that I'm afraid on the rare occasions when they do have something to say, the mechanism just isn't there for getting it said. But we keep on trying.

Clearly, a big part of the problem with our kids is their autistic tendencies, which render them literally incapable of focusing on others and how their own actions, and inactions, can affect others. It's not that they see an opportunity to be thoughtless and then go for it. They simply don't think. It's not that they sit around thinking of ways to disregard the rights and property of others. They simply don't think. It's not that they notice nice things that people do for them and deliberately decide not to thank them. They don't notice those things. They are so into and surrounded by themselves, spinning in their only little worlds, that their relationships with the rest of the universe are sort of "out there."

It's not their fault, and yet, because they perform reasonably well on some levels, we get furious with their behavior. It's hard to separate being furious with the behavior from being furious with the person exhibiting that behavior. I guess what I'm trying to say to you is that it's OK to be furious with Jack Massey's behavior, while remembering that Jack Massey himself doesn't realize how infuriating his behavior is. This won't change, honey. I wish I could say it will. No matter how old they get, there will always be "something."

Oh, maybe I shouldn't say it won't change. After all, FRAXA is funding a clinical trial of a drug that, if it works, will help our kids with learning disorders. And learning right versus wrong, acceptable versus unacceptable, and OK versus not OK behaviors is going to be all of that piece, right? After all, learning right and wrong *is* part of what we teach our children, part of learning, part of what we ask them to remember for future reference. So, let's think that indeed there will be changes for the better within the next decade. Still and all, though, there will likely always be "something."

You're fortunate, in a way, because nowadays there are so many more support systems out there to give you guidance. When I consider the FRAXA listserv and all the other groups one can join, not to mention that at least you young parents today know what's wrong with your kids, I realize that we truly were flying blind back in the 1960s and 1970s. I find that I learn so much from today's young mothers. And that means you, Megan.

Just last week, I had lunch with a young mother of a Fragile X child. She gave me a great tip that is way too late for me to use on my boys, but not too late for you. She said that when they are in, say, a supermarket and her son is being too friendly to strangers, she'll caution him by saying, "Now you're overgreeting." I know exactly what she means by that. That's never been a problem with Jack, but it sure is with Robert and I just wish someone had said to me, about thirty years ago, that if I didn't nip "overgreeting" in the bud, I'd be sorry. So now hear me, Megan, when I say it to you that it truly is a problem later on. I know it doesn't seem so now, as—if you're anything like I was—you're so thrilled that your Jack has finally learned to talk to people at all that you can't imagine shushing him as long as it's "happy talk." Right? But one fine day, what used to be happy, cheerful greetings and pleasantries will come across as irrelevant, slightly bizarre (no, make that truly bizarre), and unwelcome behavior. The saddest thing of all is that it will set him apart even more.

And now that we know what a rotten week we've both had with our Jacks, let's just hope that this coming week will be better. You know what? Your Jack's behavior doesn't sound so bad to me—though I realize that's easy for me to say. I don't mean he sounds normal. Of course he isn't. But the oppositional behavior you mentioned is truly so typical and you simply have to work around it. Even now, when we go into a restaurant and are about to sit down at the table, if I say to Robert, "Robert, honey, why don't you sit there," he will automatically sit at the place opposite the one I suggested. Automatically, without question, that's what he does. So, what I try to do, if my mind is clicking along swiftly enough, is to decide where I want Robert to sit and then tell him to sit in the seat opposite that one. What is that? Counteroppositional mothering? Whatever. You just have to do what works. Maybe you should suggest this approach to Jack's teacher. Then again, maybe not. Some teachers are not dying for input from mommy dearest. I have, however, read that there is indeed a disorder called oppositional disorder, so perhaps you could just say to her, "You know, Jack does have OD." Sometimes I think that if you can spout off the initials for something, it sounds official. Or is that just Washington?

I guess one of the reasons our boys' behavior in public has been as reasonably good as it is—and, believe me, I'm not suggesting that it's always good—is that we started taking them to church when they were toddlers. When we attended Christ Church Georgetown, in the late '60s, an angel of a woman, Dorothea Capello, had a mentally handicapped son and decided to start a Sunday school class for her child and others. Our boys loved going. Dorothea, who was and is a well-known actress (Dorothea Hammond) in the Washington theater, could keep the attention of these kids, and anyone else, by reading the DC phone book. They adored her, so this was a win-win. They developed the notion that going to church was a fun thing to do and that they'd rather go than not go.

When Robert and Jack were a little older, we moved out to Potomac where we attended another church. Others who attended there may remember it differently, but my memory is that our boys were reasonably well behaved in church. Our policy was that the minute they began to create a disturbance, we simply left and went home. I really don't think we had to do that more than a couple of times, and they learned that when you don't behave, you don't stay. Later still, when we moved back into town and Robert went off to McCall's, we attended yet another church. This one had an active Sunday school program for Jack's age group, and he also sang in the children's choir until his voice changed. I know we were lucky with the leaders at that church, who surely explained to the other children that Jack was mentally retarded and they simply had to deal with it. I can only remember one boy who was ever unpleasant to Jack and made fun of him. You're nearly always going to have that one, and you simply accept it and go on.

We all know that children tend to be so cruel to their peers—especially when they don't accept a child as a peer. Our boys were always the odd kids out, and I just got used to it, that's all. I think a mother of a child with Fragile X has to be tougher than other moms. And it's not only kids who can be cruel.

I'll never forget meeting a young woman at a cocktail party maybe twenty years ago. It was before the diagnosis of Fragile X, as I recall. I told her that I had two mentally retarded children, and she said, "Gee, you must feel like a real freak." I answered, "Now, I do." I'm glad we didn't go to her church.

Now, whenever Jack is home with us, he ushers at the Washington National Cathedral. He's been ushering there for twelve years or more. Even with all his problems and bizarre talking to himself, they kind of love him and accept him as sort of a mascot. The ushers, unbeknownst to us, had a dreadful dilemma a while back, when they caught Jack helping himself to money in the collection plate. Can you imagine, Megan? And can you imagine our horror when after the third time he did it, one of the ushers took David aside and told him that this had occurred. That really put me to bed with a "sick headache," as my grandmother used to say. We met with Mitchell Thompson and the therapist and the punishment we all agreed on was that Jack was not allowed to usher for four months. Whenever he went to church with us, he had to sit with us, which he hated. All the ushers knew and understood the situation and while they said they wouldn't have imposed this restriction, they supported David and me in our effort to drive home the point to Jack that what he did was very wrong. I think the clergy and the other ushers consider having Jack among them to be a special ministry, and it is precisely that. For that I'll be ever grateful. Needless to say, I'd rather my sons had been able to grow up to minister to others, rather than to be ministered to, but my heart knows that being messenger angels, they bring their own special messages to those they interact with, and I assume that more people than I realize have heard, on some level, those messages.

I know that although you grew up attending the Episcopal church in Omaha, you and John and the boys go to his lifelong Methodist church in Scottsbluff. It's funny because I grew up going to the Methodist church in Oklahoma City and then joined David in the Episcopal church in New York after we were married. Whither thou goest, huh? But I don't think it much matters whither we go to church, as long as we do go. One thing I love about the Episcopal church is what my daddy used to call the "canned stuff"—the rituals that remain the same Sunday after Sunday, year after year, and (albeit with modifications) century after century. I love being able to count on the service being what it is, no matter where in the world we may be traveling, and I think that our boys respond to ritualistic routine in church, just as they do at mealtime, bath time, and bedtime.

Not to put too fine a point on this, but I feel that our children have the capacity to achieve spiritual growth that soars above and transcends the constant rejection that is inherent in simply being who they are. My boys, I'm convinced, know that God loves them unconditionally and that no matter what, He's there for them. Your boys know that too, because by taking them to church and having them participate, you have put them in an environment where they'll have occasion to learn it.

Whatever you do about Jack's and Jacob's behavior problems (when did they start calling problems "issues" do you suppose?), pulleeeze take some time for you and John to be alone and to have some fun. Go to a movie, or have sex an extra time this week, or call up a couple you rarely see and ask them to meet you for dinner—out. Definitely out. Something. I realize that you almost have to set the alarm to make these things happen, but it's not merely important. It's essential. No matter what else, you and John must keep your time together special, fun, and regular. Frankly, it's a lot easier to let it slide than to make it happen. So do the hard, tough thing and have some fun, OK?

Love,
Mary Beth

PS. "Pride goes before destruction, and haughtiness before a fall." (Proverbs 16:18)
I'm afraid that too much of the time, I've been fairly complacent in thinking things are going fairly well with the boys. Then whoosh! All of a sudden, I realize it's never over. There will always be another something.

Dear Mary Beth,

As mothers, we all have certain embarrassing or humbling moments that our children bring to us. However, as a mother of special needs kids, it is ten times worse. It can be magnified beyond belief. I always say my kids are X-perts at it all!

One of many stories is still vivid in my mind. Jack had wanted to walk home from church to his grandparents' house for many months. He attended an after-school program at the church every Wednesday. Our church is three blocks from his grandparents' house. On the way is the Longfellow Elementary School that John attended, as well as Jack and Jacob. It is a beautiful walk in an older neighborhood. There are a few trees, but it is far from a forest. There is one busy street, (5th Avenue) to cross. It is two lanes, but traffic can be heavy around 5 p.m. Now, rush hour traffic in our town means there are three or four cars at the stoplight. Once I conceded to Jack's request to walk by himself, I instructed him to cross 5th Avenue up on 20th Street where there is a stoplight.

As all mothers have done, at least once in their life, I followed Jack down the street in my car. I was driving in the back alley so he could not see me. I was feeling so proud as I watched him march down the sidewalk. (Isn't it, indeed, pride that comes before the fall?) Jack must have felt so grown up and independent. I marveled at him as I watched him approach the intersection. He had been able to do many things despite his mental impairment brought on by Fragile X. But, for once, he was doing what the "normal" kids do. He pushed the crosswalk button on the tall pole and waited patiently. Little did I know, Jack was struggling with an urge that often hit him very quickly. I watched him as he stood so proudly at the stoplight. His erect posture suddenly turned into a dance. It was a dance I recognized. Not a joyful, happy dance. It was the "potty dance."

You can guess what happened next. Right there, on 5th Avenue and 20th Street, my ten-year-old boy dropped his shorts to his ankles and urinated on another church lawn, which was on the corner. I couldn't drive my car up there fast enough to stop him. After he completed this job, he continued to walk to the next block, where I finally caught up with him. I hollered at him to get into the car. I was horrified and angry. I asked him, "What were you doing?" He said, "Crossing the street." He had no clue his actions were out of line. I began to tell him, quite hysterically, that it was not acceptable to go the bathroom outdoors, let alone in public. It then occurred to me, that in the country where we live, we allow it. But it is always in the trees where no one is watching. I also told him he could be put in jail for exposing himself in public. OK, I got carried away, but I had a very important point to make.

When we finally arrived at Grandma's house, we were discussing what he could do differently the next time. I, of course, was looking for the planning-ahead component of using the bathroom before he left the church. Jack, very confidently stated that if this happened again he would just run to the woods to go the bathroom. The closest wooded area that I am aware of would be in Colorado—about 200 miles away.

Now that we're considering sending my precious Jack away to a boarding school, I feel badly about this situation. I am not pleased with the way I handled it. It is so hard to remember that they are doing the best they can. Jack wouldn't have done this if he knew the consequences. Social graces just don't have an impact on them in any way, unless a "learning experience" is included. And even then, there is no guarantee that they will be able to apply what they learned in a different environment. Life for them is a training ground. I guess it is for all of us, but the learning curve our boys have to work with is a huge handicap.

I guess it's the grace of God that allows us all to continue on. The next morning brought a new day with all new experiences. We cannot allow ourselves to become consumed with these situations that seem so overwhelming. Life goes on and we learn, with every new day, we learn.

Give my best to David.

Love,

Megan ✉

Dear Megan,

Needless to say, I laughed out loud at your story about Jack's "watering" the church's lawn. Well, at least it was another church, and not yours. That truly is a funny story. I'm sure most any parent of any normal child would have a similar story to recount. The difference is that our boys did these sorts of things at ten, rather than at three or four years old. But then, that's what being retarded is all about. Slow. Later than usual.

Reading your story, though, does make me ponder the concept of unconditional love. You and I would like to think that we love our boys unconditionally. But do we, really? I'm not sure, if I'm to be truly honest with myself. I'm afraid that my love for Robert and Jack does sometimes have conditions attached. I love Robert on the condition that his behavior doesn't embarrass me, on the condition that he measures up to my expectations. Never mind that my expectations may be divorced from reasonable hopes. I love Jack on the condition that he does the right thing. I think I know, and he should be able to judge, his concept of the "right thing." But is this fair? And can I be fair?

One thing I have learned, I think, is that some of the boys' caregivers, over the years, have been the ones who have loved them unconditionally. They don't have to love them. They have to do their jobs, but they don't have to love them. But the ones who have come to love them have done so with a love that is truly unconditional.

Anyway, these little embarrassing incidents, too, shall pass. Some of them we'll remember, you and I. Some we won't. Let's just hope that the ones we remember twenty years from now will be the ones that make us laugh out loud.

Love,

MBBB 🖂

23

What's in a Name?

Dear Megan,

Yesterday, Jack went back to work and to his group home, and Robert went back to Oklahoma this morning. At supper this evening, DB said, "Boy, isn't it nice to be rid of all those Busbys!?" He was kidding, of course. Oh, yeah? Actually, we are thrilled to get back to our little routine here.

One of our big projects for this vacation period was to solidify the practice of calling David Jr. "Robert," once and for all. We're not totally "there" yet, but we're making progress. Every time I refer to him as Robert, people who have known him all his life look at me as though I am daft. Once I give the explanation, though, everyone thinks it's great.

The explanation for the name change, which I pieced together by talking to his group home counselor, is that he went to a Special Olympics event in Ardmore, Oklahoma. Somehow, the Special Olympics people used his first name, which is indeed Robert, instead of David, and they put Robert on his name tag. Then he won the fifty-yard dash he had entered, and they announced over the loudspeaker that Robert Busby had won that race. He heard that and must have decided that, hey, this Robert fella must be a winner. From that time on, he began referring to himself as Robert. I first noticed it when I was down there the next week and gave him a birthday card to sign for Irene, the boys' nanny and special friend, who is still very much a part of our lives. He signed it Robert—not spelling it quite correctly, but I got the idea. When I asked him what this was all about, he simply said that he is Robert now. It was weeks before I got the story straight, but we all began immediately trying to accommodate his wish.

Actually, I have long regretted having named him Robert David Busby Jr. I think that naming a little boy after his father is—right from the get-go—putting a lot of pressure on him. As things turned out, David Jr. didn't really feel that pressure, but I sure did, and I hated what I had done, both to him and to his daddy. So, I love what we're doing now, calling him by the name he has chosen.

But wait a minute here. I have to ask myself why I have so quickly, completely, and wholeheartedly embraced this name change. I find myself almost giddy with delight in calling him Robert. And why? Am I, on some level, making this my thing? Is this my subconscious notion of making him over, reinventing him? Am I trying, once and for all, to rid my own mind and heart and soul of David Jr., the hand flapper and biter, the head banger? I'll never be able to put aside completely the image of that tiny toddler marching resolutely up to the wall of his bedroom, calculating the distance between his head and the wall, and then slam! He would bang his head on the wall. Not once, not twice, but he would keep it up until I grabbed him and clung to him, willing my body to control his. He never cried during these episodes. I cried for both of us.

So I wonder. Did I and do I want, by embracing the name change, to change what David Jr. was into what he might become? Robert is and will always be my precious baby with Fragile X. He no longer bites and flaps his hands, though he does rub them together a lot. He no longer bangs his head on the wall, but there is a price to be paid for the faulty wiring in his brain that allowed that long ago toddler, who couldn't talk, to communicate his frustration by insult and injury to himself.

None of my regret over having named our firstborn son after his father was made easier when David's wonderful daughter, Alison, and her husband, Bill Vareika, had a baby boy whom they named David Wesley Vareika. When Ali was pregnant with him, she and Bill decided not to find out the sex of the baby. She told me, though, that if it turned out to be a boy, they were going to name him David, after her daddy, but that I shouldn't tell DB this. She knew him well enough to know that he would be disappointed if the baby wasn't a boy, knowing about the game plan for the name plan. So, I dutifully kept the secret.

When the baby was born, it was clear that although he was a perfect-looking, full-term baby, there was a serious problem with his heart. They took him in an ambulance up to Children's Hospital Boston, where the heart team, one of the best in the country, said that there was truly no hope, that his heart was so defective that massive damage had already occurred. Alison and Bill, with heroic bravery, held and rocked their precious infant, who had been baptized David Wesley Vareika, until he died at the age of twenty-three hours.

David and I went to Newport the next day for the graveside service. Hopie, who had flown in from California to be with her sister, met us at the Providence airport with the girls' mother, Ann. As we were driving to Newport, they handed us the Newport newspaper with the obituary. David looked at it and realized for the first time that the baby had been named for him. It is one of the rare times I remember seeing David Busby cry.

I then wished more than ever that we had given Robert his very own name. But, at the same time, I was grateful that Hopie and Steve had named their two spectacular boys Patrick Busby Burleigh and Nicholas Busby Burleigh. Through them, at least, the Busby name will at least be "in there," hopefully, for a while. And David's brother, Phil, has one son who has two sons. So, the Busby name will be around there ("there" being the gene pool) for a while.

David's daughters, Hopie and Alison, are truly the joys of my life, just as I know your sisters and cousins are to you, Megan. What an incredible stroke of luck for me to have married a man who already had two wonderful daughters, both of whom have turned out to be perfect sisters to the boys. They and their husbands treat the boys as though they were just the brothers they would have wanted and enjoyed through the years. And I know that they will always be good to and watch over my boys, as will my cousin Jan. Talk about guardian angles! I'm blessed indeed.

So, while I would never, ever have initiated this name-change bit for Robert, I'm frankly thrilled that he did it for himself, and I'm making every effort to make it happen for him. There's this look of real pleasure on his face each time someone calls him Robert. It's as if he's reinvented himself, and he likes this guy Robert. I don't know, maybe he has hopes for Robert that he never had for David Jr.

I should imagine that having named Jack John Massey Jr. hasn't caused as much regret on your part as naming our Jr. has on mine. After all, calling him Jack is really a whole different sound from John. With us, it was always Little David. I swear, I don't think we began calling him David Jr. until he was about twenty-five. Here he was this totally grown—physically anyway–—"Little David." Enough, already. I would have wanted to invent a new name too, if I had been Little David. I have for years fantasized about what it would be like if someone discovered the cure for Fragile X and all of these kids could be reinvented. I think about it for about two minutes, and then I don't think about it anymore for a while. It won't be a happening thing for guys the ages of mine. Even though some researchers say that when they figure out how to treat these kids, that it could help people of all ages, I just don't go there. But that's OK. My boys are playing their parts, and not too badly, really. They're such sweet little guys—as are your boys, I know. I haven't even met them, but I love them more each time I hear from you. And you know what? I honestly, in my heart of hearts, think that there will indeed be either a cure or a truly effective treatment for Fragile X for your boys. It's that hope and that expectation that keeps me keeping on.

Hug all your boys for me,
Mary Beth

PS. "Who hath not own'd, with rapture-smitten frame, the power of grace, the magic of a name? (Thomas Campbell, 1777–1844) ✉

Dear Mary Beth,

How assertive of Robert David to change his name to Robert. It is his first name. It must be quite a confidence builder for him. I think that shows good processing skills. After all, he could have grabbed something out of the air, like "Oscar." I have nothing against Oscar, I'm just making a point. I bet you are grateful that the Special Olympics committee didn't give him the wrong name tag, with someone else's name altogether.

Speaking of names, our Jack is not a John Jr. His full name is John Thomas Massey. John's middle name is Douglas. We chose the nickname of Jack because his great-grandfather John Gordon Elliott went by the name of Jack. You may recognize that name. He owned and ran the J. G. Elliott Insurance Agency in Scottsbluff for fifty years. John still works there today.

Jacob just came out of nowhere. I should say the name "Jacob." We know where Jacob came from. We actually tried for over a year to conceive with Jack, so when Jack turned a year old we thought we'd better get busy. Well, along came Jacob, twenty months after Jack's birth.

My favorite story about the boys' names occurred when they were about seven and five. Jack and Jacob were playing with a jack-in-the box at our local men's store while I was birthday shopping for John. After a short time, Jacob said, "Don't they have a jacob-in-the-box?"

Who knows what names my boys will want to be called someday? No nicknames have occurred yet. Nothing out of the ordinary anyway. If I had it to do over, I would have just named Jack, Jack. It gets confusing for him. He didn't realize he was really a "John" until middle school. He wouldn't answer to roll call. He just looked around for his dad. Oh well, we live and we learn. I love those Massey boys regardless. All three of them.

Take good care and hope to see you soon.

Love,

Megan ✉

24

Kelly's Story

Dear Mary Beth,

I have a dear friend, Kelly Randels, whom I met in Holland. You know what that means, right? She called me because she has a son with Fragile X syndrome. Her cousin gave her my name. We instantly hit it off on the phone. She is darling. She is just starting all of the early childhood intervention services and is formulating a plan for the education of her son, Cody.

She is fortunate because she is a teacher. She has a master's degree and is teaching in an elementary school. She knows the ropes. She had many questions, but there was one I was not able to answer. The question involved having another baby. No thanks! My plate is full. As my mother says, "I have more hay than I can put up." After Jacob's birth, I mean right after his birth, I knew I was done. Jacob's delivery was a VBAC (vaginal birth after a cesarean). Jack was a C-section. So, Jacob made it out the natural way. It must be a real accomplishment for the doctors. You know it isn't good when your feet are up in the stirrups after delivery and one obstetrician is sewing you up and his partner peaks in the door and says, "What do you call this? A vaginal section?" I guess they thought it was a success since they got him out without surgery, but I beg to differ. If men had babies, they would only have one.

Anyway, I am writing because I think you can be of some help to Kelly. She is thinking about having another baby, but is interested in exploring all of her options. What do you think? Would you be interested in talking to her? I bet you would have some great wisdom to impart. It's over my head at this point. Think about it and let me know, and I will send her address on to you.

Thanks again. I'll be out in DC in the next few months. I will be sure and let you know the dates. I love having dinner with the Busbys.

Love,

Megan

Dear Megan,

So Kelly wants to have another baby? Why am I not surprised? She strikes me as a young woman who should have more than one child. But, oh, Megan, I can't believe you're asking *me*, of all people, for advice for her on this subject. I carry far too much emotional baggage to be able to give a rational response. I can only tell you that for the longest time—far longer than anyone who knew me at the time would have dreamed—I, as well as Kelly, badly—really badly—wanted to have another baby, to try again. I can remember that a couple of times I thought I might be pregnant, that there had been that "accident." About half of me hoped that I was indeed pregnant. All I can say is, thank God it was only premature ovarian failure—or early menopause—which, as I later learned, is quite common among us Fragile X carriers.

Honey, you're just going to have to suggest to Kelly that she talk to a number of other people—people far more objective than I. Also, I hope she'll talk with people a lot younger than I and even—forgive me—younger than you are. Though that excruciating, decision-heavy time still weighs greatly on my consciousness, the fact is that it was a very long time ago, literally in a different age. Well, my goodness, don't I sound old?—which is sort of the point. I am old, in terms of being able to imagine this situation for Kelly right now. I am so old that for me, "that time of the month" is the few days before I get my hair color done. So, I'm simply way beyond all this.

Back in those dark ages, of course, before we even knew about Fragile X, even knew about amnio being able to detect it, even knew about the wonderful new in vitro fertilization processes, it would have just been David and me taking one more chance that a third baby would be OK. Obviously, I would have had some chance of passing on my "good" X chromosome to that third child, but I guess one of the things that stopped us was the question of the fairness—or lack thereof—of saddling that normal child with two mentally retarded brothers to take care of for a lifetime. Talk about pressure to succeed! Boy, that would weigh heavily on any child. Big time.

So, since you asked, I guess I would have to say that as much as I dreamed of a daughter to enjoy in my old age, as much as I envied all my friends with those daughters, for the Busbys, I think it would have been the wrong decision.

David has always said it's a shame that young people are required to make so many of the major decisions in their lives when they're too young to make them. But in Kelly's case, it seems she's being forced to hurry up and make this monumental judgment before she gets too *old* to make it. If she waits much longer, it really will be too late. Then she'd just be left with woulda, coulda, shoulda. God only knows what she should do. I sure wish He would tell her, because I can't.

I can tell you one thing. Kelly is fortunate to have you for a friend. She's also fortunate in that the new preimplantation genetic diagnostic procedure (PGD) is very exciting. I'm sure Kelly and Ryan are looking into all sorts of options, including that one, and I assume you know that one of our FRAXA board members, indeed our board chairman, has gone that route. We all anxiously awaited the outcome of Debbie Stevenson's pregnancy, and the joy that she and Jeffrey have in the divine Miss Samantha St. John Stevenson is a thrill to behold. Another board member and one of the founders of FRAXA, Kathy May, went that route as well, with unsatisfactory results. She did not produce many eggs, even with the stimulation, and on the first attempt had only two embryos and three on the second attempt that the lab was able to test for the Fragile X gene. PGD testing revealed that both embryos during the first cycle carried the Fragile X gene. In the second attempt, only one embryo, a female, did not have the Fragile X gene. Unfortunately, the implanted embryo did not thrive and the pregnancy failed. After that, Kathy and John decided to settle with their great little Fragile X guy, Sam, and to let that be that.

Kathy May is indeed a marvelous example of moving on to the next phase. She moved into a long career with the Association for Retarded Citizens (ARC) of Northern Virginia. She feels that this reflects her life, in that she moved from desperately wanting a "normal" baby to seeing the beauty and value in individuals with intellectual disabilities and using her passion to fight for their civil rights. Kathy is another example, Megan, of God closing one door and then opening another.

The side effects from all the hormones one has to take during the in vitro fertilization (IVF) process can be pretty unpleasant. Better warn Ryan, if he and Kelly do go that route, that her mood swings are likely to be rather dramatic.

Let's face it: any young woman with CGG repeats high enough to have had one child with the full mutation has a fairly certain chance of having another one—unless, of course, and there's always that "unless," she lucks out and passes on her other X chromosome to the next child. I have to assume that Kelly has a really swift genetic counselor.

Of course, any girl can always be lucky enough to pass on that other X chromosome, the one she got from the other parent. My mother, for instance, had seventy repeats, and she passed on her other X to my brother, who's not even a carrier. I suppose the lucky part could be said to be that she and I were fortunate that I wasn't more affected than I am. Pretty complicated, huh? And maybe Kelly doesn't really need or want to hear all this. You know her far better than I, so you'll just have to decide what her want-to-know level is likely to be.

If Kelly opts not to go for IVF or PGD, but simply to get pregnant, then she will have to decide what she's going to do if it turns out to be another Fragile X fetus, and *no* one can help them there. They are literally on their own. I only mean by that that while of course all of those who love them will support their decision, only the couple involved can determine how much they can handle. I didn't get to be sixty-five without learning that you can't pass judgment on another parent when it comes to all sorts of things, and the decision about terminating a pregnancy is one of them. I've been asked what I would have done in this circumstance, and all I can tell you is what I would like to think I would have done, not what I *would* have done. You simply can't know until or unless it happens.

I think I would have terminated a Fragile X male, but not a female. There are just too many cases of Fragile X girls who turn out to be perfectly fine for me to imagine not taking that chance. I would bet on her. Gosh, when you look at Katie Clapp and Mike Tranfaglia's little Laura, right at the top of her class, and when I think of another young Fragile X woman I know of here in the Washington area who the last I heard was applying for med school, it just thrills me to know that getting that compensating X from the father can bump her IQ right on up there to normal, and maybe even beyond. Of course, not all Fragile X girls do have such good fortune, but what I think I would have done is to have run the risk.

Again, I don't *know* what I would have done about any of it. I don't *know* that I would have been able to go through with an abortion of a Fragile X male. We're all so smart about knowing what we would do when not really presented with the circumstances. Real smart. All I do know is that for organizations like FRAXA or the March of Dimes or any other organization that conducts research on a birth defect to take a position on abortion would be dumber than dumb. Not going there.

Bottom line is that Kelly and Ryan sound just great. I'll bet they have wonderful family support. And you should simply assure her that they will have the support of all who love them—whichever way they go. No one can play God for another human being, and anyone who would try it needs to reexamine his or her motives.

On a happier note. Let me say that the day will come when Kelly can honestly say to herself that no, thank you, I would not want to have another baby. No way. That day came for me in the Safeway in Potomac. I was pushing my shopping cart along and I heard a whiny baby nearby. The harried mother was trying to deal with the baby and still manage to get her shopping done and the baby was having none of it. I remember thinking, "Thank God that's not my baby." Then, "Thank God I don't have a baby that age." Then, "Thank God I don't have to have another baby that age." Then, "Thank God I don't have to have another baby, period." It truly was an epiphany. I think that word is ridiculously overused, but I can't think of any other. I probably broke into a smile at that point, glowing over my grocery cart and the fact that I had nothing in there more "baby" than baby carrots, because I knew I had reached a milestone.

Love to you all,
Mary Beth ✉

Dear Mary Beth,

I appreciate your thinking of my family and me as we move on to the next step in our lives. Megan showed me the letter you sent her regarding the decision whether or not to have another baby. I can relate to much of the letter, and I thank you for your suggestions and support.

When our son, Cody, was diagnosed with Fragile X at eighteen months, I was already pregnant with our second child. The geneticist met with me and explained the facts about Fragile X and that our second baby also could be affected. I was scared because my dream of having a big family was now threatened. The day after I found out I was pregnant with Cody, I bought a minivan—now what for? The possibility of not having a big family was frightening to me.

I was asked if I wanted to have an amnio performed, and I did not hesitate. By this time I was going into my second trimester of pregnancy.

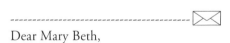

All of my family, friends, and coworkers knew I was pregnant. Life is not real while you are awaiting results like this. You worry constantly. You try to find something to keep you busy. My husband, Ryan, and I had won a trip to Las Vegas so we went there, but all I did was sit at an empty gambling table and stare at the wall. I could not relax or have a good time.

The amnio results were back in mid December, and the results confirmed our worst nightmare; our second baby, a girl, also was affected by Fragile X. We all know that Fragile-X-affected females are said to lead lives that are typically not as challenged as affected males, however, there are certainly no guarantees. What I also knew was this: I see children in my classroom who are not diagnosed with any disability, and they have daily struggles when they are learning. I knew that it is not a guarantee that all females are less affected. I am acquainted with some who are obviously affected and some who are not. And besides the chance of being challenged—as if that was not enough—I was going to consciously give my child the unfortunate status of being a carrier. I would not wish being a carrier on my worst enemy, let alone my own child. I would consciously be giving my child a lifetime filled with unanswered questions and difficult challenges.

Knowing what we know about the CGG repeat size and the percentage chance that the affected X will turn into full mutation, I knew I was doomed. My Fragile X results were showing that the repeat size on my X chromosome is 103, and through genetic testing my dad was found to be a carrier as well, and his repeats are 96. My genetic counselor showed us this chart:

No. of repeats	Percentage of chance the affected X will expand to full mutation
0–55	0
55–59	3.7
60–69	5.3
70–79	31.1
80–89	57.8
90–99	80.1
100 +	100.0

Because my repeats are 103, if I pass on my affected X, my child has a 100 percent chance of being born with full mutation. I was devastated.

When we heard the results about our second child being affected, I called Ryan and told him. Although we had discussed our decision a hundred times, he still asked me, "What are you going to do?" I told him through tears that we knew what we had to do. I then E-mailed my mom, whom I knew was going to be devastated as well. She E-mailed me back four simple words: "I am very sorry," and that was enough. I knew her heart was just as broken as mine. I too was numb and at a loss for words.

I had discussed our options with Ryan, my family, my close friend, the genetic counselor, and my obstetrician. With everyone's input we made the decision to terminate the pregnancy. We also made the decision that everyone else would be told that I had miscarried.

The results came back on a Friday and the following Monday I was in my mom's car on our way to the women's clinic. Ryan had to go to work. My dad took Cody to daycare and then he met my mom and me at the clinic. Just as my genetic counselor had warned us, there were picketers outside the clinic yelling horrible things at us. They said to me that I was going to remember this day every year at Christmastime. They were wrong. I often remember this day. We kept focused and walked up the stairs to the women's clinic. Once we were in the waiting room, we knew we were safe. My genetic counselor met us there and went back with me to speak with the doctor who would be performing the procedure. I wanted him to know that I was there because my baby was affected by Fragile X. I wanted him to know that I was different from the others he would see that day. Never would I have thought about being in this clinic for an abortion just because. I do not think that women who find themselves in an abortion clinic are bad. They are there because they are making a difficult choice. One that I would not have made had I not known my baby's condition, but a choice that is their right to make.

I was alone in the pre op room with three women who were there to terminate their pregnancies.One young woman with blue hair,leaned over to me and said, "I have three kids at home and just can't handle thinking of having another screaming kid in the house. How far along are you?" I looked at her and as politely as possible I said, "I am here because my baby has a disability. I really wanted my baby." She turned around and said nothing else to me the rest of the time.

Once I was in the operating room, I had a really hard time. The nurse kept telling me to breath and to calm down and that I was going to be fine. I felt like the room was spinning and my breathing was very rapid and out of control. I heard this little voice say, "Please don't, Mommy, I promise I will be good." I came very close to stopping the procedure, closer than anyone will ever know. But I kept telling myself that this was the right thing to do. When I walked out and into the waiting room, everyone had left except my dad. He stood and gave me a big hug and asked if I was ready. I told him yes. We left and neither of us said a word until he dropped me off at home. I told him I wanted to be alone and that I would call later. He told me to call my mom because she wanted to know that I was home. I called her and we cried. Then I called Ryan and told him it was horrible, and that I did not want to talk to anybody. I took the next few days off from work. Everyone at work was told I had a miscarriage.

Life was not and is not easy after that. I struggle often and always will struggle with the memories and what ifs. We told almost everyone that I had miscarried.

Ryan and I agreed to try preimplantation genetic diagnosis (PGD). I was confident that the PGD procedure was going to work. Why wouldn't it? I had gotten pregnant two times so easily. On the first month with Cody and on the third month with our second baby. Little did I know what was in store for me.

In January of 2003 we met with Dr. Victoria Maelin, an infertility specialist in my city. She agreed to work with the Reproductive Genetics Institute in Chicago and assisted with my ovarian stimulation. The plan was for an embryologist from Chicago to come to Omaha after my oocyte retrieval and test the embryos for Fragile X. We were never able to complete the PGD process. Over the next six months we attempted ovarian stimulation four times. Because premature ovarian failure is common in carriers of Fragile X, my ovaries were not able to perform like we hoped. I was only able to produce two to three eggs each time. My Follicle Stimulation Hormone level was 12.9, and the specialists say it is best if it is under 10. We decided not to go through an attempt to complete any of those cycles (which would have involved transferring embryos identified as unaffected), because the specialists really hope to work with at least 10 eggs. This number is necessary because an estimated half are going to be mature, then an estimated half are going to be affected. As you can see, producing two to three eggs was not sufficient for the process to be a success. Ryan and I were devastated.

I thought this was going to be so easy. I thought I was invincible. When we were making our third attempt, I E-mailed my family and close friends and explained the difficulty we were having with PGD. I told them that we were going to give it one more try and then explore the possibility of an egg donor. My cousin Alyssa Emailed me back right away and offered to be our egg donor. I was thrilled. I told her she needed to first talk about it with her fiancé, family, and close friends to see if this was something she was *sure* she was interested in doing. Immediately she replied and said she did not need to check with anyone. She said I was family and the best mom she knew, and there was no doubt in her mind that for her to be our donor was the right thing. If the tables had been turned, she knew I would do the same for her. I cried. I told Ryan what she had offered and he liked the idea. First, she had to be tested to see if she was a Fragile X carrier. Amazingly, she was not.

Alyssa flew here to meet with our infertility doctor and make the required visit with a psychologist. We successfully completed those appointments. My doctor worked with a doctor in her area to do the initial ultrasounds and to monitor her meds until her eggs were close to retrieval. In December, after Christmas, she flew here for a week and a half. My doctor was able to retrieve twenty eggs. Sixteen were mature, nine fertilized, and of those, seven survived the first three days, and of those, three were implanted and the remaining four were frozen. This attempt was not successful.The following month the four we had frozen were implanted. That cycle was also unsuccessful.

Everyone was shocked! We thought for sure this was going to be it. There was no reason why this was not working. We truly did not know what to think.

Now, seven months later, we are working with our infertility clinic yet once again. My insurance has not covered any of these procedures, which have been extremely frustrating and extremely expensive. We have spent over $35,000 at this point. We have hired an attorney who is very optimistic that he will be able to get the insurance company to pay for the procedure because of the wording in my policy. We are in the process of using an anonymous egg donor. I am requiring that the donor be tested for being a Fragile X carrier. I will never know her name. I was given the following information about her:

- height and weight
- hair and eye color
- allergies
- hospitalizations
- age
- parents' health

- grandparents' health
- ethnicity
- psychologist's report

My heart aches for another child. I want all the things that most people out there want. I want to experience the weddings of my children. I want to be a good mother-in-law. I want to be a fabulous grandma. I want Cody to have a sibling. I worry about what life will be like for Cody when I am no longer able to take care of him. I worry about how he will be treated and who will look out for him.

By the way, Cody is fantastic.He has been receiving early intervention services since he was eighteen months old. The teachers tell us they think he is doing remarkably well—and we agree. I enjoy him so much. I hate to think "What if I knew about being a carrier before I had him?" Cody is truly the light of my life. I am so proud of him. Because of him, I have had so many new doors open for me. I started a Fragile X group for our state. I have tried to raise awareness in our area. I have met so many incredible people and have gained so many friendships that I am confident will last a lifetime.

So as you can see, to have or not to have another baby is a lot more complex than one may think. I chose to write to you about a lot of very personal things. I know that there are some people who would not appreciate what I have to say, and for that I thank you for being my friend and for understanding and for being open minded. No one knows what she would do until handed a situation—I thought I knew and even then, I had second thoughts the whole time until it was too late. I only hope that by writing this I provided myself with some sense of closure and offered other women in my situation a real-life example of what it is like to be in these shoes and unfortunately, the shoes of many other women out there.

Love,
Kelly ✉

Dear Kelly,

Receiving your letter, I must say, was a humbling experience for me. In my letter to Megan, which I assumed she would pass on to you, I had rather breezily chattered on about what I would like to think I would have done on the one hand, and then on the other hand. Well you, my friend, have lived out the "on the other hand" scenario that I can only barely imagine in my worst nightmares. You and Ryan have been there. No one can presume even to imagine the pain, the anguish, the uncertainty, and the sadness that coursed through your very beings as you dealt with the tragedy of knowing you were carrying a second Fragile X baby. No one who hasn't, like you and Ryan, been there will ever know. Period.

The only way in which I can say that you've been "lucky" is in the family support that you have, and that I'm sure you appreciate. Cody's a lucky little guy to have such grandparents.

The sermon in church this morning dealt with fairness—going all the way back to the passage in Luke (10:38–42), where Jesus goes to visit the home of Martha and Mary. Martha is scurrying all over the place making preparations for supper, while Mary sits there at Jesus's feet, visiting with Him and having a great time. Finally, Martha has had enough of this and complains to Jesus that Mary never helps with the household chores. Then she really gets steamed when He says to never mind, that Mary is focusing on only one important thing and that this will not be taken away from her. The nerve! He even told poor Martha that she was worried and distracted by many things, when there was, really, only need of one thing. Excuse me, but was He interested in having supper that night or not?

When I heard that scripture read, right before the sermon, I leaned over to David and said that I had always had real trouble with that passage in the Bible. He said, "I know."

Of course, some of us carriers of Fragile X know what it is to get distracted by too many competing details and not having the luxury of sitting down and focusing on one important matter. As in multitasking. As in symptomatic carriers.

Then the visiting preacher, a wonderful Roman Catholic priest from Nevada, began his sermon by reminding us all that when we were young, we were always pointing out to our parents that a sibling didn't do his or her share of the chores, or didn't have to go to bed at nine o'clock, and that it was "not fair."

My own mind wandered off at that point to you, to the whole question of fairness. Surely, Kelly, what you and Ryan have endured in these last two years is not fair. Where is the fairness in having to decide whether to terminate a desperately wanted and planned pregnancy? Where is the fairness in having the whole experience of the termination procedure take on B movie proportions? Where is the fairness in having to undergo unbelievably invasive measures in order to achieve what is, on its face and throughout world history, the most common and simplest process in the world: having a baby?

And where, indeed, is the fairness in one couple going through what you and Ryan are willing to do and another couple not being able to afford even to consider this process? And where is the fairness in some couples, with no known genetic conditions, not even wanting children? I know two Fragile X carriers who have sisters who are not carriers but who have decided not to have children because they really don't want children. Go figure.

But do you know what else I read in your letter, Kelly? I read, "Cody is fantastic, the light of my life." Not every mother of a child Cody's age with Fragile X will or can say that, can even begin to appreciate what he *is*, rather than focusing on what he isn't. I truly don't think that, at that stage, I considered either of my boys to be "fantastic." But I know by now, I think, just who is fantastic. And you, Kelly Randels, are fantastic!

When I realize that all the while you've been going through all this during this past year, you found the time and the energy to put on a marvelous fund-raiser for FRAXA, the Mary Higgins Clark Gala in Omaha, I am bowled over with awe and admiration. Just know that you are a remarkable young woman and that you have a huge fan here in Washington, DC.

I will be acutely anxious to hear how this next donor egg attempt goes, and I will hold all good thoughts and prayers for its success, Kelly.

Love to you and Ryan,

Mary Beth ✉

Dear Kelly,

Mary Beth shared your letter with me. Now that I can finally see after wiping all the tears from my eyes, I can take time to write you back. This entire ordeal is one I do not recall your sharing quite so intimately with me. I cannot imagine your pain and suffering on that day when your pregnancy with the girl you wanted so badly was ended.

By your words, it is evident that this pain is still with you. I am so sorry. I cannot begin to know all that you went through. Pondering all of this must have been a living nightmare. Being faced with such devastating news that your dear Cody would be mentally retarded (I despise those words, but it seems that's what we hear) and being pregnant with another child must

MEGAN MASSEY (L) WITH KELLY RANDELS

have made it so overwhelming and complex. Picturing you in this situation, trying to make sense of it all, I feel a great sense of compassion for you.

Your experience just goes to show that no one ever knows what another person has gone through. We all have diverse belief systems and deal with things in different ways. My boys are now teenagers and I cannot imagine life without them, just as you cannot imagine your life without Cody. Jack and Jacob have helped to define my life and teach me many lessons. They seem to do this on a daily basis. Through them I have seen so much grace and mercy extended by others. I realize this is not always the case, but for us, I can honestly say it has been true most of the time.

Kelly, please know I love you. I do not condemn you for your decision. Obviously, I didn't get the diagnosis for my kids until they were eight and six years of age. Our circumstances vary so greatly. As a result of individual situations and our beliefs, we come to different decisions. For me, abortion is not a choice. I trust God will only give me what I can handle.

Our friendship will always be important to me. You have always given me great support for the issues I encounter with my children and family. I am so glad your cousin found my name on the Internet and gave you my phone number, right after you received your diagnosis for Cody. She must have known we would become friends quickly. She was right.

Remember the first time we met? I'll never forget it! We first met face to face in the Pittsburgh airport, on our way to attend the FRAXA Gala. No, the gala wasn't at the airport. I do remember that. It was at a swanky hotel. We shared a room, and remember the first room they gave us at the hotel was occupied? We laughed so hard and quickly ran from that place. We must have been quite a sight, carrying our luggage down the hall along with our gowns for the gala.

We must have been too cheap to get a bellman. We probably didn't know we could. After all, we carry our own luggage at home.

I was so excited to finally meet you after spending countless hours on the phone discussing our kids and dealing with the diagnosis of Fragile X. We definitely hit if off from the start. I remember my friend Jill saying to me, "You have never met her, you are sharing a room, and she will see you in your underwear!" Oh, how I love Jill too! She has a special-needs daughter adopted from China.

I remember it was a wonderful evening at the FRAXA Gala and then we stayed up almost all night talking. It was that gala that spurred you on to organize one in Omaha shortly after. You are amazing. It took me *years* before I did anything like that. I think that Omaha gala raised $80,000 or was it $100,000? And you did all that while you were completing your second master's degree. That literally bowls me over.

Kelly, I will pray that someday your hurt will subside and you will have a sense of peace with that horrific day. Maybe you already do. I hope so. It seems that writing this letter has been quite therapeutic for you. A friend of mine told me once that when something is really important you should write it down, instead of making a phone call or talking to someone in person. This allows those thoughts to be put in some perspective and that will enable us to understand more about where we are coming from. One of the most beautiful letters I have ever read was one that a mother wrote to a child she lost. If you want to do that, I would encourage you to do so. I will read it with you, cry with you, and comfort you.

Kelly, I will always count you as one of my Fragile X blessings. Holland isn't so bad. After all, we are there together.

Always know you are loved,

Megan ✉

Dear Mary Beth,

I am writing you this letter with fantastic, incredible news. I am pregnant!!! Our due date is May 25, 2005.

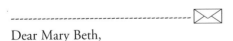

This summer we were matched up with an anonymous egg donor. We were able to use Ryan's sperm and the donor's eggs. We had the donor tested to find out if she was a Fragile X carrier, and she was not. We do not know her name, but we were given her description. She is twenty-six years old; has straight, medium-brown hair; hazel eyes AB+ blood type, she is five feet, seven inches tall; one hundred fifty pounds; and 50 percent German and 50 percent Irish. Her mother and father are in their fifties. Her maternal grandmother is seventy-nine years old; her grandfather died of a brain tumor at forty-nine. The paternal grandmother is eighty-seven years old and the grandfather is eighty-four years old. She is a first-time donor, married, and has a healthy daughter. She has three siblings, all of whom are healthy. She has no allergies and no chronic illnesses. She has a job and some college education. People at the clinic describe her as a wonderful, motivated person with a great personality.

On August 31, she had her egg retrieval. Seventeen eggs were retrieved, twelve were mature. Of those twelve, five fertilized, three did not fertilize, and four degenerated. On Friday, September 3, four of the five embryos remained and they were implanted.

I took it easy for the first twenty-four hours. My parents kept Cody overnight and on Saturday they brought him home in the morning. I wanted to get out of the house so Cody and I went with my parents to a local mall. We stopped at a few stores and then headed home.

I had to wait ten days to find out through a blood test that the pregnancy was successful. Ten days is a long time when you are awaiting results like this. It was similar to the waiting period we had with the amnio results from our second baby. You feel like your future is in someone else's hands. I did a lot of word-search puzzles and watched a lot of TV during those ten days. I went back to work on Monday and time went more quickly.

On Monday, September 13, we found out we were pregnant. I went to the clinic at 7:15 a.m. for a blood test. Unfortunately, the results take a couple of hours. I noticed on my cell phone that I had a missed call at 9:00 a.m. I checked to see who the call was from and it was from the clinic. I had mixed feelings. I wanted to ask another teacher to cover my class so I could call the clinic back, but at the same time, I was afraid it could be news I did not want to hear. I took my students to gym at 10:30 a.m. and called the clinic right away. The nurse who took my blood answered the phone and told me the results were positive. I cried, called Ryan, my mom (and asked her to phone my dad), and then E-mailed my friends and family members the terrific news.

It was a wonderful day. That evening we went to a restaurant to celebrate the news with my family. I phoned my obstetrician and told her the exciting news! She was thrilled. Coincidentally she will be ending her practice in June. With a May due date, we were just in the knick of time. She told me that even if she was not practicing, she would have been in that delivery room. She is so great!

On my first visit with my obstetrician, she asked me what advice I would have for another person going through what I (and many, many others) had gone through. The first thing I said was that one needs to understand the odds are fifty-fifty. Just because you were able to get pregnant easily on your own does not mean that you will have luck getting pregnant with infertility methods. I thought I was invincible and that having a baby with an egg donor was a sure thing. I also would suggest that the woman talk about her situation with family and friends on a frequent basis, about her feelings and thoughts. The ups and downs that one goes through under these circumstances are unbelievably, emotionally stressful. I do not know what I would have done without the support system of my family and so many of my friends.

I believe that dealing with these circumstances and the cost of infertility treatments is not only emotionally stressful but also financially stressful. Knowing what I know now, I still would have spent every dime we have spent again and again and again. At this point we have spent over $45,000 and are still not done, as bills are still coming in. It has not been easy for us. We are living paycheck to paycheck and sometimes that is not enough. When times get rough, I always say, "Things will work out; they always do." And you know what? They do.

We continue battling my insurance company over our coverage. At one point they agreed to pay for everything, only to turn around a month later (two days before the egg retrieval) and deny coverage for the whole procedure.

I reflect on your last letter and the section about being fair. None of this is fair. It is what it is. I sympathize with the people who cannot afford to try the procedures I have been fortunate enough to try. I do get sad when I think about the people who cannot have children and then to think that there are those who do not want children. For me, children are incredibly important in my life. They are a gift!

The sisters you mentioned in your letter could get together and consider having the noncarriers donate their eggs to their carrier sisters. Wouldn't that be terrific?

I remember Oprah once saying that you should discuss with your partner before you get married about having children and choosing adoption if the couple is not able to conceive. I think that is valuable advice. I would also add other options, like egg donation and sperm donation. I do, however, have to tell you this: if I would have followed the advice and spoken with Ryan about choices beyond naturally conceiving a child, Ryan would have said no, end of discussion to all the above choices. I know he would have because he did just that. He said no to these options after we learned about Cody having Fragile X and the chances of our future children being affected, including the baby I was currently carrying. He was all for preimplantation genetic diagnosis because that would have allowed us to use my eggs and his sperm; however, he was not interested in any other option. I knew that I was going to have to do two things. One was to give him time. Adjusting to so much change and information at once can be scary. The second was to give him all the facts of all of our options. He understood our choices when given the facts more than if I had shut down and not told him any of the details. Communication is key!

My point is this: you never know what you will accept or what you are capable of accepting until you are faced with the facts. Ryan was able to learn from his own uneasiness and uncertainties about the unknown, *not* the unthinkable. I have to give him credit. Not every husband would have stood by his wife's side. I know that. So, while discussing what ifs before you get married is important, it should not be the only determining factor to continue or not to continue a relationship.

We would love to try egg donor again after the birth of our baby. We would like to have two unaffected children. We think it would be incredible for the donor to be the same person, and we hope that works out. Time will tell if trying these procedures again will be an option.

I wrote a tribute to the donor for our egg donor book. I phoned the clinic and asked the staff to send it to the donor, but they declined. They explained that it is in the best interest of both parties. I understand their point, but I wanted to include the tribute in my letter to you.

A Tribute to the Egg Donor:

"Thank you" is something you say to the pizza delivery person when he brings you your pizza. "Thank you" is something you say to your friends and family when they do something nice for you. But how do you thank someone for donating an egg?

There are no words that will ever come close to showing you the amount of appreciation we have for you. What you did was absolutely one of the most amazing things you or anyone can ever do. To donate *life* is a *gift*. A gift that will never be forgotten, as so many gifts are easily forgotten. A gift that could not have been given by just anybody.

For my family, you offered us the gift of a child not affected by Fragile X. I think that what you gave us was a miracle gift. Not a day will go by that I will not think of you and what a wonderful and compassionate woman you are. I hope you know how happy and grateful we are for the wonderful opportunity you have given to us. I would love to have known you. I know I would have had you as a best friend. I would have liked the opportunity to thank you personally, however, we realize that is not the way the clinic works these things out. I do not know what I would have said because "thank you" would not have been enough.

What you have done has changed our lives. I have told everyone in my family that if something ever happened to me, they have my permission to use my organs to help others in need of the *gift* of *life*. I hope that I can help someone someday the way you have helped me. Even though you are a mother, you will never know how much what you have done means to my family and me. I had hope and you helped answer my dreams. We spent over $45,000 for all of the trials . . . And it was the best $45,000 I ever spent. I would do it all over again! Thank you, thank you!

In the meantime, Mary Beth, Cody is truly fantastic. He rubs my belly and says, "baby." I do not think he truly understands that in months to come, there will be a real baby, but it is cute! He continues to do well with preschool. He is three and a half and can count to twenty! He recognizes a few letters. I cannot believe the things he does. We continue working on shapes and colors . . . one of these days, he is going say them as if he has known them the whole time. I smile like crazy when I am with him. He is so incredibly loving, and he loves to be held and loved. I know that not all people affected by Fragile X are like this. I know that I am lucky, very lucky.

Love,

Kelly ✉

Dearest Kelly,

I am beyond thrilled to hear the marvelous news of your pregnancy. If you think back about ten years, you have to realize that this simply wouldn't have been possible. We do indeed live in a miraculous age, and I am truly ecstatic for you to be on the cutting edge of its endless possibilities.

You are right to be concerned that most people—especially people in their childbearing years—simply cannot begin to afford to spend $45,000 to have a baby. That is the tragedy—or one of the tragedies. I'm sure that being on that roller coaster with the insurance company added great stress to the whole procedure.

I have to tell you, too, that my admiration for Ryan is unbounded. When you think back to what all of our husbands had every right to expect when marrying us (and I refer here to the husbands of all Fragile X carriers), and the challenges they ended up facing, it's pretty overwhelming. The Ryan Randels, John Masseys, David Busbys, and so many more husbands, deserve some special badge of courage for accepting a horrendous loss, making the best of it, and going on as if they have just the wives and just the children they want. And you know what? I think they truly do feel that. This is because they are very big men. We're blessed indeed.

I, too, would have been disappointed for the egg donor not to have been allowed to know of my profound gratitude. But I do understand the clinic's policy. And, somehow, I know she knows. She knows that no one would go through what you and Ryan have gone through unless this was the most crucial matter in your lives. No way. She knows that. And she has the joy of knowing that she has been able to give the incomparable gift of life––not just to a child, but to a deserving family. She's making a family whole. She knows.

Please keep me posted on each and every development in the coming months. And do know, Kelly, how happy I am for you and for Ryan and Cody. The whole world is brighter today, and it's all your fault!

Much love,

Mary Beth 🖂

Dear Mary Beth,

Jaden is here! He was born on May 18, 2005, at 9:14 a.m. Less than ten pushes. They started pitocen at 6:00 a.m. and so labor was pretty short. He was twenty-one inches long and seven pounds, eight and one-half ounces. He is beautiful.

XOXOXO

Kelly 🖂

Kelly and Ryan Randels with sons Cody (L) and Jaden, 2005

Dear Kelly,

I can't remember when—or even if—I've received happier news. Congratulations to you and Ryan on a job well done! Yay! A brother for Cody! And I'm sure he'll be thrilled, once he learns that Jaden is indeed here to stay and a positive force to reckon with on a full-time basis. It's just so exciting. It sounds like all went as well as we could have hoped. And of *course* he's beautiful. So are you, and so is the world today.

Much love,
Mary Beth

P.S "One does not discover new lands without consenting to lose sight of the shore." (André Gide)

Dear Kelly, Ryan, and Cody,

Congratulations on the birth of your new baby boy, Jaden. I am praising God for this wonderful gift. You said it first in a previous letter, "children are a gift." How right you are. They are gifts from God. It seems like we have been waiting so long for this day to come. Jaden has arrived! Hallelujah!

Won't Cody have fun interacting with Jaden? Jaden will think Cody is wonderful and amazing. They will learn so much from each other. It will be so good for Cody to have a sibling. Jaden, on the other hand, will learn to be very compassionate and patient. Most siblings who have brothers or sisters with special needs do. I have seen it firsthand.

Wow! You are officially surrounded by boys. If I recall correctly, both of your dogs are boys too. It's not so bad. I have managed it for almost two decades. I actually think boys are much easier to deal with than girls. Especially when they get older. Boys get over things quickly. It seems girls tend to "hang on" to upsetting situations. Who am I to be telling you this? After all, you are the teacher and probably see it in living color. You may just need to brush up on your sporting events to keep up with the dinner conversations. Don't worry, there will be plenty of time for that!

I want to come back to Omaha soon to see your new little guy. I will be sure to call ahead before I show up at your door. I'll have to come bearing gifts, especially for Cody. He will need to feel extra special for a while. He is going to have to share his limelight.

Kelly, I am very excited for you, and know you must be overwhelmed with joy! I'll pray for some extra sleep for you and good health and happiness for all.

Love,

Megan ✉

25

Riveting Research

Dear Megan,

I agree that the latest research on Fragile X is looking more exciting than anything we've seen in years. I guess I'm a little afraid to believe that a viable treatment could truly be a possibility in the not too distant future. The fascinating thing is that it's looking very much like what the researchers have been saying for years: once they do come up with a treatment, it would most likely help Fragile X children of any age. So, your Jack, Jacob, Robert, and our Jack might indeed be helped to the extent that there could be real improvement in their cognitive skills. Now, let me be up front with you. As seductive as the reports about possible gene therapy are, it's still simply that: "possible." They're not there yet. Indeed, I think that gene therapy is still way down the road. The prospective treatments we're talking about now will not switch the FMR1 gene back on, but they will, we truly think, clear out the pathway in the brain that, in our kids, has been so messed up.

And here's another interesting thing. This, because of the ages of our boys, may be more interesting to me than to you, in that my boys are adults. As you well know, FRAXA has funded Dr. Elizabeth Berry-Kravis, at Rush University Medical Center in Chicago, in a project testing a new drug, called an ampakine, on adults with Fragile X. While that particular ampakine didn't appear to help the participants in a double-blind study, there are also some other compounds that could prove even more successful than the one Dr. Berry-Kravis was using. The great thing is that now she has the mechanism and the staffing in place to do another study, and she's gearing up to do a trial using lithium. Randi Hagerman is also planning one at University of California, Davis; now if we could get one going on the East Coast, this would provide many more interested families with the opportunity to participate.

I say, "interested families" because you know, Megan, plenty of families will in fact not be interested. Plenty of families feel that they and their kids are fine the way they are, that nothing really needs "fixing." I can't tell you how much I admire and respect those families, and there have been plenty of days when I would have loved being a member of one of them. But for David and me, the research is literally what keeps us going. It's wonderful that the Fragile X community is a large umbrella and that there is a warm and welcoming spot for each and every affected person.

Speaking of families, Drs. Randi and Paul Hagerman at UC Davis, are on to something so fascinating. They, as you know, do great work with families of children with Fragile X and also families with children with autism. In workups on some older male carriers, they were surprised to note that in some of them, there were Parkinson-like symptoms as well as some memory deficits. This is important for all women who are carriers to know, because if it's determined that they got the gene with the Fragile site from their fathers, this syndrome, called Fragile X-associated tremor/ataxia syndrome (FXTAS) could be something to look out for in their fathers down the road. And male carriers who suffer Parkinson-like symptoms might be given different treatments if it is determined that those symptoms are a result of FXTAS.

FXTAS was one of the topics covered at an NICHD conference this past year on premature ovarian failure (POF), which was put together and chaired by Dr. Larry Nelson, an NICHD researcher who studies reproduction. As you and I both well know, many carriers of Fragile X have very early menopause. Katie Clapp says that it's likely that we release more of our eggs at once, hence, they get used up faster. This is another reason for my own belief that it would be oh so useful for young women to know whether or not they are carriers, because it would certainly be a factor in decisions on when to start a family. In my day, nobody waited to start having babies until age thirty, let alone thirty-five—whereas nowadays, it's commonplace to do so. So much to research, so little time; in some cases, so few eggs, so little time. Someday, I hope some researcher will look into whether there is a large number of sets of fraternal twins born to carriers of Fragile X. Not that all of those twins would have Fragile X, but they could be carriers.

I know you're aware of the newborn screening projects that are being launched by both Dr. Donald Bailey at the University of North Carolina at Chapel Hill, and Dr. Roger Stevenson at the Greenwood Genetic Center in South Carolina. These are both extremely important in helping families obtain early intervention services for their children with Fragile X, and to help the Centers for Disease Control and Prevention and others to know what the prevalence is. One school of thought seems to be, "Well, if we can't cure it, why test for it?" I'm sure you agree with me though, Megan, that we need to have the screening mechanism in place so that when (notice I don't say "if") there is a viable treatment, the system will be ready. Also, the sooner we know, the better, both for "early intervention" and for family planning.

A whole other research pathway, the one that is the very most exciting to me, is being explored by Dr. Mark Bear at MIT and Dr. Kim Huber at the University of Texas Southwestern Medical Center at Dallas. There is a pathway in the brain that is overactive in the Fragile X mouse model and, presumably, in humans with Fragile X as well. They call it the mGluR pathway, because it is regulated by specific glutamate receptors (mGluRs). This implies that drugs that dampen the mGluRs (called mGluR antagonists) can be therapeutic for Fragile X. Some of them are being tested in mice, with early promise.

Bear and Huber observed that a form of synaptic plasticity, which is called long-term depression, or LTD (and this, Megan, has nothing whatever to do with the kind of depression that makes one sad), is exaggerated in the brains of mice that don't have the Fragile X protein. This LTD is triggered by metabotropic glutamate receptors, known as the mGluRs I mentioned before. Another brain process is called long-term potentiation, or LTP. LTP helps build connections between brain cells, and LTD helps to destroy unnecessary connections. I am way out of my depth here, but as I get it, the lack of the Fragile X protein prevents the LTD and the LTP from happening correctly, in tandem, to make the brain function normally. Good scientific explanation, huh? But this work is significant in the quest for finding a treatment. Indeed, there is a compound that is currently being used on mice to test this theory, and the hope is that the next step will be to gain approval for human trials.

The theories behind Mark Bear and Kim Huber's work have been supported by Dr. Steve Warren at Emory University in Atlanta, who—as you know—codiscovered, with Dr. David Nelson of Baylor University and Dr. Ben Oostra in the Netherlands, the Fragile X gene in 1991. Warren, Nelson, and Oostra remain giants in Fragile X research. Steve Warren, especially, has encouraged Mark Bear and Kim Huber right along in their exploration of the mGluR theory, and FRAXA has been pleased to contribute to their research projects. Also FRAXA's principal researcher, Rob Bauchwitz at Columbia University in New York City, uses his mouse laboratory to monitor all research.

The research is moving so quickly now that I feel breathless, trying to absorb it all. Of course, it would help a lot if I had the kind of mind that could absorb it. I'll admit I find it daunting. Indeed, there are times when reading researchers' abstracts, I want to yell, "Hey, just wake me when it's over and you have the cure!" But in the meantime, honey girl, we've got to deal with these kids, to get through the next day, the next IEP, the next IP, the next job placement process, the next whatever. There's always a "next."

And then, Megan, when we consider all of these potential treatments, still in the stage of being tested on mice, as promising as some of them look and sound, we have to ask ourselves, "What would this mean?" Gosh, it's staggering to contemplate, isn't it? I ordinarily discipline myself a little more than I am doing today because I'm afraid I might sit around filling out applications for Yale for my boys. Yeah, right. Not bloody likely.

I don't know about you, but if one of these potential treatments should pan out to be successful, all I can imagine hoping is that my boys might be able to focus a little better on what they're supposed to be doing—whether it's a job or cooking dinner or a telephone conversation. I wouldn't expect more. We would not be talking Yale: We would also not be talking high school equivalency.

I can't help assuming that their personalities would be exactly the same. Jack would be our social animal, loving to go out and have a great time, with a generally upbeat personality. Robert would likely continue to be a bit oppositional in attitude, and a bit moody. But his already pretty good organizational skills would, I'd like to think, be enhanced, and he would continue his efforts (selective though they may be) to be helpful to those around him. In Robert's orderly little world, everything would continue to be in its place.

Most of all, though, I wonder what they would think about, what they would feel strongly about, whether they would be kind and generous young men? Could they better comprehend what they read? Could they ever learn to keep a checkbook? Probably not. But that's OK. I can't keep a checkbook either.

I've been thinking about the parable in the gospel according to Luke—17:11–19. Jesus was approached by ten lepers who asked him to heal them. He did just that, and they went happily on their way. All but one, that is. He was a Samaritan, who came to pay tribute, praising God and thanking Jesus for his help. Jesus said something to the effect that it was interesting that only the "foreigner" took the trouble to praise God and thank him for what he, Jesus, had done for all of them in curing their leprosy.

I would like to think, and I have to think, that if Robert and Jack were to be healed, that they would somehow know that for all their lives, they have been "foreigners"—handicapped people in a normal world. I would like to think that they would be grateful for their new blessings, received as a result of the brilliant work of many researchers who have labored in the Fragile X vineyard for lo these many years. I would like to think that they would continue to praise God, as they always have in their own sincere ways, and that they would be humble in their newfound abilities to think more clearly.

I assume that the deficits that have been compounding themselves over forty years are such that, for my boys, there won't be major changes in their functioning levels. I don't for one minute think that all of a sudden they'll be filling out those college applications. If, however, they could even be able to process elementary information with a bit more efficiency, their possibilities would be greatly enhanced. And their mom would be a happy camper. I also know one thing for sure: Robert and Jack will always be their mama's sweet, good boys.

One other joy, in my dreams, that I would contemplate would be the lessening of "the look" that they get from strangers who notice their bizarre behavior and don't know what to make of it. Dealing with the look has become a way of life for us all, and I know you deal with it every day too—as does every parent of a handicapped child. It just goes with the territory, and that is territory I'd be happy to cede elsewhere. Except who would take it? Oh, I truly do envy those parents who view their handicapped children as special gifts. I love my boys with my life and to the very center of my soul, but I so wish they'd had an opportunity to play on a level playing field. I so wish I could listen to Garrison Keillor extol the virtues of Lake Wobegon, "where all the children are above average," and not feel tears stinging my eyes.

You know what, though, Megan? This is all fantasy talk for me. I rarely think in these what-if terms. I sure don't talk this way to anybody. Only another Fragile X mom could hear me say things like this and not think I'm nuts. But you're another Fragile X mom. And we can dream our dreams. For dreams are the stuff of achievement. And just you wait, Megan girl: one fine day, one of these researchers is going to achieve our dearest hope, the cure. And in the meantime, there will be the treatment.

OK, I'm off now to do my seriously delinquent errands. I need to "research" dinner possibilities at the Safeway and then come back home to prepare the dinner "treatment" for David Busby.

Love to you,

MBBB ✉

P.S "Discovery consists of seeing what everybody has seen and thinking what nobody has thought." (Albert Szent-Gyorgyl)

Dear Mary Beth,

Riveting research? It is indeed, but I admit, I used to be one of those families you referred to. You know, the ones who may not immediately step up to the plate in order to join in the clinical trials of potential Fragile X treatments? It used to scare me just a bit, and I thought my kids were just fine the way they were. I still think their fine, *but*—time changes your perspective. If there was a waiting line for these trials and the benefits were far greater than any side effect, I would be there. In fact, if I were in that line, I would try to maneuver my way to the front! I teach Jack and Jacob never to do it, and they do it anyway and often succeed. But in this instance, I would allow it. As the boys get older, dealing with their Fragile X gets more difficult.

OK, I'll be honest with myself. It becomes a lot more difficult. When you have a grown adult, taller then Mom, handsome and kind, nicely dressed, yet conversing with others like a ten-year-old, it's hard. I know I'm preaching to the choir here, but all of this is really beginning to hit home for me.

Believe it or not, I have found myself swaying back and forth on this treatment decision. I'm not even guaranteed this will ever happen, but I think about it. Maybe it is wishful thinking, but I do believe someday it will become our reality. John and I would have a monumental choice to make. Could we allow both boys to participate in a study? Let's say a drug was approved by the FDA for use in people with Fragile X. Would we put both of the boys on it? If we could only try one child, whom would we pick? How could we decide that? How would it work? Would my boys wake up one morning and be able to figure it all out? If they did, I would want some treatment too. You mentioned if your boys were to be healed, they may somehow know that for all their lives, they were foreigners in our normal world. I don't think Jack and Jacob would see it that way. They would just think life got easier, because it would.

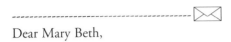

Oh, Mary Beth, "the look" is a terrible thing. The stares I have gotten are amazing. That could be another topic of discussion that would take up much of our correspondence time. But, it doesn't solve anything. Those people are just uninformed. John and I have certainly come a long way with that reaction from strangers. Now we find it fun to just let the kids go and see how the general public responds. Just sitting back and watching others react can be entertaining. I can join those people and put on that "Where is their mother?" facial expression instantly.

Jack was playing cards once on a plane with the man sitting next to him. You know that feeling well, don't you? Should I go over and explain the situation or just let them figure it out? Now, I'm all about watching the learning curve of others. I heard this man say loudly to Jack, "Hey, you're cheating." I thought to myself, "Yes sir, he sure is and he doesn't try to hide it." Honesty is the best policy.

Jack also enjoys eating at restaurants, but he prefers his own table or sitting at the bar. He may even try to join others even if he doesn't know them. We have drawn the line there. That would make for an interesting evening. So far anyway, we haven't allowed it.

Well, Mary Beth, even with all this talk, and considering our hopes and our dreams for our boys, they're still our boys with Fragile X. And you know what? If they didn't have it, I wouldn't have you. So, we will forge ahead and keep that hope that someday, somehow, all of this will be history. The mystery of Fragile X solved. I'm counting on it. I just hope I will still be sane enough to know it happened.

Take good care.

Lots of love to you and David,

Megan ✉

26

Cooking as Therapy

Megan, dear,

OK, here's my Four-Bean Chili recipe, and I really do hope you'll make it the next time there's a football or basketball game to watch with friends. I'm sure you'll make yourself get around to doing it, eventually, if only because you know how I love sharing recipes.

Just last night at dinner, David and I were talking about why I seem to be overwhelmed with all I have (or think I have) to do. He said that it occurs to him that I spend too much time marketing and cooking. I don't market every single day, but I do lots of days. I spend from 7:00 to 8:00 in the evening, while he's in the library watching the *NewsHour with Jim Lehrer*, in the kitchen cooking dinner—also watching the *NewsHour*. He said that maybe we should figure out a way to live without my doing that. I literally drew in my breath in horror. To give up cooking our dinner would be an unspeakable sacrifice for me. I truly cherish that time in the kitchen and I love putting food on the table. Always have. And I'm never happier than when wearing an apron. I told a neighbor this, when I was talking with her on the phone about what she would bring to our annual neighborhood potluck supper. I could hear this intake of breath as she said, "Really?" But I swear, Megan, it's true.

Come to think of it, I think one reason I do a lot of things with chopped onion—like chili—is that I really love chopping. I don't even have, and don't want, a Cuisinart. I just really find that sort of activity satisfying. And I've only ended up in the emergency room once with a finger cut while chopping onions. The other time was for (stupidly) slicing cheese with a killer knife.

I remember being so astonished when my mother gave up cooking. I'm sure it was gradual, but to me it seemed pretty sudden. All at once, I realized that she never, ever was cooking dinner anymore. They went out to the cafeteria every night, except Sunday when they stayed home and had sort of an hors d'oeuvres supper in front of their fireplace and the TV. I don't think we'd go out for dinner that much even if we had a cafeteria down the block, one of the few things our neighborhood in Washington lacks. Of course, I'm nowhere near as old as my mother was when she stopped cooking, not by a long shot. But when I asked her, a few years before she died, if she enjoyed cooking in earlier years, she said she didn't remember liking it or not liking it—that she just did it. Well, I do like it. A lot. So I'll figure out another way to save time. Hmmm.

Anyway, here's the recipe—with love,
MBBB

PS. "The French cook, we open tins." (John Galsworthy, 1867–1933)

FOUR-BEAN CHILI

This is a great thing to do when you don't feel like going out to the market. As long as you have a little hamburger meat in the freezer and a nice big onion and some garlic, you can do it. You will, of course, keep cans of these other ingredients in your pantry at all times, right? Of course you will.

1 1/2 teaspoons salt
1/2 pound ground beef *
2 cups coarsely chopped onion
2 teaspoons minced garlic
1 tablespoon chili powder
1 1/2 teaspoons ground cumin
1/8 teaspoon cayenne pepper, or 1/2 teaspoon crushed red pepper
1 can (15 ounces) diced tomatoes
1 can (15 ounces) black beans
1 can (15 ounces) dark red kidney beans
1 can (7 ounces) garbanzo beans (chickpeas), drained and rinsed
1 can (7 ounces) pinto beans
1 can (3 1/2 ounces) diced green chilis
1 can (8 ounces) tomato sauce
1/2 cup water

Put the salt in a nonstick pot or slow cooker and turn the heat to medium-high.(The pot I like to use is a 5 quart non-stick pot that fits into its own slow cooking element when the stovetop part is done.) Add the meat, crumbling it with your fingers. Stir until browned. Add the onion and stir until translucent, then add the garlic and stir a few seconds more.

Add the rest of the ingredients. Simmer for at least 30 minutes. I like to take it off the stove and put it on the slow cooking element of my pan. Then I can just go off and leave it until I'm ready to serve. I do that with all soups and stews.

Serves 4.

*Use more or even less, depending upon whether you like a meaty chili. You can even make it with ground turkey, or without meat at all—if you want a vegetarian meal—or if you don't have any ground meat in your freezer. Actually, now that we're into counting carbs, I'm using more meat and less beans. That's the fun thing about this recipe. You can play with it. But be sure to use plenty of the seasonings.

Needless to say, by the time you put all this together, your kitchen counter will look like Can City. Count 'em: seven cans !! Well, I've never aspired to emulate French cuisine, much as I love it.

Dear Mary Beth,

I guess we are opposites in some ways. Just thinking of cooking as therapy is hard for me to grasp. My family would say I need therapy for my cooking! It is pretty funny, really, because they are truly somewhat leery of my cooking. It's kind of a joke, but they continue to tease me!

My older sisters think I'm not much of a cook. In fact, my sister Kristy came out for Thanksgiving last year and showed up a day early so she could assist with the preparations for Thanksgiving dinner. She must have been fearful of what she might have to eat.

It's not too bad a reputation to have. When we all vacation together they do most of the meals. I'd better not interfere with those plans. Every kitchen needs a supervisor. I'm great at pouring wine.

I do like to cook, but not many people believe it. John is happiest at suppertime when it's quick and easy and he can go outside and get to work. He'd eat TV dinners or hot dogs anytime.

I'll really blow them all away with the chili recipe. I may just tell them I made it from scratch. They won't believe it.

I'll let you know if it works.

Thanks again for sharing.

Megan ✉

Dear Megan,

Well, if you make this chili, it *will* be from scratch. Just because it has canned beans and tomatoes in it doesn't mean you have to use dried, then soaked, then cooked beans, and tomatoes from your garden. I promise, this is easy and good. Make it for a football-watching party and see how your stock goes up among those Big Red fans—though of course, "Big Red" for the Busbys means Oklahoma University, not Nebraska. Wonder who stole that name from whom? Well, we won't settle that one anytime soon, will we?

Love,

MBBB ✉

27

Transition for Jack Massey

Dear Mary Beth,

Hey, as Bob the Builder says, "We did it. We did it!" And Jack is still alive to tell about it. He is doing well. John, Jack, and I arrived in Kentucky on Friday afternoon and that evening was not a good scene. He cried all the way through our dinner at Chili's. He loves Chili's. He ordered nothing and ate nothing. He fought back tears and asked us please not to send him to the school. I have never seen Jack cry like that in all my life. I was at the table with tears running down my face. I would have run out and taken him with me back to Scottsbluff in a New York minute. But, John was the tough one. He stood strong, was very firm, but extremely loving. I would be lost without him. I don't know how many other husbands, none as a matter of fact, who could have done what he did this weekend. If I was him, I might have said, "See ya . . . I'm out of here." I am so grateful for John.

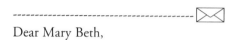

Anyway, on Saturday morning when we arrived at the school Jack said, "Oh, I remember this place. I will like my school." Did he think we were just going to leave him on the street corner? He must not have been picturing the Stewart Home School behind all of those tears. The correct memories of his previous visit obviously came back to him quickly. He jumped out of the car and ran into the administration ~~B~~building by himself to see Sandy Bell. She is the director of the school. He gave her a big hug and really seemed to settle into the idea that he was staying. He went to see his room with one of the dormitory supervisors. Jack just marched right off and left us with Mrs. Bell in our meeting. He returned about ten minutes later and sat in on the rest of our conversation. He was so well behaved. Jack had talked a lot about being independent and living on his own. Maybe now he was starting to like the idea. Supervised independence was the key. Stewart Home could do it.

We went back to survey his room and make a list of all the items we would need to make it just right. We had sent out quite a few things ahead of time, and the school set up his room. So, when he opened the door, it really did resemble a room he recognized. That was a great suggestion on Sandy Bell's part. Jack has his own room, no roommate. All of the rooms are private. Next we were off to Applebee's. After all, it was lunchtime. It's amazing how food comforts the soul and makes Jack feel so much better, and his mother too. After all, Jack must have been starving after not eating anything the night before.

JOHN AND JACK MASSEY AT STEWART HOME SCHOOL, ADMISSION DAY

Frankfort really is a nice town. We stayed at the Hampton Inn, which is just two miles from the school. The staff there is very familiar with Stewart Home and their kids. We were treated so nicely by everyone. The whole town must be able to spot these kids coming. There was a newly finished Starbucks across the street. I don't mean to sound prideful, but I think the Lord put that there for me too. We were within walking distance from Wal-Mart, Home Depot, Lowe's, and a Panera Bread Company. I sound like a child, but Scottsbluff folks get pretty fired up over all these choices.

After lunch we were off to Wally World to buy all the stuff we needed for the room. Jack was thrilled over the fact that he would have his own television and VCR/DVD player in his room. He wouldn't even have to share the remote with his brother. He picked out movies like *Barney*, *Dora the Explorer*, and *Elmo*. I usually discourage those at home, but that day, whatever he wanted was fine with me.

When we went back to the school to unload the car, we had plenty of extra help. All of the students swarmed around us, grabbing packages and lifting boxes out of the car. I drew the line when one man picked up the television. We could move that one ourselves!

Everyone was so excited to watch the "new boy" move in. They all wanted to be a part of this special time. I must tell you, Mary Beth, I use the word "kids" loosely. The ages of the students on his dorm floor range from fifteen to seventy-one years. They certainly don't look it. I can't help but wonder if being protected from all the stresses of the world keeps you younger. Jack has taught me many things in my life, and his ability to see everyone's hearts and not judge by appearance has been one of his best gifts to me. It takes a while to get adjusted to this type of environment. Everyone is very affectionate. The best way for me to describe it is they have no social filter. Whatever they want to say or do, they just do immediately. (I must admit I have had that problem before.) I believe we all have a purpose on this earth and the Stewart Home School provides an opportunity for these students to shine like the stars, inspire others, and grow in knowledge and develop new skills.

The assembling of bedside tables, TV stands, and other items took about three hours. The extra help actually made the job more difficult. We had about seven guys circled around John trying to assist with the screwdriver, screws, and brackets. John was so patient. At times I wanted to scream and kick them all out. If John felt that way, he never showed it. We persevered and completed the job. I will have to send you a picture of that moment. I

New friends (L to R): Anthony Duncan, Jack Massey, Tim Beaumont, and Will Johnson at Stewart Home School

have one. Jack was in and out of the room during this whole process. He loved going into other people's rooms as well. He never mentioned going home again. He must have figured it out, or decided that this was going to happen, and he would have to accept it. What a trooper. Our boys are so resilient.

Jack stayed with us in the hotel for the weekend, and on Monday morning we went to the school to meet with Sandy Bell and all of his teachers. While we were unpacking the last few items, I began to cry. Not too much As my dad says, "The sun must have been in my eyes." Jack stood tall in his room and looked at me and said, "I'm going to class." He didn't even have his schedule yet. He said, "Mom, I'm going to computers." This was one of his favorite classes when he visited this summer. The academic director, David Sellwood, appeared and said it was fine for him to go. He walked off with Mr. Sellwood to the academic building, marched down the stairs, and that was the last time we saw him. He wasn't coming home until Thanksgiving.

We met with all of his teachers, and they are fabulous. His counselor is Lisa Tindell. She is young and very committed to her job. She adores Jack and wants to get him involved with lots of sports and with a special group of higher-functioning boys. Academics will be a large focus as well as developing social skills and vocational skills. The coaches for different sports were actually arguing over who would get Jack on their team. That would never happen here in Scottsbluff.

Jack Massey goes happily off with SHS academic director David Sellwood (L)

I am now convinced that we have done the right thing for our son. Stewart Home School will be a place for Jack to grow and experience some success. We had a big meteorite shower before Jack went to school and he told me he wished he could go back to Kentucky. Sometimes I think he says those things just because he knows I want to hear it. But, he got his wish. When we returned from our *long* trip home Monday night (twelve hours total travel time) I went to sit in our hot tub, which is out on the patio. I was gazing at the beautiful, wide-open western sky and thinking about Jack. He would usually always come and join me in the hot tub. As I was sitting there, what falls out of the sky but a shooting star! Jack was with me. I believe God is faithful and His plans work out. We will miss Jack terribly, but the opportunities for him will be endless. He will grow in so many ways.

I can't thank you enough for being there for us and showing us the way. You were a great support. We appreciate all of your thoughts and prayers. Stewart Home School is truly a gift that I am thankful for.

Hopefully, we will see you soon. The next FRAXA Gala can't be soon enough.

Take good care.

Love,

Megan ✉

Oh, Megan,

This is such a marvelous report, and I can't tell you how much you and John and Jack have been in my thoughts and prayers this past week. I'm so happy that it went as well as it did. Just think how much better it is that the tears came on the first night and not the last. And how!

I feel so good about the choice you have made for Jack, and before long, he will be thinking of it as *his* choice.

You know people always tell a young couple that their lives will never, ever be the same again, once their first child is born? Well, I think it's much the same once that first child goes off to boarding school. Oh, sure, he'll come home for vacations and perhaps even back home to live again one day; and you still have Jacob at home. But the dynamics of the household will change; and whether you make these changes positive or negative is your choice—yours and John's.

I agree that mentally handicapped people tend to look younger than their years, and I have wondered, as you have, whether the lack of the normal stresses we feel may account for that, at least in part. If my boys didn't have so much gray hair, they would look a lot younger than they do.

We just got home this afternoon from Oklahoma where we had the best Busby reunion ever, we think. Everyone had a great time, especially our boys, of course. They look forward to this all year long. We sent Jack back to Washington on the plane on Monday, after which David and I started out driving. Before we left Ada, we joked with Robert that we had to hurry home, in order to be there when he arrives by plane next Monday for his annual Labor Day visit.

So, all is well here. The air-conditioning went right on like a champ, and the dishwasher will be repaired on Saturday. Life is good.

Speaking of the good life, it sounds like Frankfort, Kentucky has about everything you could want in a town. How large a town is it? We went through there once to have lunch with our dear friend Linda Breathitt, who now lives here in Washington, but we didn't get to see much of the town. I only remember that it was very appealing and that it's the capital of Kentucky. I'll be able to visualize you and Jack there, whenever you go to visit. And I'll visualize you and Jack laughing at Chili's. Those tears of the night you arrived in Frankfort are already history, but it's important to remember them as part of the saga of helping Jack to take one more step toward independence. Congratulations, my dear friend, for having taken this momentous step, and taken it with such grace and courage and love for your precious son.

Much love to you and John,
MBBB

P.S. "And soon the night of weeping shall be the morn of song." (From "The Church's One Foundation," third verse).
PPS. "When one door closes, another opens; but we often look so long and so regretfully upon the closed door that we do not see the one which has opened for us." (Alexander Graham Bell, 1847–1922) ✉

28

Mary Beth's Excellent Adventure Dream

Oh, Megan!

I just have to share this with you. It's Sunday morning and I just woke up. Normally (if David doesn't wake up first and do all of this), I plug in the coffee, go down in the elevator to get the *Washington Post* and the *New York Times*, then crawl back into bed with my coffee and the *Washington Post*. David gets the *Times* first, and then we switch. This morning, though, I have to write to you first, before I fetch the papers, before I forget the dream I just had.

I dreamed that Katie Clapp was here and that we went to a meeting out at the NIH where a huge breakthrough on Fragile X was announced. I mean, we're talking The Big One. It was the day that the article was to be published. There were all these people there who wanted to talk to Katie, and I was just sort of trying to keep her schedule straight. Lisa Kaeser of the NICHD was sort of helping us. We were trying so hard not to make anybody mad at us for not talking to the right people in the right order.

I remember a male researcher at the meeting. He was tall, with dark reddish hair and a mustache. Can't think who it might have been. He didn't resemble anyone I know. He was so generous in his enthusiasm for the work about to be published—even though he knew that this work was going to render his own work less important than he had hoped.

I remember standing there chatting with two female researchers. Somehow, they were discussing what miserable lives they had had in high school because they were science nerds and didn't fit in. I laughed and said that we all certainly did have our little problems, and that I had had to drop Algebra 2, having barely passed Algebra 1 because I simply couldn't get it. Several of us stood there laughing and noted that of course in those days, nobody knew I was a carrier for Fragile X and that some Fragile X carriers were symptomatic in various ways, including math deficits.

At some point in this dream, I almost woke up, but I wouldn't let myself completely wake up. I kept my eyes closed and willed the dream to continue. It became sort of a twilight dream—half asleep and half awake.

There were other people who seemed to be almost like transparent cutouts, and they would sort of fade in and out, sometimes in sharp focus, sometimes only soft suggestions of who they might be. They weren't walking, just floating, a dizzying array of the many characters in the saga of Fragile X research. Most of them I could clearly recognize, while a few—perhaps suggestions of researchers yet to emerge into our orbit—remained softly indistinct.

Oh, and dear Linda Crnic, looking as pert and radiant as if she truly were still with us, as well as the late Dr. Mario Rattazzi, with his droll smile. Gosh, Megan, even though he and Linda are both gone now, they were right here in spirit with me this morning.

I remember feeling sad that both Mike Tranfaglia and David Busby weren't out there at the NIH with us, because it was such an exciting day, a day I wanted never to end.

I remember that Katie and I kept hugging each other a lot.

Gosh, this dream was so real.

I remember that Katie and I got our handbags mixed up, that she had accidentally put stuff in my bag and I in hers, and that I was concerned to get my wallet back because I knew I barely had enough money in it to pay for the parking at the NIH lot, and Katie and I had to get back downtown to meet David at what was to be some kind of press conference. I was wondering what Katie would say at the press conference and whether the press would take note of this astounding breakthrough.

Then *you* walked into the dream, Megan. You were wearing a raspberry-colored suit made of soft wool and your hair was even blonder than it really is—very, very blonde. You walked in and immediately sorted out all the stuff that was in Katie's and my handbags. It was as if you had heard that we were so frazzled that we were about to lose it, so you came to the rescue. Maybe that's your nurse's training working in my subconscious, huh?

Oh, Megan, honey, I know this was only a dream, and parts of it were only twilight dreams. But you know what? It's barely a dream, it's almost a reality. What you and I must do is to keep on truckin', keep on pushing, keep on believing, keep on hugging each other and our kids, keep on loving those kids for who and what they are, keep on wading through all the trauma of their fragile lives with the courage and strength to do what's right for them, and keep on remembering that their fragile lives will—down the chain of generations—be lives that helped lead to the cure for Fragile X.

That's what you and I have to do. And with God's help and a lot of hard work, we will. We will.

Now *you* have a good day too, OK? I'll write more to you after church, because I'm full of (some might say "a tad manic with") excitement, as this day begins. Stay tuned.

Much love,
MBBB ✉

Dearest Megan,

This is one of those crisp, clear fall Sundays when you know that God truly is in His heaven, even if all's not right with the world and maybe won't be for a while.

We just returned from church. There was an attractive young woman whom I've seen at the Washington National Cathedral many times. Usually, she has her son with her. He's handicapped with what appears to be cerebral palsy. Clearly, he can't sit up alone. She brings him in his wheelchair and takes him up to Communion. She leaves the wheelchair a little off to the side and carries him up to the Communion rail. Just last week, I remember noting to myself that he's getting big enough now so that it's difficult for her to lift him out of the wheelchair and get him up to the rail for Communion. I would imagine he's about twelve by now. Today, she was there alone. When we offered each other the sign of peace, I turned around and saw her a few rows behind me. She smiled and nodded. I assume she feels she sort of knows me because she's seen us there with Jack. There's this soft, unspoken bond between moms of handicapped kids, isn't there?

When I saw this lovely young mother alone, I began to speculate on whether the child's father might be taking him for the weekend, or whether another family member or friend was pitching in today, to give her a little time and space. I also began to feel guilty for *ever* giving in to the feeling that *I* am burdened. I can only imagine the constant, relentless burden of this woman's life. I won't say, "this poor woman," for that would be demeaning and denigrating to what I'm sure is her notion of her life and her role as a mother. But, boy, am I lucky. And so are you, Megan girl. Don't forget it. Ever.

Another remarkable happening occurred at the Cathedral today. This was children's recognition Sunday, and they had two students from the Cathedral schools read the scriptures. The boy must have been about ten or eleven, and I have to admit he did a great job of reading from Genesis. I was struck with his resemblance to Robert at the same age—in his looks, that is. I was also struck with the realization that this didn't bother me. Believe me, Megan, there was a time—until quite recently, really—when seeing a boy who looked so much like Robert, but who was clearly "a star," would have sent me up and out of my seat and down the aisle in tears. A lot of things reduced me to tears for a lot of years. I won't say it never happens now, but the occurrences have become few and far between.

Robert will never read the scripture at the Washington National Cathedral. And Jack will always be sort of a "mascot" usher. But these boys—and Jack and Jacob as well, for sure—are teachers in their own ways. They can teach others to be leaders in promoting tolerance. They can inspire researchers to pursue their own goals. They can demonstrate to their many teachers and caregivers just how crucial their work is. By some strange twist—or, more accurately, by the roll of the genetic dice—our children have been chosen. They don't feel "chosen" and, believe me, there have been far, far more days and years when I have felt a sense of our being cursed more than any notion of their or my being chosen. But they are chosen, Megan. They have been chosen to lead others toward the inevitable research breakthrough that will enhance the lives of all of those who are affected by Fragile X. I know you sense this, Megan, and so do I. We're blessed indeed.

And now that I'm feeling so blessed and chosen to do all this important stuff, I'll toddle on down to the kitchen and make Black Bean Soup for supper. DB would say that making good soup is a noble calling as well. Haven't made it in a while, but sometimes we feel like it on a chilly Sunday evening. Besides, I happen to have on hand all the stuff I need to put it together.

While I'm chopping the onions and carrots, I'll relish revisiting my excellent adventure dream of early this morning, and I'll visualize you once again in that scrumptious-looking raspberry suit. Now I've come down off of my high and the dream was, after all, just that. But, Megan, I know in my heart that one fine day, this cherished dream has the seeds of what's out there, what's possible, what's bound to come to pass. One fine day, Megan. One fine day.

Love again,
MBBB

PS. Lest you worry about the woman at church without her son, I should tell you that I saw her in the vestibule afterward and said something about having missed seeing her son. She said he was at home with her mother, that he was OK but might be coming down with a cold. It's kind of strange that as many times as she and I have seen one another, we've never exchanged names. But there is this bond between her and me. It's as if we have this secret little society, one that not just anyone can join and that no one ever wants to join. The members, for the most part, don't even know each other's names. But how fortunate for her that she has her mother nearby to help out with her son.

PPS. "The beautiful part about helping someone up a hill is that you get closer to the top yourself." (Ann Landers)

Dear Mary Beth,

I would give your adventure dream four stars. If I could have that raspberry suit, I would give it five. Isn't it heartwarming to know that some day this may be a reality? We have to hold on to that. We must never give up hope.

Your lady friend in the church, reinforces my theory that two moms with special-needs kids have such an instant bond. I feel it all the time when I'm in those situations. We understand without speaking a word. We just seem to know. I think that is another reason all of us carriers, or even affected moms, hit it off so miraculously. Sometimes it is a bond of silence, yet it pulls you toward the other person. It is true empathy.

Bill Greenough, the FRAXA researcher, told me once that he would love to study Fragile X carriers sometime. He thinks we are all so highly motivated and never hesitate to speak out. He is amazed to see how quickly we are all attracted to one another. I'm really not amazed. Let's face it, we have a lot in common! I know I didn't get the nickname "motormouth" as a youngster for nothing. I was born with it!

Well, Mary Beth, another morning is coming to an end and I still have all my errands to run. I'm meeting with lots of school administrators this week trying to get a good idea of what their transitional program for Jacob is all about. That job seems like it will never end. Have a great week and tell David hello for me.

Love,
Megan

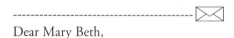

29

On Marriage and Divorce

Dear Mary Beth,

Since we have returned from the FRAXA Gala in Boston, I have wanted to tell you about our twentieth wedding anniversary. We actually celebrated in Boston the night after the gala. We went to a quaint Italian restaurant for dinner. I felt like we were dating again. Sitting in a quiet restaurant, the waiter was so attentive, the menu was divine, and the atmosphere was practically silent. No kids, no spilled milk. We were seated next to a small window on the second floor looking out onto the old streets of Boston.

John surprised me with three beautiful rings. They are small bands; two of them are circled with diamonds, the other with sapphires. Sapphire is my birthstone. I was really caught off guard. He reached in his pocket and set the wrapped box with a royal-blue bow on the table. I had no idea what was in the box. At this point the waiter became even more astute. I think he thought we were getting engaged. It must have been dark in there or my wrinkles would have given that away.

John and Megan Massey

Oh my, if the waiter only knew. We've had quite an exciting twenty-five year history together. You are asking, "Twenty-five years?" Well, Mary Beth, John and I met my freshman year in college when I was only seventeen. At that time I never would have dreamed our present journey. Especially, the unplanned trip to Holland. If the waiter would have cared to listen, I think he would have been impressed with our story and maybe even learned a thing or two.

We have been so blessed to have a strong mutual commitment to one another. Our belief system is a common bond. I have never doubted John's devotion or love. It is genuine. We trust one another implicitly. We enjoy each other's company and have many of the same interests. We share many friends who have strong marriages as well. You and David included. We enjoy traveling alone and with other couples. We are fortunate in that sense. I understand that is not always the case.

My father used to tell me that someday I would know someone who was divorced and that it may well be a close friend or relative. I would adamantly deny that statement and say, "Dad, it wouldn't happen. All of my family and friends are very happily married." Well, guess what? My Dad was right. We have experienced it in our own family.

John's brother and sister-in-law have divorced. They were two of our favorite people. Actually, they still are, and as Jack would say, "It's just a little different." Dallas is a close friend, like a sister. Jim is fabulous too. We obviously share the same in-laws, including twenty years of holiday dinners, birthdays, and other occasions. When the kids were young those gatherings could be quite a fiasco. My children could liven up any joint. Four boys in all! The four of us raised our kids together. Jim and Dallas both went through all the searching with us to find a diagnosis for our kids.

The whole thing was devastating to watch. What divorce isn't? It was downright consuming at times. It is amazing how we suffer along with others. I am reminded of a verse in 2 Corinthians 1:4: "God comforts us in all our troubles so that we can comfort others. When others are troubled, we will be able to give them the same comfort God has given us." Looking back now over the whole process, I know I could have done much better in that department.

It seemed the conflicts went on for years before the divorce was final. John's brother ended up moving just north of us. We all live out in the country on a farm of over one hundred acres. Now Jim is on the north end, we are in the middle, and Dallas is to the south. It has worked out nicely for their children. They can literally go back and forth without ever leaving the farm. They used to travel on bikes, and then it was four-wheelers and dirt bikes. Now they are in cars. We rarely saw them walk. Does any child travel by foot anymore?

Jack and Jacob did pretty well with the whole thing. Of course, they knew none of the details, just that Jim and Dallas were no longer able to solve their differences. This was a tough concept to reinforce because you encourage your children to do just the opposite. Jack and Jacob had questions about it often. Sometimes they were difficult to answer. My friend Helen told me, "Just reassure them that you will not divorce." It was good advice and it avoided any complicated answers. John and I have always joked with each other that in our home, whoever files for divorce first gets the kids!

I remember one day when Jacob came home from playing at Uncle Jim's and said, "Mom, I think Dad should get his own house and you can live here. Then I would have two homes." He loves it at Uncle Jim's. It is a great place to hang out with no mom to police meals or activities.

Now, it seems, so many kids come from broken homes. It must be the norm these days. It is not uncommon to hear Jacob say that one of his friends is staying at his dad's this weekend and his mom's the next. He kind of likes to keep track of it all.

Now Jim is remarried, so the kids learned the whole process. We attended his wedding and both boys hid their faces when the bride and groom kissed. I must say time seems to make all of these things better. I knew my children would have to learn some life lessons, and I guess this is just one of them.

I am grateful for my marriage. It is something I will never take for granted. I recently read a book by Dr. Laura Schlesinger, *The Proper Care and Feeding of a Husband.* It really spoke to me about being a submissive wife and yielding to one another. (There are days when John may think I skipped that chapter.) But, it is much easier to praise your spouse while you in turn are also being lifted up. Love and respect for one another is the key. As a matter of fact, the guidelines to a successful marriage are outlined quite nicely in Ephesians 5:22–33. Many people see that as a "wretched verse." I like Beth Moore's interpretation from her women's Bible study, *To Live Is Christ: the Life and Ministry of Paul.* She is actually from Texas and her ministry is women's Bible studies. You can check out her Web site, Living Proof Ministries, at www.lproof.org. She has written numerous books and has a video series with her studies. I feel as if I know her personally.

This is how she explained it and I agree with her. This portion of scripture revolves around the biblical roles of three distinct figures intimately involved in marriage: wives, husbands, and Christ. The attitude of all Christians is to be submissive to each other. Love one another. She says Paul regarded husbands and wives as spiritual equals but with functional differences. To apply her example to my life, John has to worry about things I don't. He has to come up with answers when I can't. He doesn't want to drive around town, be the bus driver, delivering the boys where they need to be, or sit at doctors' appointments, take care of school issues, grocery shop, clean toilets (OK, I do get some help once a week with that chore), and every other matter moms take care of. We each have our own areas of expertise. John will sometimes say to me, "Don't ask me about the boys' medicine, you're the nurse." If we disagree, I speak up. Just ask him. Through voicing our opinions thoughtfully, we can have a discussion and come to an agreement. Once in a while our agreement may be to disagree until one of us has a change of mind, or submits to the other's judgment.

Beth Moore continues to explain that in Ephesians, Paul's primary directive to women dealt with submission, while his primary directive to men dealt with love. As she said, "Could it be he was targeting the area most likely to be our weakness? Submission does not mean slavery."

As Moore says, she has a husband she can look to for counsel and direction. She can rely on her husband for toughness when she is too soft, and for sound logic when she is too emotional. Mary Beth, I think we are both abundantly blessed with our spouses. We could say the same thing about them.

When a woman is truly loved, lifted up, and treated with goodness and her husband is devoted, it becomes rather easy to submit. We are all equal in God's eyes.

THE MASSEY FAMILY (L TO R): JACK, JOHN, MEGAN, AND JACOB

Well, speaking of husbands, we are about to watch Nebraska play football on TV, so I better go. It is an important activity in our part of the world.

Take care Mary Beth, and again, thanks for listening.

Love,

Megan ✉

Megan, dear,

How I loved visualizing you and John celebrating your twentieth anniversary at that charming Italian restaurant in Boston. And whichever one of you chose the restaurant had gotten that act together. Massachusetts is of course known for its outstanding Italian food—and wouldn't you know that the first thing I would focus on is the food. I keep wondering what you and John ordered that was divine. Chances are that you no longer remember the menu but, needless to say, you do remember what was special and meaningful about the evening.

Your taking the time to reflect upon the marriage that you and John have built together is a good thing. Just last evening, David and I were talking about what fun we're having at this stage in our lives, and we were wondering how many people truly do focus on and appreciate the good times at the very time when they are so good. We've always tried to do that, though likely not often enough.

I'm sure you wonder, as I do, what made your marriage work and Jim and Dallas's not work. On the face of it, you all had it all going for you, but then you and John were hit with the Fragile X whammy and realized that you had landed in Holland instead of Italy. I'm sure you've heard the statistic that 80 percent of marriages with a handicapped child end in divorce. Actually, I've heard quite recently that this statistic isn't accurate, that those marriages are only as likely to fail as any other—which means about 50 percent. So I don't know. Statistics, as you know, aren't my strong suit. I suppose that what we can conclude is sort of negative in that, in fact, we simply don't know what makes a marriage click, what can strengthen one marriage and cause another to crack.

It would be a toss-up to determine whether statistics or Bible study would be my weaker suit. I have never really studied the Bible. I only listen to the lessons as they are read in the church service, following the text in the bulletin. I was interested in your opinion, and that of Beth Moore's, on

Paul's take on marriage in the fifth chapter of Ephesians. I envy, in a very real sense, women who subscribe to his guidelines, and I truly rejoice for you and others for whom they work. I guess I've always wondered how Paul, as an unmarried man, could have been so certain what makes a marriage work. But you know what, Megan? This is why there are so many different churches in the world. Why, in Pauls Valley, Oklahoma, alone—a town of eight thousand people—there are thirty-eight churches. With all the options out there, there is no reason for anyone to say or feel that there isn't a church for that individual. The right church is there, if only a person will let that church into his or her life. And you know what else? Knowing what makes you and John happy makes me happy too. I have no doubt that where there is any kind of built-in problem that confronts a couple, having a shared faith can literally move mountains. I know it has for us.

What I'm sure that all parents of handicapped children can agree on is that those marriages present additional challenges because of the guilt and recrimination that go along with having a child with special needs. As well as David and I may have weathered my abject misery over having "caused" us to have two mentally retarded sons, I would be less than honest to suggest that it's gone away, that it's history. It's very much alive—and unwell, perhaps—as part of who and what I am.

I will—if I'm to be honest—admit that even today, I feel reluctant and guilty about asking David to pick up one of the boys, take a boy back to the group home, or be in charge of a boy if I'm out of town or otherwise engaged. That reluctance is surely borne in part by my generational sense that dealing with almost all aspects of the children's schedules, care, and feeding is the mother's responsibility. Daddy's responsibility, in my day, was to have a job, to bring home the proverbial bacon, to deal with the big issues, like whether the United States should pay its United Nations dues. It's also, however, my sense that if not for my gene that caused "all this," those boys would be picking themselves up, would be getting to their own doctor appointments, would be making their own dinner plans. That guilt will not go away, because Fragile X will not go away. It may—and I think will—be cured one day for future generations, but for the Busby family, it will not go away. It's a happening thing, and so is my guilt.

I can only imagine the anguish of other parents of children with special needs. Perhaps some of those marriages weren't in the best shape even before they had children. Who knows? All you and I can do is to be grateful for what we have, and with lots of nurturing, will be able to keep as long as our health holds. At my age, that's the real key to happiness.

Feeling sad for those with less happy marriages makes me feel a little guilty, as I'm still basking in the glow of our fortieth wedding anniversary, which we celebrated with family and extended family. We tend only to celebrate the big ones, when it comes to birthdays and anniversaries.

We were actually in Ireland on our anniversary in June of 2002, attending the wonderful wedding of the son of our dear Minneapolis friends, the Struyks. The Rehms from Washington and the Reisters, other Minneapolis friends, took David and me out for a splendid dinner in Dublin on our anniversary, which was the day after the wedding. As perfect as that celebration was—and it truly was—we still wanted to celebrate here at home with our family and a few extended family members, which we did a few weeks later. What came through to me, with all that David and I said and all that others said that evening, is how spectacularly fortunate we were to have found each other in the first place. Here is what I said to him that night in my toast:

Our Fortieth

There are, of course, many reasons for one marriage working and another one failing to do so. I think that one reason ours has endured, and happily so, is that we each had—from the beginning—clearly defined roles.

Mary Beth and David Busby on their 40th anniversary, Dublin, Ireland
Photo by Diane Rehm

David is the CEO and CFO of our little partnership. Ah, but I'm the COO. And David has constantly reassured me, over these forty years, that I'm a pretty darned good chief operating officer and that, indeed, he'd be hard pressed to carry out his duties as chief executive officer and chief financial officer without me beside him as the COO. I'm sure he'd admit to having had occasional problems with my list of priorities. And he hates my filing system. But, hey, it all gets done.

My fulfillment of my duties has allowed David to focus his free time on the Middle East, while I focused on things like our combined middle girth.

Most of all, we have had almost incredibly good luck. How could either of us have known of our good fortune in his having been married before, with his two spectacularly wonderful daughters? How could I have imagined the joy that Hopie and Alison would bring to my life, as they grew up to be caring, fun, interesting women who would bring five extraordinary grandchildren to our lives?

How could we have known that our dear Robert and Jack, who

Busby Family Reunion, 2001
(Top row, L to R: Tim McGeary, Bill Vareika, Nick Burleigh, Steve Burleigh, Patrick Burleigh. (Bottom row, L to R): Robert Busby, Christian Vareika, Alison Vareika with an arm around Hope Vareika, David and Mary Beth Busby, Jack Busby, Hope Burleigh.

have had challenges and who have brought us challenges, would also bring to us that rarest and most valuable of opportunities: that of being able to participate—even in a minor role— in a project that can make a difference. Who knew?

One thing I *did* know, back in 1962 as we prepared to marry, is that David Busby would, to the end of our lives, be devoted to me and to the bonds of our marriage. He's never given me any reason to doubt his devotion. He's never given me an occasion to regret our marriage—except during those years when I wished I had never imposed myself and my genes on any man on earth, ever, and he's given me myriad reasons to love being married to him. His sense of humor gets me through every day with moments of fun and laughter. His can-do attitude keeps me moving and growing and believing that all things are possible. His abiding faith keeps me hopeful, and his conviction that each day is a new day keeps me wondering what's next. And so long as being married to David Busby is what's next, I'm blessed indeed. And I'm happy. My cup runneth over. So, happy anniversary, my darling David.

Hopie and Alison, unbeknownst to me, had dug out my little cookbook that I sent out to friends at Christmastime about ten years ago. In it were some of my Christmas letters, plus a lot of recipes and a few other odd things—including a letter that I sent to the *Washington Post* in response to its request that readers who consider themselves to have happy marriages write in and tell why they feel their marriages are good. The *Post* never printed my letter, but I kind of liked it and I was pleased that the girls remembered it and liked it enough to read it at our anniversary celebration. I'm enclosing it too, Megan, and then I promise this is the last you'll ever hear from me on this subject. For a good while, anyway.

This was written by me on July 2, 1992.

To: *The Washington Post*

This responds to your request to hear from people who consider themselves to have good marriages—having, I gather, heard plenty from people with troubled relationships.

Last weekend, we were at the christening of my husband, David's, baby granddaughter, Hope Emily Anne Vareika, and at the luncheon which his former wife hosted following the ceremony, some reference was made to the fact that he and I had just celebrated our thirtieth wedding anniversary. People said, "My, imagine that," "I can't believe you've been married thirty years," etc. David joked to his former wife that in another ten years, he's going to throw in the ten years he was married to her and give a golden anniversary party. Both she and I thought that was a grand idea and said we'd have ten years to plan the menu. The point is that divorce, like marriage, is a relationship—not only between a man and his wife, but also between everyone else who has been affected by that union. I think too many people think they can simply marry a person and march off into the sunset with that person, not realizing that a certain amount of baggage goes along for the ride.

So, then, why wouldn't all "young" marriages be happy? After all, young people don't have a lot of baggage to carry, do they? Oh, you bet they do. A large portion of the baggage is packed before they are born, with their parents' lifestyles and genes, and they grow up sorting it all out as best they can, using the examples set for them.

Another reason for so many marriages being unhappy is that many people choose partners who are simply not right for them. They may bring to the marriage the same amount of baggage, but it's not the same stuff. Who, for instance, carves the turkey? Who does the dishes? Do the kids go to church? Which church? Who drives? Do the kids get spanked? If so, who does it? Who likes air-conditioning, who likes open windows? How do they spend their money?

They may not like to do the same amount of work, they may not think the same things are funny, they may not worship the same God, they may simply not care about the same things outside the relationship. In short, they may not realize that all of the things outside the relationship are, indeed, inside the relationship. So much of this is luck. Indeed, I would submit that there's more luck involved in a happy marriage than we would like to think.

David and I have two sons, both of whom are mentally retarded. Talk about bad luck! This is the kind of thing that has destroyed myriad marriages. The guilts and recriminations that accompany the day-to-day dealing with such children are devastating to most any relationship. How have we kept tragedy from ravaging our marriage? By letting each other be sad and overwhelmed and by giving each other space, with an abundance of love, humor, tolerance, caring, and mutual respect buffering the space on all sides.

Allowing "space" is a very tricky wicket, and there, again, I think the whole Luck thing comes into play. Not all couples like, need, or want the same amount of space. Space, for some, is emptiness; for others, it's the very breath of life, without which nothing can work. Both David and I fall more into the latter category (talk about good luck!), and we rejoice that we do. We cherish our time together, and we treasure our time apart.

It also helps that whenever I get a parking ticket, David is sure it was the cop's fault, that whenever I overdraw my bank account, it's the bank's fault, that when our insurance almost gets cancelled because I forgot to pay the bill, it's the insurance company's fault for being so pushy, that whenever our library is a total mess of piles of catalogues and magazines, it's the postman's fault for bringing too many. But I don't think either of us is on any pedestal. People on pedestals are up there all alone, in empty space, breathing thin air. Both David and I are just down here, truckin' along, having fun, and keeping on keeping on.

My niece will be married later this month. I hope that I will be able to restrain myself from telling her that I hope she and her husband will be as happy as David and I have been for these past thirty years. That's so boring and trite. It's also true.

Most sincerely,
Mary Beth Busby

And those, Megan girl, are my views on marriage. I'm sure they wouldn't be at all useful to most people. They may, indeed, not be relevant to anything or anyone you know. But I have to tell you that as I reread what I said back in 1992, it all looks truer and truer to me today.

And talk about luck! Who ever could have dreamed our spectacularly good luck in finding our life's work when we still have time to do it? The joy has been finding new friends like you and John and all of our treasured FRAXA friends, plus being able to retain the old and dear friendships of a lifetime, plus Hopie and Alison and their marvelous families and—always and ever—darling Robert and Jack. These cherished treasures make our life good beyond measure. There is no measure for our good fortune. There can only be recognition of it and rejoicing in the coming joys of the unknown morrow.

So much love to you, always,
Mary Beth

PS. "Where does the family start? It starts with a young man in love with a girl—no superior alternative has yet been found." (Sir Winston Churchill)
PPS. And how, dear Megan, could I better end this letter than with "Old Wives," which is my all-time favorite poem. It was written by my dear friend,

E. J. Mudd. I suppose E. J.'s lyrical wisdom is waxing wonderful to me these days, as David and I now approach our forty-third wedding anniversary. The import of her words may not yet ring true to you, a "young" wife. But tuck it away, honey, because as the years progress, it will. Trust me, it will.

Old Wives

What did we think, when we promised to love and cherish
those barely known men, til death did us part—and all that?
I think what we heard was the first set of terms—
for richer, for better, in health.
Who bothered to look through the mist of tulle
at the contrary side of the vows—for poorer, in sickness, for worse?
Who ventured a question—How poor? In what sense poor?
How sick? Where sick? For how long?
For worse? Were there limits to worse?
Well, never mind now, after all these years.
We've seen it from both sides now.
The point is that all of us promised we would,
and some of us actually did.

—E. J. Mudd

30

January Blahs and Blues

Dear Mary Beth

I can hardly believe I am writing this letter to you. Today I lived through another experience I never planned on. You know, all the moments you dream about when raising your children? The places you will go and the things you will see. The opportunities that you will give them and the things they will learn. I knew with Jack and Jacob we would do a few things differently, just as they do things differently in Holland from the way they do in Italy, but I never could have dreamed up this day. This day was not even on the radar screen.

This morning, I took Jack to the Denver airport, so he could fly to Cincinnati and then go on to his school in Kentucky. The Denver airport is about a three-hour drive from home. He watched movies on the DVD player and slept. I drove and prayed a lot. I was about to put my baby on a huge airplane that would fly him back to school. There in Cincinnati, a representative from the Stewart Home School would meet him and take him back to school in Frankfort. I had a special letter from Dr. Stewart that was going to allow me to obtain a pass to go through security and escort Jack to his plane.

This all sounded so easy. We checked in at the airline counter, and I presented my letter. This letter, by the way, explained everything. It talked about Jack having Fragile X and that he was mentally impaired and should not be left alone in the airport under any circumstances. It had the flight times (which turned out to be incorrect) and other valuable information. I requested that Jack fly as an unaccompanied minor.

The man behind the counter asked me, "How old is your son?"

"Fifteen," I replied.

"Oh," the man said. "He doesn't need to fly as an unaccompanied minor when he is fifteen. He can fly on his own." He really hadn't even looked at Jack. He was staring at the computer and typing as if he had a thesis deadline or something. I was annoyed. It seemed he had no concern for my son. I told him that Jack was mentally impaired and needed to be dealt with as requested in the letter.

He then asked me, "Have you paid for this?" After taking a deep breath, I calmly told him that the school had arranged it. He seemed rather put out, but then he went ahead and processed the paperwork.

Mary Beth, I don't think the airline gave him an ounce of extra attention. All I got was a false sense of security that my son would be fine. I was trying to do the right thing. It's not as if I turned my son loose in the airport. Now there's an interesting thought. I could write a whole book on that possibility.

After we got through the paperwork hurdle, we were off to security. At that point, a woman checked our passes. She spoke very broken English, which of course is fine, but we simply don't see much of this in the Midwest. She asked Jack how old he was and he didn't understand her. He looked at me and back at her with a puzzled expression on his face. He mumbled, "I don't know," and went on to the security table where you put the things you're carrying on the plane. She asked me, "What's the matter with him? Doesn't he talk?" At that point, I was ready to scream. I told her he had a mental handicap and was doing the best he could. We made it through security and got on the passenger train to the concourses. Jack asked me, "Which train do we get on?" "Well," I answered, "One says Position Closed, and the other says Concourse A, B, and C. What do you think?" He made the right choice and we were on our way. With each stop, he would holler, "Don't get off here, we need Concourse C." Sometimes I just wanted to pretend I didn't know him.

When we arrived at Concourse C, the doors opened and we headed up the escalators. Jack says, "Now we get on the bus." People looked at him in amazement because in the Denver airport, there is no bus. To Jack's credit, though, I think there is one in Cincinnati.

We had almost two hours before his plane departed. I went to use the restroom on the way to the gate. Jack said, "I'll wait right here." Guess what? He didn't. He was gone. He was nowhere to be seen. I really didn't panic too much. I wondered which way to go first, the gate? The candy store? McDonald's? After all, I had two hours to find him. Maybe he was looking for that nonexistent bus! I decided to go to the gate, because I knew he had the gate number memorized. As I walked down the long corridor, there he sat, waving his arm, just as proud as could be. I didn't say anything. I was going to have to say good-bye soon, and that was hard enough.

Next came boarding the plane. The flight attendant began letting passengers board the plane by zones. Jack could read his ticket and when he heard them call zone five, he jumped up. "I'm going to miss you," he said with tears in his eyes. "I will miss you too, honey," I said. I tried to hug him, but he wanted no part of that. In fact, he was very insistent that I leave. He wanted to do this all by himself. In hindsight, I should have just hidden behind a pole and watched. Jack made it up to the front of the line where he was told he had to wait to be boarded. Finally, a man escorted him onto the plane. I watched his every step and was leaning around people in front of me so I could watch him disappear. So many things were running through my mind: "What are you doing? He is a fifteen-year-old with the mind of a six-year-old, and you just put him on a plane by himself? Why not just keep him at home for the rest of his life, where you can keep track of him?"

Then I remembered what a gift it is for him to be able to grow, to become independent and learn life skills in a place that is so well equipped to give him the lifestyle he needs. As I am deep in thought and my face is covered with tears, I am interrupted by the paging of missing passengers for the flight. And who do you suppose they are looking for? Yep. "Passenger Massey."

That was the icing on the cake. Had I written a check at the ticket counter for this meet and greet status, I think I might have demanded a refund. Instead, I calmly walked to the desk and told them they had just put Passenger Massey on the plane.

"Oh, thank you," the man said, as he looked at his computer and continued to type.

Well, God is faithful and Jack made it safe and sound to Stewart Home School. His representative called me to let me know. Jack was none the worse for wear. He knew all along that he would make it. I even tried going through other scenarios with him in case his representative wasn't there. He would have none of that. "Stop it," he would say. "Don't talk about it, they will be there." Oh, to have the faith of a child. Jack is right: it always works out for him. He is in such a protected environment. But when you throw him out in the big world, like I did today, he seems so innocent and naive.

As I drove out of the airport, I tried to call our dear friend, Mary Jane Clark. I know she is looking at sending her David off to school someday. I left her a teary message saying this was really the pits. I know I have so much to be grateful for. Jack was a trouper. He was so brave and courageous. He never wavered from the plan. He never looked back as he walked down that ramp. He is an incredible young man, if I do say so myself. I was very proud of him.

This day was just another reminder that as the parent of two handicapped children, I am not in Italy. I am in Holland, and Holland is where I must stay. Jack loves it in Holland and Jack loves it at the Stewart Home School. He is thriving and maturing. Jack knew all along his schedule for the day, and it went just fine. He didn't even call home when he got back to school. He was home.

Someday all of this will get easier. I know I will survive. You are living proof that I can. You and David are such blessings to us. We love you both.

Now that I am finally getting this letter about the Thanksgiving travel sent off, it is almost time for Jack to fly home for the Christmas holidays. He will be confident, and filled with excitement. I can learn from that attitude. As they say in *The Lion King* musical, "Hakuna Matata," or, "No worries, be happy!"

Take good care and have a very Merry Christmas.

Love,

Megan ✉

Dearest Megan,

I'm longing to hear from you on how you survived the holidays. Not that I expected to hear from you during all the craziness, any more than you expected to hear from me. This is my first day "back," and naturally, I still have catchup items galore.

Are Jack and Jacob back in their respective schools yet? I had an E-mail from a young friend with three small children, and the heading was, "'Tis the Season to be Over!!!!" How true it is! There is absolutely no time of the year I love as much as the Christmas holidays, and absolutely no time I'm readier to reach than January 5, or whenever it's over. I don't think there's a parent alive who doesn't feel that way. I know you and John will be happy to get back to your everyday work.

Before I tell you about yesterday morning, I simply have to tell you about the last time Robert was home and traveled back to Ada after his Labor Day visit. I didn't tell you about this before, frankly, because you and John had—just two weeks before that—taken Jack to the Stewart Home School, and I didn't want to scare you out of your wits. With your having now gone through a couple of these trips home for Jack, however, I figure maybe you can handle this. But fasten your seatbelt, honey girl.

Busby Family Christmas, 1977 or 1978

On post–Labor Day travel day, Robert and I arrived at the airport in plenty of time. We went to the counter to check in, so that I could get a pass to accompany him to the gate. So far, so good. Until the agent took Robert's e-ticket, looked at it, checked the computer, and informed me that Robert was on the "No Fly" list. I said, "What? You mean the list they put terrorists on?" She didn't answer. She said, "Just a minute. I need to make a phone call." Which she did. Then she came back over and said, "It's OK. He can fly." I said, "But wait a minute. Why would he have been on that list?" She said something to the effect that "you never know." Hmmm. You can imagine what a warm feeling that gave me. She gave him a boarding pass, but she took a big red Magic Marker and put a big red mark across it, which I gather is some sort of scarlet letter, the signal for the people at security to give him a full search. Which they did. This didn't really bother Robert. He's pretty used to that. My son the terrorist.

When we got down to the gate, I told the gate attendant what had happened and asked if she could shed any light on the subject. She really couldn't, except to say that only last names are on that list and that you never know how someone gets on it. Wonderful. Does this mean that all Busbys who fly are going to get this treatment? She gave me a card with an eight-hundred number and an E-mail address for the Transportation Security Administration (TSA) and said that I might want to take this up with that agency. I came home, intending to do just that. But I simply couldn't make myself pick up that phone. In fact, two days later, I still didn't have the nerve to pick up that phone. Finally, David did it. He called and was told something like, you have to have flown three times before your name can be removed from the list. The person said I should write an E-mail to the TSA, which would put me in touch with its ombudsman. I did.

Needless to say, I was not anxious to have Robert arrive at the Oklahoma City airport to come home for Christmas, only to be told that he couldn't fly. Can you just imagine, Megan? Not an option. Then a day or two later, someone from TSA sent me a return E-mail telling me where to send a letter by snail mail, which I did, enclosing the E-mail I had sent to TSA. Then two weeks after that, I got a call from the ombudsman, asking for Robert's birth date. She said that I would be receiving a packet in the mail. The packet arrived about ten days later. The main things TSA needed were on an enclosed list, and most of them were things Robert doesn't have––things like a driver's license and passport. The only two things we could provide were his birth certificate and his photo ID. And this is where we are at this moment. Waiting to see if Robert is still on the "No Fly" list. My son the terrorist. Oh, yikes!

Megan, it's so lucky that you can get a nonstop flight for Jack from Cincinnati to Denver. Even though you have the three-hour drive from Scottsbluff to the Denver airport, that makes a *huge* difference, not having to ask the airline to do the meet-and-greet business, where an agent meets him and helps him find the next flight. Not a lot can happen on a nonstop flight. Unless you're Robert, of course. Then the possibilities are endless.

As I agonize over this "No Fly" stuff, I keep wondering if this could be a result of the trip Robert took in July to Los Angeles to visit Hopie and Steve. They were truly so dear to invite him, and he was ecstatic over going, as he has boundless adoration for both of his sisters and both of their husbands. Big excitement. The trip out there, to my knowledge, went without incident. But while he was in Los Angeles, Hopie and Steve took him to Disneyland one day, and he got a little sick. Not real sick. Just a little sick. She took him to the infirmary, where the nurses were—I gather—dressed up like fairies or something, and everyone made a fuss over him as they would a very young child. He adored all this, and decided that being sick in Los Angeles was definitely a good thing. He was loving this, big time.

The next day, he acted vaguely sick, though neither Hopie nor Steve really thought he was. But as he was scheduled to fly back to Oklahoma the following day, Hopie got really nervous as the day went on and Robert continued to lie around, feeling poorly. She finally decided that she had better take him to the little clinic nearby to get him checked out. The folks at the clinic, where Robert was delighted to be, found nothing wrong and pronounced him perfectly well enough to travel.

The next morning, when Hopie went in to get Robert up and ready to go to the airport, he dashed into the bathroom and tried like the dickens to throw up. Didn't work. Nothing to throw up. At that point, Hopie informed Robert that he was not, repeat not sick, that he was fine, that he was flying back to Oklahoma that day, and to get his act together. Once he realized that, he was fine all the way to the airport and got on the plane without incident.

Fast-forward to later that same day when Robert got off the plane in Oklahoma City—in a *wheelchair*, please! Do you love this? Tracy, the young woman from McCall's who met him, said that the flight attendant who brought him off the plane said that he had seemed a little sick. Yeah, right. Tracy also said that when they got down to baggage claim, the minute he saw his suitcase, he jumped out of the wheelchair and that was the end of his "illness." Can you stand it?

What I can't help wondering is if perhaps the airline simply decided that Robert Busby was such a pain-in-the-ass and they don't need his high-maintenance business, thank you very much. Hence, the "No Fly" list. Well, I guess we'll find out eventually.

Hopie and Steve, putting the most charitable face on this whole episode, said that Robert is really bright in so many ways, even in his ways of being incredibly manipulative. Indeed, Steve wrote me the dearest letter, telling about how Robert helped him lay some tiles in their kitchen. It's very interesting to hear what someone else sees in Robert that I don't see.

OK, fast-forward to this week, when "'Tis the season to be *over*!" So here's what happened yesterday. Yesterday morning, David and I divided up the chores. I took Robert to the airport, and David took Jack to work at his job at the Marine Barracks, where he is now a mess attendant. We were proud of Jack for being cheerful about working most days during the holidays. We felt strongly that he needed to pitch in and go that extra mile, especially because he does get a fair amount of time off for various trips during the year. This was one week when most of his fellow work-crew members were taking off, so I have to assume he was helpful to his wonderful boss, Carole Allen, who combines the qualities of nurturing concern and toughness—more nurturing than tough, I suspect.

Robert had been so quiet all day the day before he left that I would have been worried had he not done this same bit so many times in the past. I think he falls into silence partly because he knows it's his last day home for a while, partly because he's reluctant to leave, and partly because the holidays have been such fun. With so much going on, I know that a part of him thinks that if he was able to stay here at home in Washington, it would be party time all the time. Which it wouldn't be. But wonderful as the idea is, it's too much for him, as it is for everyone else. Hence, the silence, as he's mentally preparing to go back to Oklahoma and is changing "mode."

My dear friend Ellen, bless her heart, took Robert to a movie that last afternoon and he was silent to the point of being rude. Ellen and I both wondered if it might have been because he's no longer taking the antidepressant he was on for several years, but I rather doubt it. He was in such grand spirits during the entire holidays until that very last day. I think it was more the postholiday blues—namely, situational, rather than clinical.

I'll admit that by letting him go to the movie, I violated my own cardinal rule, which is to plan nothing, and I mean truly *nothing*, on his last day at home. No movie, no lunch out, no shopping, no dinner out, nothing. That way, Robert knows that the holidays are so over, so history, that everyone else is now back in their little grooves, wherever those grooves are, and there's not much going on here. Just Mom and Dad doing their little everyday stuff. Boring, boring. Ready to get on that plane and head back to his little groove in Ada, Oklahoma.

In the late afternoon, day before yesterday, we called his group home, which we always do the day before he goes back. For one thing, I have to find out for sure who is meeting him, so that I can let the airline know. Then, too, it's good for him to talk to people there, to help him get back into that mode. I'm always amused that during that phone conversation, he begins once again to talk "Okie." He'll say things like, "Yes, ma'am." Whichever staff member at McCall's is on duty—whether it be Pat or Diana or Jennifer—she always talks to Robert about how they all miss him and how he needs to get on back. They're so marvelous and they always know what to say that will amuse Robert. Then one or two of the residents will often get on the phone, and I love hearing our end of those conversations. He'll hang up and be a little more ready to go to his home the next day.

Megan, you may have already learned with your Jack how difficult it is to get off for the airport. I swear, no matter how many years we do this, it seems not to get better. There is always the hassle of getting him packed. He always wants to carry about three separate little bags on the plane with him, and we always go through the business of sorting out what he really needs to carry and what can go in the suitcase. And no matter how early on the day or evening before travel we get all this settled, the next morning I go up and discover that he's changed everything back the way he first wanted it. Then we negotiate all over again. Yikes! With his oppositional behavior, this negotiation is a major challenge.

I don't know about your Jack, but on the morning of departure, Robert tends to function more slowly than is possible to imagine. Slow to get up, slow to get in the shower, slow to shave, slow to dress. Slow to get down for breakfast. Slow to get his bags downstairs. It's like pulling teeth.

But here's the fun part. As we were arriving at the airport, Robert asked me, "Do you need your purse?" I said, "No, not yet. It's in the backseat. I'll get it when we get parked." End of subject.

After we parked and I reached in the backseat for my purse and tote bag with the newspapers I always carry when I know I'll have sitting-around time, I realized—to my horror—that all I had thrown back there was the tote bag. Omigod, I thought, no purse. No driver's license for my ID in order to get a pass to accompany him to the gate. No money to pay for parking, which costs a fortune at National Airport. No credit card, no ATM card, no nothing. Clearly, Robert had known perfectly well that I had gone off without my purse; otherwise, why would he have asked me if I needed it? And didn't he pick a fine time to mention it—just as we were arriving at the airport. The good news is that Robert had about $35, so he made me a small loan to pay for the parking.

The people at the check-in counter were nice beyond belief, and they waived the rule in order to give me a pass, even without my ID. It was a good thing I was able to go to the gate with Robert, because the flight was more than an hour late leaving, and we were concerned that he might miss his connection in Houston. We called McCall's to warn the person meeting him of this possibility, but happily it all ended well and he got back in fine fettle. When we talked with him last night, he was high as a kite—just where I want him on his first night back at his group home. Believe me, this is not always the case.

The thing I keep thinking about is that Robert knew perfectly well that I had left my purse at home. I guess this is literally what it means to be retarded. You do get around to asking a question like, "Do you need your purse?" You just don't get around to asking the question when it would be useful. But you do get there. Eventually.

Bottom line, Megan. There is never enough time on the morning of departure for the airport. And you will be frazzled beyond belief. So frazzled that you may leave your purse at home. But he'll get off and you'll survive.

I guess that even at this stage, I'm constantly amazed at the serenity with which both of my boys assume that everything will work out OK—"everything" like getting to the airport with no ID and no money. None of this bothered Robert. What, him worry? He simply *assumes* that someone will always be there to help him. I suppose, actually, that this is a nice way to view the world, huh?

I swear, the assumptions our boys make is worrisome as all get out, isn't it? I remember once when I was taking Jack somewhere in the car and I was muttering about the tight schedule I was on and how I didn't see how I could possibly do this and that and thus and so and get it all together by such and such time. Jack listened to this fretting for a minute and then said, "Don't worry, Mom. You'll think of something." I lost patience with him and said, "Yeah, well, how do you know I'll be able to think of something? I may not be able to think of anything at all!" And I thought, well, this is either very good news or very bad news—the fact that my boys have not a doubt in the world that I—or whoever is in charge, will always be there to work everything out for them. Bless their hearts, they're so trusting.

Jack went back to his group home on the van after work yesterday, but I'll likely go out there on Saturday and bring him home for the weekend. It always pleases us when he prefers spending weekends at his home, and sometimes this is the case. Not often enough, however. Even on weekends when we don't do anything, he likes being here.

After I left the airport yesterday, I came home, got my wayward purse, and then went out to Rockville and shopped till I pretty near dropped, which was not all that long. I simply had to get new bathroom rugs—like a year ago. Then I treated myself to a drop-by at Bruce Variety store in Bethesda, where for thirty-five years, I have gone for things I couldn't find anywhere else—everything from ribbon to pure cotton socks. I'll bet Scottsbluff still has at least one marvelous variety store, and I hope so, because every woman owes it to herself, now and then, simply to wander into a variety store and amble up and down the narrow aisles, browsing for nothing much.

My excuse for going there yesterday was that I needed some heavy black thread to sew on coat buttons—a heavy-duty shopping agenda, right? As I was moseying toward the thread section, my wandering eye flitted by cosmetics. I could scarcely believe what I saw. It was Lady Esther Face Powder! My grandmother used Lady Esther Face Powder and, I swear, it looked like the same box with the little pink and blue flowers on it that she always had on her dressing table. Better still, I could literally smell that powder. I furtively picked up a box and opened it, to see if I could smell it—already assuming "they" had removed any trace of fragrance from it, as has happened with every other cosmetic product on the face of the earth. But no! It had that same powdery fragrance that I loved as a child at my grandmother's house, and that I still loved yesterday at Bruce Variety. Naturally, I picked it up, paid my $5.19—Bruce's didn't have the thread I was after—and sailed out the door in ecstasy.

Finding an insignificant little thing like the Lady Esther powder can—however briefly—let me forget things like misplaced handbags, frantic rushes, security traumas, my son the terrorist, the agony of parting, the still-present guilt over "sending my baby away." I can forget it all for one brief, fragrant moment that takes me back to the 1940s, to my grandmother's dressing table. These small, unexpected encounters with my childhood are rare but oh so delicious to counter the January blues and blahs.

Am I a nutcase, or what? But I've always been this way. A browsing trip through Bruce Variety or the Rite Aid drug store, or a hardware store, or the Container Store, just picking up little nothing essentials, is a mood lifter for me. It literally fights the January blahs and blues.

I have a fondness for Bruce Variety or various reasons—besides the fact that I can find nearly everything in the world there. When Robert was about eight, David had the boys in there with him and after they got home, he realized that Robert had swiped a little rubber ball. We decided to make a big deal out of it, and David put him back in the car, went back to Bruce's, and made Robert return the ball. The clerk got the picture right away and was very nice about it, while assuring Robert that this was not an OK thing to have done.

You might think that after that traumatic experience, I would never have darkened the door of Bruce's again, but I rarely think of it anymore. I mention that in order to assure you that the horribles—those incidents that make parenting our kids stressful beyond all understanding—do fade with time and tide. Besides, there are too many things I'm always needing at Bruce Variety to stand on too much emotional ceremony.

I swear, I don't think Robert has ever gotten over his thing about loving little rubber balls to carry around with him. When we went through the airport security yesterday, he of course had to take everything out of his pockets and put it all in one of those little baskets. As usual he had some little rubber balls about the size of ping-pong balls, along with myriad other things, in his pockets. If it's not the little rubber balls, it's a whole bunch of little plastic Native American figures, with headdresses and all—plus a lot of photographs, keys, you name it. When they gave him back his basket of items, there were only three balls, and Robert insisted that he had had one more. With a zillion people behind us, and what with my near panic over the whole security episode so far, and with my desire not to make any more waves, I told him that it didn't matter and that he would survive with only the three. He was not thrilled, and gave me his ax-murderer glare, but we went on to the gate. As we were waiting at the gate, here came the security guard with that fourth ball, saying they had found it. While I of course thanked him profusely, Robert looked at him accusingly, like, "Well, I told you I had another one."

Some years, the January blahs and blues are worse than others, and it's too early in January to know about this year. But you know what, Megan? I think this month, and this year, will be quite OK. Better than OK. I'm feeling so up about the ongoing research on Fragile X that I'm going to wave my magic wand and will any hint of blahs and blues to be quickly overtaken by my overwhelming sense of gratitude to my supportive friends and gratefulness for my so-far good health to continue the tiny little bit of work I can do to help further the effort. And now if all of our researchers will have continued good health, hey, there's no stopping them.

Now we can all get on with our work. David has a gut feeling that exciting research breakthroughs are imminent. So, let's hold that thought and get to work raising some more research dollars because, dear Megan, I'm in the mood for a banner year. I know you are too. And I'm in the mood to tell you once again how very much you enhance my life. You and your boys are truly the future, in terms of really being able to benefit from what is being learned, what is being done, what is being tried, and the future—God willing—may be sooner than we know.

When I went to camp as a child, we used to sing a round that went, "Make new friends, but keep the old; one is silver and the other's gold." Do you remember that one? You, Megan would—in that context—be one of my silver friends. But oh, my dear, you are sterling silver of the finest quality. I love knowing you and having you in my life. Marvelous as Italy is and would have been to experience, you are right: we are in Holland, and Holland is where we must stay. Being there with you makes it a fine place to be.

Have a great year, Megan, and do know that I send

Much love,

MBBB

PS. "Hope smiles on the threshold of the year to come, whispering that it will be happier." (Alfred, Lord Tennyson, 1809–1892)

PPS. "For last year's words belong to last year's language. And next year's words await another voice. And to make an end is to make a beginning." (T. S. Eliot, 1888–1965) ✉